T0305682

## Voices on the second edition

"Professor Kacapyr's work in the field of econometrics—specifically, his work in making the subject more understandable to aspiring economics students and enthusiasts—is incredible. His style is straightforward and engaging, delivering the subject matter so effortlessly that it is a pleasure to read and immerse yourself in the text."

—**Krasimir Kehayov**, Goldman Sachs

"Direct and to the point, Professor Kacapyr provides an effective exposition of the essentials of econometrics in both technical terms and prose. The second edition [...] is a rugged and reliable resource for instructor, learner, and practitioner. Kacapyr targets economics majors, but this book is also suited for use in courses in business, statistics, and social sciences, where the same skills are applied."

—**Wade L. Thomas**, SUNY Oneonta

"I really like this book as a supplement to the required text in my course. It's at the exact level that my students need, and the exercises are great practice for them."

—**Cynthia Bansak**, St. Lawrence University

# Essential Econometric Techniques

Now in its third edition, *Essential Econometric Techniques: A Guide to Concepts and Applications* is a concise, student-friendly textbook which provides an introductory grounding in econometrics, with an emphasis on the proper application and interpretation of results.

Drawing on the author's extensive teaching experience, this book offers intuitive explanations of concepts such as heteroskedasticity and serial correlation, and provides step-by-step overviews of each key topic.

This new edition contains more applications, brings in new material including a dedicated chapter on panel data techniques, and moves the theoretical proofs to appendices. After Chapter 7, students will be able to design and conduct rudimentary econometric research. The next chapters cover multicollinearity, heteroskedasticity, and autocorrelation, followed by techniques for time-series analysis and panel data.

Excel data sets for the end-of-chapter problems are available as a digital supplement. A solutions manual is also available for instructors, as well as PowerPoint slides for each chapter.

*Essential Econometric Techniques* shows students how economic hypotheses can be questioned and tested using real-world data, and is the ideal supplementary text for all introductory econometrics courses.

**Elia Kacapyr** is Professor of Economics at Ithaca College, USA.

# Essential Econometric Techniques

## A Guide to Concepts and Applications

*Third Edition*

**Elia Kacapyr**

Routledge
Taylor & Francis Group

NEW YORK AND LONDON

Cover image: © Jorg Greuel/Getty Images

Third edition published 2022
by Routledge
605 Third Avenue, New York, NY 10158

and by Routledge
4 Park Square, Milton Park, Abingdon, Oxon, OX14 4RN

*Routledge is an imprint of the Taylor & Francis Group, an informa business*

First edition published by M.E. Sharpe Inc 2011
Second edition published by Routledge 2015

*Library of Congress Cataloging-in-Publication Data*
A catalog record has been requested for this book

ISBN: 978-1-032-10122-4 (hbk)
ISBN: 978-1-032-10121-7 (pbk)
ISBN: 978-1-003-21375-8 (ebk)

DOI: 10.4324/9781003213758

Typeset in Sabon
by MPS Limited, Dehradun

Access the Support Material: www.routledge.com/9781032101217

# Contents

# 1 The Nature of Econometrics

## WHAT IS ECONOMETRICS?

Literally, econometrics means "economic measurement." Therefore, gathering data and generating economic statistics such as gross domestic product and the consumer price index could be considered econometrics. In practice econometrics is about testing economic hypotheses with statistical techniques. Respected econometricians have given us a variety of definitions. One favorite, perhaps because of its brevity, is from Henri Theil: "Econometrics is concerned with the empirical determination of economic laws" (Theil 1971, p. 1).

Economics is comprised of innumerable laws, theories, hypotheses, assumptions, and suppositions. Econometrics is subjecting any of these to empirical verification. Empirical means "by observation or experience." Rather than argumentation or debate, econometrics is about testing economic ideas to see if they hold true.

Students may say that econometrics is like a mash-up of their statistics course with an economics course. That is not a bad description of an econometrics class; only it conceals the main point—econometrics is about testing a proposition of some sort.

Data mining is a field similar to econometrics. The difference is that data miners say, "Let's see what the data reveal about this idea." Econometricians say, "Let's get the data and test if this idea holds true." This may seem like a trifling difference, but it turns out to be important. Data miners comb the data for interesting relationships. Econometricians use the data to test if a specific idea can be rejected or not.

DOI: 10.4324/9781003213758-1

## THE ECONOMETRIC METHODOLOGY

Econometric tests are based on scientific method:

(1) Ask a question, or state a theory
(2) Design a way to test the idea
(3) Conduct the test
(4) Reject or do not reject the idea

In econometrics, the steps are more explicit:

(1) State the idea to be tested
(2) Specify the econometric model
(3) Collect the data
(4) Estimate the parameters of the model
(5) Use the model to test the idea
(6) Forecast with the model

As an application of the econometric method, consider Keynes' law of consumption:

> The fundamental psychological law, upon which we are entitled to depend with great confidence both *a priori* from our knowledge of human nature and from the detailed facts of experience, is that men are disposed, as a rule and on average, to increase their consumption as their income increases, but not by as much as the increase in income.
>
> (Keynes 1936, p. 96)

Now apply the steps of the econometric methodology to test this law.

(1) State the theory, law, or hypothesis

It is impossible to state Keynes' law more eloquently than the master economist himself. However, it may be stated more succinctly: when income goes up, consumer spending goes up, but not by as much.

(2) Specify the econometric model

This step requires writing the idea in mathematical form. One of the simplest forms is the equation of a straight line: $y = mx + b$. To state

Keynes' law in linear form, let the y stand for consumer spending (CONS) and the x stand for consumer income (INC):

$$CONS = m(INC) + b$$

The tradition in econometrics is to replace the b with $\beta_0$ and the m with $\beta_1$ so that the same equation looks like this:

$$CONS = \beta_1(INC) + \beta_0$$

Now write the $\beta_0$ first and drop the parentheses:

$$CONS = \beta_0 + \beta_1 \ INC$$

The econometric model (CONS = $\beta_0 + \beta_1$ INC) assumes the relationship between CONS and INC is linear, in slope-intercept form. $\beta_0$ is the vertical intercept of the straight-line relationship between CONS and INC. The slope of the line is $\beta_1$. The econometric model is merely a mathematical way of stating the theory that is being tested.

Notice that Keynes' law implies that $0 < \beta_1 < 1$. That way if INC increases by one dollar, CONS will increase, but by less.

There is an important addition to all econometric models, the error term (u):

$$CONS = \beta_0 + \beta_1 \ INC + u$$

The error term is explicit recognition that the relationship between CONS and INC is not exact. Suppose the income of two people increases by $100 each. Keynes' law posits that both people will increase spending by less than $100. Yet it is not expected that both people will increase spending by the exact same amount. One person may be closer to retirement and therefore save more of the increase. Another person may have pressing needs and spend the entire amount. The error term allows for these differences.

## (3) Collect the data

In this step, data on CONS and INC are gathered. Several alternatives present themselves. The Bureau of Labor Statistics annually surveys households concerning their income and expenditures. CONS and INC could be obtained for each household last year. This is cross-sectional data—information across entities (households) at a point in time (last year).

Table 1.1 Cross-Sectional Data

| Household | CONS | INC |
|-----------|------|-----|
| 1 | $76,234 | $83,234 |
| 2 | $22,346 | $23,457 |
| 3 | $56,873 | $57,876 |
| 4 | $44,829 | $35,987 |
| ⋮ | ⋮ | ⋮ |

Another possibility is to use macroeconomic data from the Bureau of Economic Analysis. Here we have CONS and INC for the entire nation over the years. The data are per capita and adjusted for inflation. This is time-series data—information on one entity (the USA) over time (1960 to last year).

Table 1.2 Time-Series Data

| Year | CONS Per Capita | INC Per Capita |
|------|-----------------|----------------|
| 1960 | $11,122 | $12,630 |
| 1961 | $11,166 | $12,860 |
| 1962 | $11,539 | $13,281 |
| 1963 | $11,843 | $13,583 |
| ⋮ | ⋮ | ⋮ |

Lastly, some data sets combine both cross-sectional and time-series data. If the same households were surveyed over the years, then we would have what is known as panel data—information across entities (households) and over time (1960 and 1961).

Table 1.3 Panel Data

| Year | Household | CONS | INC |
|------|-----------|------|-----|
| 1960 | 1 | $38,432 | $46,774 |
| 1961 | 1 | $40,573 | $47,314 |
| 1960 | 2 | $20,445 | $22,439 |
| 1961 | 2 | $19,294 | $23,471 |
| 1960 | 3 | $34,768 | $35,925 |
| 1961 | 3 | $34,631 | $36,112 |
| ⋮ | ⋮ | ⋮ | ⋮ |

Notice that Household 1 was surveyed in 1960 and 1961, as were Households 2, 3, and so on. Panel data sets have elements of cross-sectional and time-series data.

In any case, data collection involves obtaining a vector of data on CONS and a vector of data on INC. It is critical that the data match in the sense that if one vector is seasonally adjusted, then so is the other. If one vector is per capita, then so is the other.

A scattergram is a particular type of graph of the data set. Remember the econometric model of Keynes' law:

$$CONS = \beta_0 + \beta_1 \ INC + u$$

The variable on the left of the equality sign (CONS) is measured on the vertical axis. The other variable is measured on the horizontal axis. This scattergram uses the time-series data set on the USA from 1960. INC is real per capita disposable income. CONS is real per capita consumption spending.

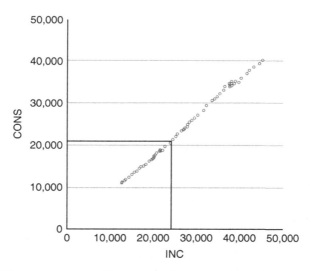

**Figure 1.1** The scattergram of income and consumer spending.

Each dot on the scattergram represents the CONS/INC combination for a particular year. The delineated observation is 1984 when INC was $24,014 and CONS was $20,535.

(4) Estimate the parameters of the model

In this step values for $\beta_0$ and $\beta_1$ are obtained. If a line was drawn through the points on the scattergram, $\beta_0$ would be the vertical intercept. $\beta_1$ is the slope of that line.

There are many possibilities for placing a line on the scattergram. For instance, one could simply draw a line freehand. This might be called the "freehand" technique. The value of $\beta_0$ could be read off the scattergram if graph paper were used. It is the vertical intercept. The slope of the line is $\beta_1$ and could be calculated.

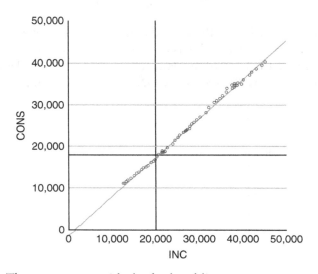

**Figure 1.2** The scattergram with the freehand line.

It appears as if the line may intersect the vertical axis at around $-1,000$. Therefore $\beta_0 = -1,000$.

The slope of this line, as calculated from the graph, is less than one. The slope of the line can be calculated by taking any two points on the line and forming the ratio of the change in the vertical distance over the change in the horizontal distance between those two points.

One point on the line has already been identified, CONS = $-1,000$ and INC = 0. This is the vertical intercept. A second point can be discerned by noticing that when INC = 20,000, coming up to the line and over to the vertical axis gives CONS = 18,000. The slope of a line is the vertical change between these two points divided by the horizontal change.

$$\text{Slope} = \beta_1 = \frac{\text{Vertical change}}{\text{Horizontal change}} = \frac{-1000 \text{ to } 18,000}{0 \text{ to } 20,000} = \frac{19,000}{20,000}$$

$$= 0.95$$

The freehand technique has estimated the parameters of the model to be $\beta_0 = -1,000$, and $\beta_1 = 0.95$. Therefore, the econometric model of Keynes' law of consumption is estimated to be:

$$\text{CONS} = -1,000 + 0.95 \text{ INC} + u$$

One problem with the freehand technique is that different people may see different lines. A more scientific approach is needed. Indeed, much of the next chapter will be concerned with developing such a technique—ordinary least squares.

(5) Test the theory, law, or hypothesis

Using ordinary least squares, rather than the freehand technique, to estimate $\beta_0$ and $\beta_1$, yields:

$$\text{CONS} = -1216 + 0.96 \text{ INC} + u$$

The results between the two techniques are not much different in this case. They verify Keynes' law of consumption because $\beta_1 = 0.96$, which is greater than zero but less than 1. The equation above makes it clear that if INC increased by $1, then CONS would be expected to increase by $0.96. The 0.96 is an estimate of the marginal propensity to consume in the United States. Given an extra dollar, the typical American will increase consumer spending by 96 cents.

It seems that Keynes was right about this. However, statisticians are very loath to "accept" theories. Instead, they would say this econometric study has "not rejected" the theory. If the analysis was done with data from another country or using a different data set, then the results would have been different. The new results could produce a $\beta_1$ that is greater than one or less than zero, which would reject Keynes' theory.

Another issue is that 0.96 seems quite close to 1. And 0.96 is merely an estimate, so it is possible that in reality the value of $\beta_1 = 1$. If so, it implies that when income increases, consumer spending increases just as much. Keynes' law is rejected since it states that if income increases, then consumer spending will increase by less.

There are statistical tests to determine if it is likely that the true $\beta_1 = 1$ when an econometric model yields a value of 0.96. These tests are a critical component of econometric research. When such a test is applied in this particular case, it suggests that the true $\beta_1 < 1$ and therefore Keynes' law is not rejected.

(6) Forecast with the model

An econometric model can be used to make predictions. For example, in 2010 INC was $32,335. Plugging that value into the model and assuming for the moment that u = 0:

$$\text{CONS} = -1216 + 0.96(\$32,335) + u = \$29,826$$

The predicted value of CONS is $29,826. The actual value of CONS in 2010 is $29,871. The forecast error is

$$
\begin{array}{cccc}
\text{Actual value} & - & \text{Predicted value} & = & u \\
\$29,871 & - & \$29,826 & = & \$45
\end{array}
$$

In 2010, u = $45, not 0. The econometric equation predicts a value that is $45 less than the actual value for CONS in 2010.

## MANY APPLICATIONS

The econometric methodology outlined in the chapter has been used to test an incredible array of theories and ideas. The popular book *Freakonomics* (Levitt and Dubner 2009) details some of the more exotic applications: Did legalization of abortion lower the crime rate? Is a backyard swimming pool more dangerous to little children than a gun? Do street-level drug dealers make less than the minimum wage?

Some of these issues do not appear to be within the realm of economics, but they are. Remember, economics is about how people make choices to maximize their satisfaction. All of the applications in Freakonomics concern people responding to incentives.

Many disciplines have adapted the econometric methodology to their own specific fields. Thus we have biometrics, psychometrics, sociometrics, and more. Sabermetrics is the analysis of baseball with this very same methodology. No matter the field or discipline, the object is to test hypotheses with statistical techniques.

## TERMS

Cross-sectional data—Information across entities at a point in time.

Econometrics—The empirical determination of economic laws, theories, and hypotheses.

Error term (residual or disturbance)—This variable is attached to the end of an econometric model. It captures the difference between the observed value of the Y-variable and the value predicted by the econometric model.

Ordinary least squares—A technique for estimating the structural parameters of an econometric model. This technique minimizes $\Sigma e_i^2$.

Panel data—Information across subjects and over time. It is a combination of cross-sectional and time-series data.

Scattergram—A chart showing observed values on two variables where one variable is measured on the vertical axis and the other variable is measured on the horizontal axis.

Time-series data—Information on one entity over time.

## CHAPTER 1 PROBLEMS

(1) Given the following regression: CONS = –1218 + 0.97 INC + u
  (A) What is the predicted value of CONS in 1960 given INC = $9,735 in 1960?
  (B) Actual CONS in 1960 equals $8,837. Give several reasons why the forecast may be off from the actual.

(2) Given the following regression: CONS = –1218 + 0.97 INC + u
  (A) What is the predicted value of CONS in 2005 given INC = $27,340 in 2005?
  (B) Actual CONS in 2005 equals $26,476. Give several reasons why the forecast may be off from the actual.

(3) (A) Specify an econometric model to test the theory that an increase in the money supply has no effect on real GDP.
  (B) What does this theory imply about the value of $\beta_1$?

(4) (A) Specify an econometric model to test the theory that an increase in the interest rate on automobile loans will lower car sales.
  (B) What does this theory imply about the value of $\beta_1$?

(5) A professor gathers data on student performance in college and the number of alcoholic drinks students consume to determine if alcohol consumption affects performance in college. Can this research be classified as econometrics? Explain why or why not.

(6) Data are collected on rainfall and temperature in the Bordeaux region of France to determine if weather can be used to predict the quality of the wine produced in a particular year. Can this research be classified as econometrics? Explain why or why not.

(7) Mark the following data sets cross-sectional, time-series, or panel data.

(A) Unemployment Rate in Various Nations in 1998

| Nation | Unemployment Rate |
|---|---|
| Albania | 10.7% |
| Algeria | 11.4% |
| Argentina | 11.4% |
| Armenia | 16.4% |
| ⋮ | ⋮ |

(B) Unemployment Rate in the USA

| Year | Unemployment Rate |
|---|---|
| 1960 | 5.5% |
| 1961 | 6.7% |
| 1962 | 5.6% |
| 1963 | 5.6% |
| ⋮ | ⋮ |

(8) Mark the following data sets cross-sectional, time-series, or panel data.

(A) Unemployment Rate in the USA in 1960

| Month | Unemployment Rate |
|---|---|
| JAN | 5.2% |
| FEB | 4.8% |
| MAR | 5.4% |
| APR | 5.2% |
| ⋮ | ⋮ |

(B) Unemployment Rates in US States in 1976

| State | Unemployment Rate |
| --- | --- |
| Alabama | 6.8% |
| Alaska | 7.5% |
| Arizona | 9.7% |
| Arkansas | 7.0% |
| ⋮ | ⋮ |

# 2 Simple Regression Analysis

## THE BASIC IDEA

Consider the hypothesis that X affects Y negatively—that is, when X increases, this generally causes Y to decrease, and when X decreases, this typically results in Y increasing. The econometric model to test this hypothesis might be:

$$Y = \beta_0 + \beta_1 X + u$$

If $\beta_1$ is negative, then the hypothesis is supported. An econometric model implies cause-and-effect. The notion being tested here is that a change in X causes a change in Y in the opposite direction.

The next step is to collect data on Y and X. Here are the data and a scattergram of them. Notice that the variable causing the effect, X, appears on the horizontal axis and the variable being affected, Y, appears on the vertical axis.

| X | Y |
|---|---|
| 1,514.567 | 11.20333 |
| 1,560.333 | 11.57667 |
| 1,593.433 | 12.83000 |
| 1,620.733 | 13.16333 |
| 1,664.600 | 13.98333 |

(*Continued*)

DOI: 10.4324/9781003213758-2

| X | Y |
|---|---|
| 1,694.067 | 14.92000 |
| 1,737.767 | 14.61667 |
| 1,777.133 | 15.01000 |
| 1,815.133 | 14.51000 |
| 1,849.000 | 13.75333 |
| 1,891.133 | 11.87667 |
| 1,994.133 | 11.84333 |
| 2,045.000 | 11.57000 |
| 2,076.933 | 12.34333 |
| 2,114.700 | 12.41000 |
| ⋮ | ⋮ |

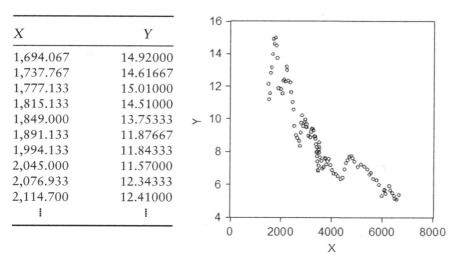

Figure 2.1 The scattergram of X and Y.

Fitting a straight line through the points on the scattergram amounts to the same thing as estimating $\beta_0$ and $\beta_1$ in the econometric model. $\beta_1$ is the slope of the line and $\beta_0$ is where the line touches the Y-axis.

The "freehand" technique roughs in a line by hand. Another possibility is to take the point furthest to the left on the scattergram and the point furthest to the right and draw a line connecting those two observations, ignoring all the other points. Both of these techniques are simple and easy to apply but lack rigor.

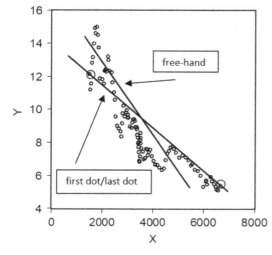

Figure 2.2 The freehand and first dot/last dot lines.

The first dot/last dot technique takes the observations farthest to the left and right and connects them. Those two observations are circled.

The freehand/freehand technique roughs in a line that fits well according to the person drawing it.

Neither the freehand nor the first dot/last dot method are adequate for econometric research. The preferred technique is to fit a line so that the vertical distances from the points to the line squared is minimized—that is, fit a line such that $\Sigma u^2$ is minimized.

Fitting a line that minimizes $\Sigma u^2$ is known as ordinary least squares. Before considering that technique and its merits, it is necessary to understand econometric notation.

## NOTATION

Although it may seem fussy, notation is important in econometrics. All of the subscripts, carets, and bars symbolize concepts. If the notation is incorrect it could cause confusion.

To test the notion that X affects Y negatively, we have written the following econometric model:

$$Y = \beta_0 + \beta_1 X + u$$

This equation is called the "econometric model," "structural equation," or "regression function."

Subscripts are typically added to indicate that this is the "*ith*" of n observations on X and Y:

$$Y_i = \beta_0 + \beta_1 X_i + u_i$$

The term $u_i$ indicates that there will be n error terms, where n is the number of observations. $Y_i$ is known as the "dependent variable" or "y-variable." $X_i$ is called the "independent variable" or the "x-variable." $\beta_0$ and $\beta_1$ are referred to as "structural parameters."

If it is possible to obtain all the data on Y and X, error-free, then $\beta_0$ and $\beta_1$ can be calculated using the formulas shown in the next section. However, in most instances only a sample of the observations on Y and X is available. Hopefully, the sample scattergram will be generally the same as the full-sample scattergram. It will have fewer observations and it is unlikely to yield the exact same values for $\beta_0$ and $\beta_1$ than the full sample. To indicate this situation, carets (^) are placed over the values that are mere estimates of the true values.

$$Y_i = \hat{\beta}_0 + \hat{\beta}_1 X_i + e_i$$

In addition, the $u_i$'s turn into $e_i$'s because the true error terms cannot be obtained without the true $\beta_0$ and $\beta_1$. Some econometricians reserve the term "errors" for the $u_i$'s and call the $e_i$'s "residuals" or "disturbances." Other econometricians are not so careful and use all three terms synonymously.

| Population Regression Function | Sample Regression Function |
| --- | --- |
| $Y_i = \beta_0 + \beta_1 X_i + u_i$ | $Y_i = \hat{\beta}_0 + \hat{\beta}_1 X_i + e_i$ |

$Y_i = \hat{\beta}_0 + \hat{\beta}_1 X_i + e_i$ is the "sample regression function" because it is based on a sample of the entire population of data on X and Y. Carets, often called hats, are placed over $\beta_0$ and $\beta_1$ to indicate that these are estimates, not their true values. The $e_i$'s are estimates of the $u_i$'s.

$Y_i = \beta_0 + \beta_1 X_i + u_i$ is the "population regression function." The true values of the structural parameters, $\beta_0$ and $\beta_1$, can only be obtained if all the data on Y and X are available.

Almost all the concepts in econometrics go by more than one name. This is exemplified by the sample regression function:

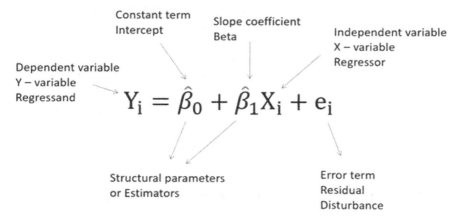

Figure 2.3 Terms used to describe econometric notation.

Yet another expression of an econometric model involves the predicted values of the dependent variable. Here the sample regression function is used to form predictions of $Y_i$:

$$\hat{Y}_i = \hat{\beta}_0 + \hat{\beta}_1 X_i$$

Since the residual is not included, the Yi's are not the actual values but the values predicted by the sample regression line. The caret over the Yi's indicates that they are predictions. The population regression line has predicted values as well:

$$\hat{Y}_i = \beta_0 + \beta_1 X_i$$

Most of the ideas tested in econometrics do not allow for population regressions functions. Consider the macroeconomic idea that lower interest rates cause increased spending by businesses on plant and equipment. A simple econometric model of this theory is:

$$INV_i = \beta_0 + \beta_1 INT_i + u_i$$

where INV is investment (business spending on plant and equipment) and INT is the interest rate on corporate bonds.

$\beta_1$ is negative if the theory is correct. To test if $\beta_1$ is indeed negative, suppose data on investment spending by 100 firms is obtained along with the interest rate each firm faces. Some firms will face lower interest rates because they are larger or more creditworthy. Other firms will face higher interest rates because of the industry or geographic region they operate within. However, it will be impossible to survey all the firms in the macroeconomy to which the research pertains. There are 100 observations in the sample data set.

Lacking data on the entire population means a sample regression function will be in hand and an estimate of $\beta_1$ can be obtained. This estimate is $\hat{\beta}_1$. It is unlikely that $\hat{\beta}_1$ will exactly equal $\beta_1$ because the sample scattergram has fewer observations. Hopefully, the sample scattergram will reflect the same general shape and splay of observations as the population scattergram. If so, then $\hat{\beta}_1$ will be a better estimator of $\beta_1$.

## THE ORDINARY LEAST SQUARES TECHNIQUE

Given a sample regression, the objective is to obtain values of $\hat{\beta}_0$ and $\hat{\beta}_1$ such that $\Sigma e_i^2$ is minimized. When a line is fit with this criterion in mind, it is called "ordinary least squares." This amounts to fitting a line between the observations on a scattergram so that the squared vertical distances from the points to the line are minimized. $\hat{\beta}_0$ is the vertical intercept of the line and $\hat{\beta}_1$ is its slope.

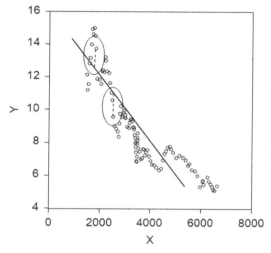

**Figure 2.4** The ordinary least squares line.

Ordinary least squares is fitting a line such that the sum of the squared vertical distances from the line to each observation are minimized:

$$\text{Minimize } \Sigma e_i^2$$

Two highlighted observations show their vertical distances from the regression line.

The equation of the regression line is

$$\hat{Y}_i = \hat{\beta}_0 + \hat{\beta}_1 X_i$$

$\hat{\beta}_0$ is the vertical intercept and $\hat{\beta}_1$ is the slope of the regression line.

There are good reasons for choosing to calculate $\hat{\beta}_0$ and $\hat{\beta}_1$ so that $\Sigma e_i^2$ is minimized. Certainly, this criterion is more rigorous than the freehand technique and does not waste as much data as the first dot/last dot method. The salient qualities of the ordinary least squares line will be pointed out in later chapters. At this point two advantages will be mentioned.

The ordinary least squares line is unique. Only one line will minimize $\Sigma e_i^2$. This is not true of some other criteria such as calculating $\hat{\beta}_0$ and $\hat{\beta}_1$ so that $\Sigma e_i = 0$. It turns out that there are an infinite number of lines that would fit this latter criterion in any given situation. The distances of the observations that lie above the line are positive distances. The distances of the observations that lie below the line are negative distances. An infinite number of lines can be placed so that the positive distances exactly match the negative distances and $\Sigma e_i = 0$.

With the ordinary least squares method all the distances from the line become positive because they are first squared. It is not possible for $\Sigma e_i^2$ to equal zero unless all the observations lie on the regression line. The ordinary least squares line not only minimizes $\Sigma e_i^2$ but also is one of the infinite lines that have $\Sigma e_i = 0$.

Another possibility is to fit the line so that $\Sigma|e_i|$ is minimized. Once again, all the distances become positive, and it is impossible for $\Sigma|e_i|$ to equal zero unless all the observations lie on the line. In most cases this criterion will yield a unique line. Unfortunately, the resulting estimates of $\hat{\beta}_0$ and $\hat{\beta}_1$ will not have the desirable statistical properties of the ordinary least squares estimates.

The ordinary least squares technique is easy to implement. In order to fit a line such that $\Sigma e_i^2$ is minimized, all one needs to do is calculate

$$\hat{\beta}_0 = \overline{Y} - \hat{\beta}_1 \overline{X}$$

and

$$\hat{\beta}_1 = \frac{\Sigma(X_i - \overline{X})Y_i}{\Sigma(X_i - \overline{X})^2}$$

In these formulas $\overline{Y}$ and $\overline{X}$ refer to the means of Y and X, respectively. $\hat{\beta}_0$ is the vertical intercept and $\hat{\beta}_1$ is the slope of a line that minimizes $\Sigma e_i^2$. The formulas shown here are derived in an appendix to this chapter. Let's put the formulas to work.

Consider the hypothesis that grade point average (GPA) is affected by the amount of time a student spends studying (HOURS). An econometric model of this hypothesis is:

$$GPA_i = \hat{\beta}_0 + \hat{\beta}_1\ HOURS_i + e_i$$

To keep the calculations to a minimum the sample has only three students: n = 3. Here are the data and the scattergram:

| Student | GPA | HOURS |
|---------|-----|-------|
| 1 | 2 | 2 |
| 2 | 3 | 4 |
| 3 | 3 | 2 |

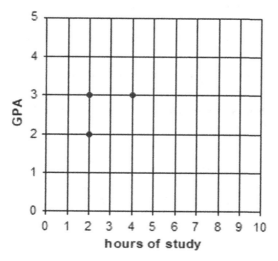

**Figure 2.5** The scattergram of hours of study and GPA.

First calculate the numerator of

$$\hat{\beta}_1 = \frac{\Sigma(X_i - \bar{X})Y_i}{\Sigma(X_i - \bar{X})^2}$$

$$\Sigma(X_i - \bar{X})Y_i = (2–2.667)(2) + (4–2.667)(3) + (2–2.667)(3) = 0.667$$

Now the denominator of the equation:

$$\Sigma(X_i - \bar{X})^2 = (2–2.667)^2 + (4–2.667)^2 + (2–2.667)^2 = 2.667$$

So that:

$$\hat{\beta}_1 = \frac{\Sigma(X_i - \bar{X})Y_i}{\Sigma(X_i - \bar{X})^2} = \frac{0.667}{2.667} = 0.25$$

Now plug the value of $\hat{\beta}_1 = 0.25$, into $\hat{\beta}_0 = \bar{Y} - \hat{\beta}_1\bar{X}$:

$$\hat{\beta}_0 = \bar{Y} - \hat{\beta}_1\bar{X} = 2.667–0.25(2.667) = 2.0$$

The regression results can be reported as

$$GPA_i = 2.0 + 0.25\ HOURS_i + e_i$$

The structural parameters can be interpreted as follows:

$\hat{\beta}_0$ = 2.0—A student who reports 0 study hours is expected to have a
   GPA equal to 2.0.
$\hat{\beta}_1$ = 0.25—If hours increases by 1 unit, then GPA is expected to
   increase by 0.25 units.

$\hat{\beta}_0$ is the vertical intercept and $\hat{\beta}_1$ is the slope of the regression line:

| Student | GPA | HOURS |
|---------|-----|-------|
| 1 | 2 | 2 |
| 2 | 3 | 4 |
| 3 | 3 | 2 |

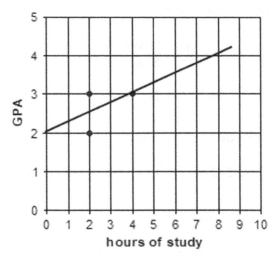

**Figure 2.6** The ordinary least squares regression line.

The three residuals can be calculated by re-writing

$$GPA_i = 2.0 + 0.25\ HOURS_i + e_i$$

as

$$e_i = GPA_i - 2.0 - 0.25\ HOURS_i$$

Then

$$e_1 = 2 - 2.0-0.25(2) = -0.5$$
$$e_2 = 4 - 2.0-0.25(3) = 0.0$$
$$e_3 = 2 - 2.0-0.25(3) = \underline{0.5}$$
$$0.0$$

As mentioned previously, $\Sigma e_i = 0$. The $\Sigma e_i^2 = -0.5^2 + 0.0^2 + 0.5^2 = 0.5$. How do we know that there is not another line that yields a lower $\Sigma e_i^2$? Because the formulas for $\hat{\beta}_0$ and $\hat{\beta}_1$ were derived, they would minimize $\Sigma e_i^2$. The derivation of these formulas in the appendix makes it clear that this line is unique.

## EXAMPLE: ECONOMIC PERFORMANCE AND CORRUPTION

To test the hypothesis that corruption negatively affects a nation's economic performance, consider the following econometric model:

$$GDP_i = \hat{\beta}_0 + \hat{\beta}_1 COR_i + e_i$$

COR measures corruption in a nation on a scale of 0 (least) to 10 (most) and GDP measures output in dollars per capita. The data set is cross-sectional with $n = 4$:

| Nation | COR | GDP |
|--------|-----|------|
| Brazil | 5.9 | 6,100 |
| Bulgaria | 6.7 | 4,100 |
| Chile | 3.1 | 12,500 |
| China | 6.6 | 3,600 |

Applying the ordinary least squares formulas, we obtain:

$$\hat{\beta}_1 = \frac{\Sigma(X_i - \bar{X})Y_i}{\Sigma(X_i - \bar{X})^2} = \frac{-20,652.5}{8.55} = -2,416.20$$

$$\hat{\beta}_0 = \bar{Y} - \hat{\beta}_1\bar{X} = 6,575-(-2,416.20)(5.58) = 20,045.33$$

The structural parameters of the model are now estimated and can be filled in:

$$GDP_i = 20,045.33 - 2,416.20 \ COR_i + e_i$$

The negative value for $\hat{\beta}_1$ indicates that COR and GDP are negatively related. More specifically,

$\hat{\beta}_1 = -2,416.20$ may be interpreted as follows:

When COR increases by 1 unit, GDP is expected to decrease by 2,416.20 units.

$\hat{\beta}_0 = 20,045.33$ is interpreted as follows:

When COR = 0, GDP is expected to equal 20,045.33 units.

The four residuals of this model are calculated to be:

$e_i = Y_i - \hat{Y}_i = Y_i - (\hat{\beta}_0 + \hat{\beta}_1 \ X_i) = 6100 - (20045.33 + (-2416.20 \times 5.9))$

$\quad = 310.27$

$e_i = Y_i - \hat{Y}_i = Y_i - (\hat{\beta}_0 + \hat{\beta}_1 \ X_i) = 4100 - (20045.33 + (-2416.20 \times 6.7))$

$\quad = 243.23$

$e_i = Y_i - \hat{Y}_i = Y_i - (\hat{\beta}_0 + \hat{\beta}_1 \ X_i) = 012500 - (20045.33 + (-2416.20 \times 3.1))$

$\quad = -55.10$

$e_i = Y_i - \hat{Y}_i = Y_i - (\hat{\beta}_0 + \hat{\beta}_1 \ X_i) = 3600 - (20045.33 + (-2416.20 \times 6.6))$

$\quad = -498.39$

The residuals sum to zero as is the case with every ordinary least squares line. Proportionally speaking, these residuals are rather small. What causes the residuals to be large or small? The residuals are the result of the following four categories of factors:

(1) Important variables excluded—There are many variables that affect GDP per capita in a given nation. The money supply and fiscal policy come to mind. The effects of monetary and fiscal policy are captured in the residuals. Not accounting for these important factors results in larger disturbances.

(2) Randomness—Even if no important variables are omitted from consideration, large disturbances occur when the dependent variable is erratic. For example, it is extremely difficult to predict daily changes in stock prices. They have a large random component. This will lead to larger residuals.

(3) Measurement error—If errors were made when measuring COR or GDP, then larger residuals will result. COR and GDP are measures that are estimated. To the extent that these estimates are poor, we can expect larger error terms.

(4) Minor variables excluded—Undoubtedly, many minor factors impact GDP in a given nation. For instance, whether particular holidays fall on the weekend can affect production and GDP. Hopefully, these often-immeasurable forces will cancel each other out. To the extent that they do not, larger regression disturbances will result.

## A NOTE ON ECONOMETRIC SOFTWARE

The calculations in this chapter are only reasonable because the number of observations is small. When n becomes larger than four or five, calculating $\hat{\beta}_1$ becomes cumbersome. Fortunately, there is software programmed to do exactly these types of calculations.

Standard econometric software packages can easily handle all of the calculations and techniques presented throughout this textbook. Some packages are free, some have lower-priced student versions, and some are expensive. Some of the programs are more sophisticated, but that usually means they are more complicated to use. Standard spreadsheet programs can calculate $\hat{\beta}_0$ and $\hat{\beta}_1$, but most of the other concepts presented going forward will require a dedicated statistical package.

Part of learning econometrics is learning to use one of these software packages. Indeed, the ability to operate an econometrics package and interpret the results is a valuable skill.

## TERMS

Dependent variable (Y-variable)—In an econometric model, this variable appears to the left of the equality sign. It is affected by the independent variable.

Econometric model (structural equation or regression equation)—A mathematical expression that captures the essence of the cause-and-effect relationship between two variables.

Error term (residual or disturbance)—This variable is attached to the end of an econometric model. It captures the difference between the observed value of the Y-variable and the value predicted by the econometric model.

Independent variable (X-variable)—In an econometric model, this variable appears to the right of the equality sign. It is affected by the dependent variable.

Normal equation—An equation that comes up in the derivation of the formulas for the ordinary least squares estimators.

Ordinary least squares—A technique for estimating the structural parameters of an econometric model. This technique minimizes $\Sigma e_i^2$.

Population regression function—An econometric model estimated with error-free data that includes the entire population of interest.

Sample regression function—An econometric model estimated from sample data.

Stochastic variable—A variable that can take on different values depending on the sample data. $\hat{\beta}_0$ and $\hat{\beta}_1$ are stochastic variables, as are the $e_i$'s.

Structural parameter—In an econometric model, $\hat{\beta}_0$ and $\hat{\beta}_1$ are the structural parameters.

## CHAPTER 2 PROBLEMS

(1) Which of the following is (are) NOT correct?

| | | |
|---|---|---|
| (A) $Y_i = \beta_0 + \beta_1 X_i + e_i$ | (D) $Y_i = \hat{\beta}_0 + \hat{\beta}_1 X_i + e_i$ | (G) $Y_i = \beta_0 + \beta_1 X_i$ |
| (B) $\hat{Y}_i = \beta_0 + \beta_1 X_i + e_i$ | (E) $\hat{Y}_i = \hat{\beta}_0 + \hat{\beta}_1 X_i + e_i$ | (H) $\hat{Y}_i = \beta_0 + \beta_1 X_i + u_i$ |
| (C) $Y_i = \beta_0 + \beta_1 X_i + u_i$ | (F) $Y_i = \hat{\beta}_0 + \hat{\beta}_1 X_i + u_i$ | (I) $\hat{Y}_i = \hat{\beta}_0 + \hat{\beta}_1 X_i$ |

(2) Which of the following is (are) NOT correct?

| | | |
|---|---|---|
| (A) $Y_i = \beta_0 + \beta_1 X_i + u_i$ | (D) $Y_i = \hat{\beta}_0 + \hat{\beta}_1 X_i + u_i$ | (G) $Y_i = \beta_0 + \beta_1 X_i$ |
| (B) $\hat{Y}_i = \beta_0 + \beta_1 X_i + u_i$ | (E) $\hat{Y}_i = \hat{\beta}_0 + \hat{\beta}_1 X_i + u_i$ | (H) $\hat{Y}_i = \beta_0 + \beta_1 X_i + e_i$ |
| (C) $Y_i = \beta_0 + \beta_1 X_i + e_i$ | (F) $Y_i = \hat{\beta}_0 + \hat{\beta}_1 X_i + e_i$ | (I) $\hat{Y}_i = \beta_0 + \beta_1 X_i$ |

(3) The savings (Sav) and number of children (Child) of four families are given below:

| Child | Sav |
|-------|-------|
| 2 | 0.03 |
| 2 | 0.874 |
| 0 | 0.374 |
| 1 | 1.2 |

(A) Calculate the values of $\hat{\beta}_0$ and $\hat{\beta}_1$ so that $\Sigma e_i^2$ is minimized for $sav_i = \hat{\beta}_0 + \hat{\beta}_1 \, child_i + e_i$

(B) Interpret the values you obtained.

(C) Sketch the ordinary least squares line in the graph.

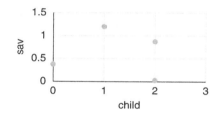

(4) The hours of preparation (Prep) and exam scores (Exam) of four students are given below:

| Prep | Exam |
|------|------|
| 1 | 70 |
| 3 | 80 |
| 1 | 80 |
| 3 | 90 |

(A) Calculate the values of $\hat{\beta}_0$ and $\hat{\beta}_1$ so that $\Sigma e_i^2$ is minimized for $exam_i = \hat{\beta}_0 + \hat{\beta}_1 \, prep_i + e_i$

(B) Interpret the values you obtained.

(C) Sketch the ordinary least squares line in the graph.

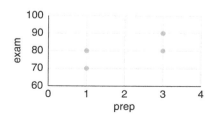

(5) (A) Calculate the values of the structural parameters for a regression of X on Y given:

| Y | X |
|---|---|
| 1.8 | 2 |
| 1.7 | 5 |
| 1.5 | -2 |
| 0.6 | 5 |
| 25.4 | 6 |

(B) Calculate the five $e_i$'s and show that the $\Sigma e_i^2 = 0$ in this case.

(6) (A) Calculate the values of the structural parameters for a regression of X on Y given:

| Y | X |
|---|---|
| 1.8 | 1.2 |
| 1.7 | -8.4 |
| 1.5 | 4.8 |
| 0.6 | 3.5 |
| 25.4 | 2.2 |

(B) Calculate the five $e_i$'s and show that the $\Sigma e_i^2 = 0$ in this case.

(7) Distinguish between the population regression function and the sample regression function.

(8) Mark the following statements TRUE or FALSE:

(A) When a line is fit to observations on a scattergram so that $\Sigma e_i^2$ is minimized, then $\Sigma e_i = 0$.

(B) When a line is fit to observations on a scattergram so that $\Sigma e_i^2$ is minimized, then sometimes more than one line meets this criterion.

(C) An infinite number of lines meet the criterion that $\Sigma e_i^2 = 0$.

(D) An infinite number of lines meet the criterion that $\Sigma e_i = 0$.

## APPENDIX TO CHAPTER 2

## DERIVING THE ORDINARY LEAST SQUARES ESTIMATORS

Given $Y_i = \hat{\beta}_0 + \hat{\beta}_1 X_i + e_i$ minimize $\Sigma e_i^2$

Since $e_i = Y_i - \hat{\beta}_0 - \hat{\beta}_1 X_i$ minimize $\Sigma(Y_i - \hat{\beta}_0 - \hat{\beta}_1 X_i)^2$

To find the equations for $\hat{\beta}_0$ and $\hat{\beta}_1$ that minimize $\Sigma(Y_i - \hat{\beta}_0 - \hat{\beta}_1 X_i)^2$, take the partial derivative with respect to $\hat{\beta}_0$ and set it equal to zero:

$$\frac{\partial \Sigma(Y_i - \hat{\beta}_0 - \hat{\beta}_1 X_i)^2}{\partial \hat{\beta}_0} = 2\Sigma(Y_i - \hat{\beta}_0 - \hat{\beta}_1 X_i)(-1) = 0$$

Dividing both sides of this equation by $-2$ leaves $\Sigma(Y_i - \hat{\beta}_0 - \hat{\beta}_1 X_i) = 0$

Distribute the summation sign: $\Sigma Y_i - n\hat{\beta}_0 - \hat{\beta}_1 \Sigma X_i = 0$; n is number of observations i.

Move the second and third terms to the other side: $\Sigma Y_i = n\hat{\beta}_0 + \hat{\beta}_1 \Sigma X_i$

The result is known as a "normal equation."

Repeat the process only this time with respect to $\hat{\beta}_1$. Begin by taking the partial derivative of the expression we wish to minimize with respect to $\hat{\beta}_1$ and set it equal to zero:

$$\frac{\partial \Sigma(Y_i - \hat{\beta}_0 - \hat{\beta}_1 X_i)^2}{\partial \hat{\beta}_1} = 2\Sigma(Y_i - \hat{\beta}_0 - \hat{\beta}_1 X_i)(-X_i) = 0$$

Divide both sides of this equation by $-2$: $\Sigma(Y_i - \hat{\beta}_0 - \hat{\beta}_1 X_i)(X_i) = 0$

Distribute $X_i$ and the summation sign: $\Sigma Y_i X_i - \hat{\beta}_0 \Sigma X_i - \hat{\beta}_1 \Sigma X_i^2 = 0$

Move the second and third terms to the other side: $\Sigma Y_i X_i = \hat{\beta}_0 \Sigma X_i + \hat{\beta}_1 \Sigma X_i^2$

The result is known as a "normal equation."

There are two normal equations and two unknowns, $\hat{\beta}_0$ and $\hat{\beta}_1$. The first normal equation can be solved for $\hat{\beta}_0$:

$$\Sigma Y_i = n\hat{\beta}_0 + \hat{\beta}_1 \Sigma X_i$$

$$n\hat{\beta}_0 = \Sigma Y_i - \hat{\beta}_1 \Sigma X_i$$

$$\hat{\beta}_0 = \frac{\Sigma Y_i - \hat{\beta}_1 \Sigma X_i}{n} = \bar{Y} - \hat{\beta}_1 \bar{X}$$

This result can be substituted into the second normal equation, which is then solved for $\hat{\beta}_1$:

$$\Sigma Y_i X_i = \hat{\beta}_0 \Sigma X_i + \hat{\beta}_1 \Sigma X_i^2$$

$$\Sigma Y_i X_i = (\bar{Y} - \hat{\beta}_1 \bar{X}) \Sigma X_i + \hat{\beta}_1 \Sigma X_i^2$$

Distribute the $\Sigma X_i$: $\Sigma Y_i X_i = \bar{Y}\Sigma X_i - \hat{\beta}_1 \bar{X}\Sigma X_i + \hat{\beta}_1 \Sigma X_i^2$

Now factor the last two terms on the right: $\Sigma Y_i X_i = \bar{Y}\Sigma X_i + \hat{\beta}_1 (\Sigma X_i^2 - \bar{X}\Sigma X_i)$

Rearrange the terms: $\hat{\beta}_1 (\Sigma X_i^2 - \bar{X}\Sigma X_i) = \Sigma Y_i X_i - \bar{Y}\Sigma X_i$

To isolate $\hat{\beta}_1$, divide both sides by

$$(\Sigma X_i^2 - \bar{X}\Sigma X_i): \hat{\beta}_1 = \frac{\Sigma Y_i X_i - \bar{Y}\Sigma X_i}{\Sigma X_i^2 - \bar{X}\Sigma X_i}$$

A more convenient expression for $\hat{\beta}_1$ is:

$\hat{\beta}_1 = \dfrac{\Sigma(X_i - \bar{X})Y_i}{\Sigma(X_i - \bar{X})^2}$ which is equivalent to the expression for $\hat{\beta}_1$

derived earlier.

# ALGEBRA OF SUMMATION SIGNS

Most students have had little experience doing algebra when summation signs ($\Sigma$) are involved. Only a few rules are required to get through all the derivations and proofs in this book.

**FOILing:** To expand the following expression: $\Sigma(X_i - \bar{X})(Y_i - \bar{Y})$ FOIL it out. FOIL stands for First; Outer; Inner; Last.

$$\Sigma(X_i - \bar{X})(Y_i - \bar{Y}) = \Sigma(X_i Y_i - X_i \bar{Y} - \bar{X} Y_i + \bar{X}\bar{Y})$$

**Distribution:** To distribute the summation sign through the parentheses in the following expression: $\Sigma(X_i Y_i - X_i \bar{Y} - \bar{X} Y_i + \bar{X}\bar{Y})$

Bring the summation sign before each of the four terms: $\Sigma X_i Y_i - \Sigma X_i \bar{Y} - \Sigma \bar{X} Y_i + \Sigma \bar{X}\bar{Y}$

The first term ($\Sigma X_i Y_i$) cannot be simplified further. It signifies multiplying each $X_i$ by the corresponding $Y_i$ and then summing up all the products.

The second term ($\Sigma X_i \bar{Y}$) may be re-written as $\bar{Y}\Sigma X_i$. This is because a constant ($\bar{Y}$ is the mean of the $Y_i$'s) can be pulled out and placed before the summation sign.

Similarly, the third term ($\Sigma \bar{X} Y_i$) becomes $\bar{X}\Sigma Y_i$.

The fourth term ($\Sigma \bar{X}\bar{Y}$) makes no sense. It requires the summation of the product of two constants ($\bar{X}\bar{Y}$). There is nothing to sum up. In cases like this, where the summation sign is placed before a constant or constants alone, it turns into an "n," where n is the number of observations. The fourth term becomes $n\bar{X}\bar{Y}$.

In summary, the summation sign may be distributed through the parentheses in

$\Sigma(X_i Y_i - X_i \bar{Y} - \bar{X} Y_i + \bar{X}\bar{Y})$ to obtain $\Sigma X_i Y_i - \bar{Y}\Sigma X_i - \bar{X}\Sigma Y_i + n\bar{X}\bar{Y}$

**Substitution:** The expression $\Sigma X_i Y_i - \bar{Y}\Sigma X_i - \bar{X}\Sigma Y_i + n\bar{X}\bar{Y}$ can be simplified further by making some substitutions. $\Sigma X_i$ is equal to $n\bar{X}$. Using this substitution, the second term in the expression becomes $\bar{Y}n\bar{X}$. The third term becomes $\bar{X}n\bar{Y}$. This results in: $\Sigma X_i Y_i - \bar{Y}n\bar{X} - \bar{X}n\bar{Y} + n\bar{X}\bar{Y}$.

**Cancellation:** Notice that the last three terms in the expression $\Sigma X_i Y_i - \bar{Y}n\bar{X} - \bar{X}n\bar{Y} + n\bar{X}\bar{Y}$ are equivalent. One of the two negative terms will cancel the fourth term, which is positive, leaving $\Sigma X_i Y_i - \bar{Y}n\bar{X}$.

# 3 Residual Statistics

## MEASURES OF GOODNESS-OF-FIT

The ordinary least squares technique fits a line that minimizes the squared distances from the observed data points. Econometricians want to know if the line runs close to most of the data points or not. Is the fit snug or at least adequate for testing the idea under consideration?

Econometric software can plot the scattergram and the regression line. However, graphs can be deceiving because scaling can make even a good fit look poor or a poor fit appear adequate.

Graphically the regression from the last example in Chapter 2 appears to have rather small residuals. The vertical distances from the dots (observations) to the regression line appear minuscule.

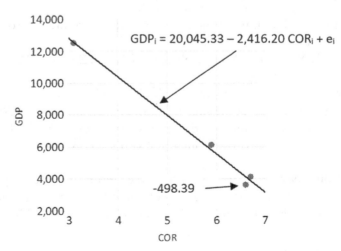

Figure 3.1 The scattergram COR and GDP with regression line.

DOI: 10.4324/9781003213758-3

While this example appears to have larger errors:

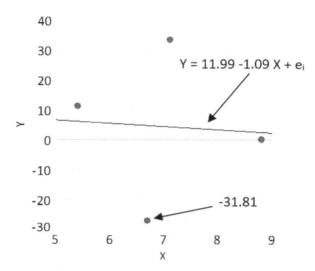

Figure 3.2 The scattergram X and Y with regression line.

But these diagrams can be deceptive because of the scaling. The largest residual in the top diagram is –498.39, while the largest residual in the bottom diagram is smaller at –31.81. On the other hand, –31.81 is farther away from its regression line in percentage terms than –431.39 is from its line. It is not clear that the graphs can be trusted.

It would be useful to have a statistic that discerns when the errors are small (a good fit) or large (a poor fit). There are several popular statistics for this purpose. We will discuss two of them.

$$\text{Standard Error of the Regression (SER)} = \hat{\sigma} = \sqrt{\frac{\Sigma e_i^2}{n - 2}}$$

This statistic is an estimate of the average absolute distance of an observation from the population regression line. The population regression line is unknown. Nevertheless, it is possible to estimate if the data points are scattered relatively close to that unknown line or not. The SER is such an estimate.

In the top diagram, the SER equals 451.03. For the bottom diagram, the SER equals 30.75. However, 451.03 is not large considering it is the residual when estimating the Y-variable that averages around 6,000. The SER of 30.75 is quite large considering the scale of the Y-variable in that regression is around 17. In other words, the thing being predicted (the Y-variable) is around 17 and the predictions of the econometric model are typically off by 30.75.

The SER is useful only when compared to the magnitude of the dependent variable. If the SER of a given regression equals 451.03, there is no way of assessing if this is large or small unless it is put in relation to something else. A rule of thumb is if the SER is less than half of the mean of the absolute value of the dependent variable, then the fit is adequate.

The first diagram represents an adequate fit since the SER < ½ the absolute value of the mean of GDP, which is 6,575. The interpretation here is that the typical distance of an observation from the population regression line is 451.03. This is rather small given that the dependent variable has a mean of 6,575.

The second diagram represents a poor fit since the SER > ½ the absolute value of the mean of Y, which is 17.93. The interpretation in this case is that the typical distance of an observation from the population regression line is 30.75. However, 30.75 is rather large given that the absolute value of the dependent variable is centered on 17.93.

The second measure of goodness-of-fit is the coefficient of determination.

$$\text{Coefficient of Determination } (r^2) \quad r^2 = 1 - \frac{\Sigma e_i^2}{\Sigma(Y_i - \bar{Y})^2}$$

The coefficient of determination (or r-squared) is the most popular measure of goodness-of-fit. It ranges between 0 and 1, where 1 is a perfect fit and zero is a horizontal regression line through random observations at $\bar{Y}$.

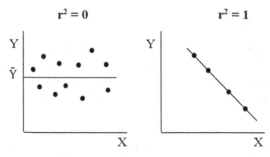

**Figure 3.3** Examples of $r^2 = 0$ and $r^2 = 1$.

Going back to the two drawings at the beginning of this chapter and depicted here, the first has an $r^2 = 0.99$. The interpretation is 99% of the variation in GDP is explained by COR. The second drawing has an $r^2 = 0.004$; only 0.4% of the variation in Y is explained by X.

Both the SER and $r^2$ give the same indication: the regression between COR and GDP has an adequate or very good fit, while the regression of Y on X has a poor fit.

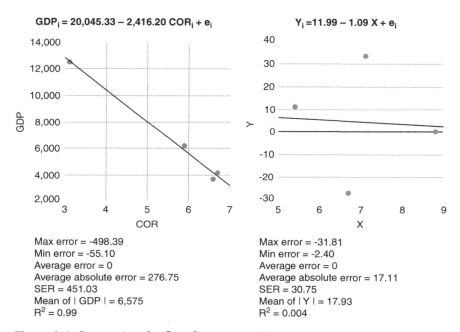

$$GDP_i = 20,045.33 - 2,416.20\ COR_i + e_i$$

$$Y_i = 11.99 - 1.09\ X + e_i$$

Max error = -498.39
Min error = -55.10
Average error = 0
Average absolute error = 276.75
SER = 451.03
Mean of | GDP | = 6,575
$R^2 = 0.99$

Max error = -31.81
Min error = -2.40
Average error = 0
Average absolute error = 17.11
SER = 30.75
Mean of | Y | = 17.93
$R^2 = 0.004$

**Figure 3.4** Comparing the fits of two regressions.

It can be disappointing to discover that a regression line has a poor fit. If the SER is large or $r^2$ is low, it may seem like the econometric model is not working well. That may indeed be the case. The residuals are the portion of the Y-variable that is not explained by the X-variable.

However, some Y-variables are rather erratic and very difficult to predict. In these situations, obtaining an $r^2$ of 0.09 may be excellent compared to what other researchers have been able to achieve. What makes for an adequate fit depends on the nature of the idea being tested.

## THE STANDARD ERRORS OF $\hat{\beta}_0$ AND $\hat{\beta}_1$

$\hat{\beta}_0$ and $\hat{\beta}_1$ vary in repeated sampling. Imagine gathering sample data on Y and X and calculating $\hat{\beta}_0$ and $\hat{\beta}_1$. Now gather another random sample on Y and X from the same population and re-run the regression. It would be highly unlikely to get the exact same values for $\hat{\beta}_0$ and $\hat{\beta}_1$. As new samples are used to run regression after regression, how much do $\hat{\beta}_0$ and $\hat{\beta}_1$ vary? The standard error of $\hat{\beta}_0$ is an estimate of how much $\hat{\beta}_0$ typically varies in repeated sampling.

$$\text{Standard Error of } \hat{\beta}_0 = SE(\hat{\beta}_0) = \sqrt{\frac{\hat{\sigma}^2 \Sigma X_i^2}{n\Sigma(X_i - \bar{X})^2}} \, ;$$

$$\text{where } \hat{\sigma}^2 = \frac{\Sigma e_i^2}{n-2} = SER^2$$

Similarly, the standard error of $\hat{\beta}_1$ is an estimate of how much $\hat{\beta}_1$ typically varies in repeated sampling.

$$\text{Standard Error of } \hat{\beta}_1 = SE(\hat{\beta}_1) = \sqrt{\frac{\hat{\sigma}^2}{\Sigma(X_i - \bar{X})^2}} \, ;$$

$$\text{where } \hat{\sigma}^2 = \frac{\Sigma e_i^2}{n-2} = SER^2$$

Going back to the example of corruption's impact on economic growth, the results can now be reported more fully:

---

$$GDP_i = 20{,}045.33 - 2{,}416.20 \ COR_i + e_i$$
$$(889.14) \quad (154.27) \qquad \leftarrow \text{ standard errors}$$
$$SER = 451.03 \quad |G\bar{D}P| = 6{,}575.00 \quad r^2 = 0.99 \quad n = 4$$

COR measures corruption in a nation on a scale of 0 (least) to 10 (most).
GDP measures output in dollars per capita.

$\hat{\beta}_0 = 20{,}045.33$: If COR = 0, then GDP is expected to equal 20,045.33.

$\hat{\beta}_1 = -2{,}416.20$: If COR increases 1 unit, then GDP is expected to decrease 2,416.20 units.

$SE(\hat{\beta}_0) = 889.14$: In repeated sampling, $\hat{\beta}_0$ is expected to vary 889.14 on average.

$SE(\hat{\beta}_1) = 154.27$: In repeated sampling, $\hat{\beta}_1$ is expected to vary 154.27 on average.

---

SER = 451.03: The typical distance of an observation from the true regression line is expected to be 451.03.

$\overline{|GDP|}$ = 6, 575.00: The absolute mean of GDP is 6,575.00 indicating the fit of the regression is adequate since the SER is less than half this amount.

$r^2$ = 0.99: 99% of the variation in GDP is explained by COR.

n = 4: Four observations were used to estimate the regression model.

These results indicate that $\hat{\beta}_0$, which is an estimate of $\beta_0$, equals 20,045.33. However, if the regression was run repeatedly with new data from the same population, $\hat{\beta}_0$ can be expected to vary by 889.14 on average. This does not mean that $\hat{\beta}_0$ cannot come out to be zero in one of the regressions, but that would be a surprise since $\hat{\beta}_0$ typically varies by 889.13 in repeated sampling and its estimated value is 20,045.33.

$\hat{\beta}_1$, which is an estimate of $\beta_1$, equals –2,416.20 with a standard error of 154.27. In repeated sampling, $\hat{\beta}_1$ is expected to vary on average by 154.27.

The regression has an SER equal to 451.03, indicating an adequate fit since the SER < ½ the mean of $|$ GDP $|$. $r^2$ is equal to 0.99, which means 99% of the variation in GDP is explained by COR. Finally, n = 4 says four data points were used to estimate all these statistics.

## REPEATED SAMPLING

The concept of repeated sampling will be used extensively going forward. It is the notion that the structural parameters, $\hat{\beta}_0$ and $\hat{\beta}_1$, could be estimated tens of thousands of times using fresh data from the same population each time. The values obtained each time would be different, unless lightning strikes in the form of sheer coincidence. That is what it is meant by the term "stochastic": $\hat{\beta}_0$ and $\hat{\beta}_1$ vary in repeated sampling. They are stochastic parameters.

The interpretations of the $SE(\hat{\beta}_0)$ and $SE(\hat{\beta}_1)$ involve repeated sampling. If the $SE(\hat{\beta}_1)$ = 154.27, then in repeated sampling, $\hat{\beta}_1$ is expected to vary on average by 154.27.

## TERMS

Coefficient of determination ($r^2$)—A statistic that measures how well a regression line fits the data.

Repeated sampling—Estimating the structural parameters of a regression over and over with fresh data each time.

Standard error of an estimator—A statistic that estimates the amount a structural parameter will vary on average in repeated sampling.

Standard error of the regression (SER)—A statistic that represents the typical distance of an observation from the population regression line.

Stochastic parameter—An estimator that will obtain different values in repeated sampling.

## CHAPTER 3 PROBLEMS

(1) (A) Calculate the values of the structural parameters for a regression of X on Y given:

(B) Interpret the value you obtained for the intercept.

(C) Interpret the value you obtained for the slope coefficient.

(D) Calculate $r^2$ for this regression.

(E) Interpret the value of $r^2$ for this regression.

(F) Calculate the SER for this regression.

| Y | X |
|---|---|
| 1.8 | 2 |
| 1.7 | 5 |
| 1.5 | -2 |
| 0.6 | 5 |
| 25.4 | 6 |

(G) Interpret the value of the SER for this regression.

(H) Calculate the standard error of the intercept term.

(I) Interpret the standard error of the intercept term.

(J) Calculate the standard error of the slope coefficient.

(K) Interpret the standard error of the slope coefficient.

(2) (A) Calculate the values of the structural parameters for a regression of X on Y given:

(B) Interpret the value you obtained for the intercept.

(C) Interpret the value you obtained for the slope coefficient.

(D) Calculate $r^2$ for this regression.

(E) Interpret the value of $r^2$ for this regression.

(F) Calculate the SER for this regression.

| Y | X |
|---|---|
| 1.8 | 1.2 |
| 1.7 | -8.4 |
| 1.5 | 4.8 |
| 0.6 | 3.5 |
| 25.4 | 2.2 |

(G) Interpret the value of the SER for this regression.
(H) Calculate the standard error of the intercept term.
(I) Interpret the standard error of the intercept term.
(J) Calculate the standard error of the slope coefficient.
(K) Interpret the standard error of the slope coefficient.

(3) Given the following: $GDP_i = \hat{\beta}_0 + \hat{\beta}_1 COR_i + e_i$

| Nation | COR | GDP |
|--------|-----|-----|
| Ukraine | 7.4 | 2,200 |
| UK | 1.4 | 21,200 |
| USA | 2.5 | 31,500 |
| Vietnam | 7.4 | 1,770 |

Where COR measures corruption in a nation on a scale of 0 (least) to 10 (most) and GDP measures output in dollars per capita.

(A) Calculate the values of the structural parameters for the regression above.
(B) Interpret the values of the structural parameters.
(C) Calculate $r^2$ for this regression.
(D) Interpret the value of $r^2$ for this regression.
(E) Calculate the SER for this regression.
(F) Interpret the value of the SER for this regression.
(G) Does this regression have a good fit? Explain.
(H) Calculate the standard error of the intercept term.
(I) Interpret the standard error of the intercept term.
(J) Would you be surprised if the intercept term equaled 26,776.70 if you re-ran this with data on four different countries? Explain.

(4) Given the following: $GDP_i = \hat{\beta}_0 + \hat{\beta}_1 COR_i + e_i$

| Nation | COR | GDP |
|--------|-----|-----|
| Bulgaria | 6.7 | 4,100 |
| Canada | 0.8 | 22,400 |
| Chile | 3.1 | 12,500 |
| China | 6.6 | 3,600 |

Where COR measures corruption in a nation on a scale of 0 (least) to 10 (most) and GDP measures output in dollars per capita.

(A) Calculate the values of the structural parameters for the regression above.

(B) Interpret the values of the structural parameters.

(C) Calculate $r^2$ for this regression.

(D) Interpret the value of $r^2$ for this regression.

(E) Calculate the SER for this regression.

(F) Interpret the value of the SER for this regression.

(G) Does this regression have a good fit? Explain.

(H) Calculate the standard error of the slope coefficient.

(I) Interpret the standard error of the slope coefficient.

(J) Would you be surprised if the slope coefficient equaled −3,342.80 if you re-ran this regression with data on four different countries? Explain.

(5) Label the following statements TRUE or FALSE:

(A) A large SER and very low $r^2$ can be the result of the Y-variable being very random.

(B) If $r^2 = 0$, then $\beta_1$ must $= 0$.

(C) If $r^2 = 1$, then $\beta_1$ must $= 1$.

(D) If SER $= 0$, then $r^2$ must $= 1$.

# 4 Hypothesis Testing

Once $\hat{\beta}_0$ and $\hat{\beta}_1$ are calculated, statistical inferences can be made about the true $\beta_0$ and $\beta_1$. For instance, suppose $\hat{\beta}_0 = 0.12$. Is that close enough to zero to suggest that the true $\beta_0 = 0$? The answer depends on the standard error of $\hat{\beta}_0$. If the $\mathrm{SE}(\hat{\beta}_0) = 0.03$, it means $\hat{\beta}_0$ typically varies by 0.03 in repeated sampling. Adding and subtracting 0.03 from 0.12 gives 0.08 to 0.15. Zero is not in that range.

This means if the regression is run many times with different samples from the same population, it is unlikely that $\hat{\beta}_0$ will turn out to be zero or negative in many instances. Therefore, even though $\hat{\beta}_0 = 0.12$ may seem close to zero, it is too far away from zero to suggest that the true $\beta_0 = 0$.

However, it is impossible to say with certainty that $\beta_0 \neq 0$ without access to the data on the entire population. Instead, the veracity of the claim that $\beta_0 = 0$ can be inferred with hypothesis testing. Hypothesis testing procedures allow researchers to discern how likely it is that a given estimator is equal to some specified value. That procedure is outlined in the box here.

---

**The five-step hypothesis testing procedure**

(1) State the null and alternative hypotheses
(2) Choose the level of significance
(3) State the decision rule
(4) Get the numbers
(5) Reject or do not reject the null hypothesis

---

DOI: 10.4324/9781003213758-4

The regression results outlined here will be used demonstrate various hypothesis tests. Thirty students in an econometrics class were asked about their overall grade point average (GPA) and study time (ST) in order to test the idea that college students can increase their GPA by studying more.

---

$$GPA_i = 2.87 - 0.02 \ ST_i + e_i$$
$$(0.21) \ \ (0.06) \quad \leftarrow \text{standard errors}$$
$$SER = 0.45 \quad |\overline{GPA}| = 2.81 \quad r^2 = 0.004 \quad n = 30$$

$GPA_i$ is grade point average of the ith student
$ST_i$ is average daily study time of the ith student

---

Here is a strict interpretation of the regression results:

$\hat{\beta}_0$ = 2.87—A student with zero study time is expected to have a GPA = 2.87.

$\hat{\beta}_1$ = −0.02—A 1-unit increase in study time is expected to lower GPA by 0.02 units.

SER = 0.45—The typical distance of an observation from the regression line is 0.45 units.

$|\overline{GPA}|$ = 2.81—The average GPA of the 30 students is 2.81.

$r^2$ = 0.004 0.4% of the variation in GPA is explained by study time.

n = 30—The regression was estimated with a sample of 30 students.

According to the SER, the fit of the regression is adequate: SER < ½$|\overline{GPA}|$. However, the fit is poor according to $r^2$: $r^2$ < 0.7. The two measures of fit give conflicting indications. This is not unusual and most econometricians would rely on the indication from $r^2$.

## TEST OF SIGNIFICANCE

A test of significance is used to determine if the population parameter is probably equal to zero or not. Let's perform a test of significance on $\hat{\beta}_1$ = −0.02 to determine if $\beta_1$ is likely to equal zero using the five-step procedure:

(1) State the null and alternative hypotheses

The hypothesis we wish to test is the null hypothesis. The alternative hypothesis is the implication if the null hypothesis is rejected.

$$Ho: \beta_1 = 0 \quad Ha: \beta_1 \neq 0$$

Notice that both the null and alternative hypotheses involve $\beta_1$, not $\hat{\beta}_1$. It is known for certain that $\hat{\beta}_1 \neq 0$. Given that $\hat{\beta}_1 = -0.02$, can we infer that the true $\beta_1$ equals 0?

(2) Choose the level of significance

The level of significance is sometimes called the "critical level" of the test. It represents the probability that the test will result in a TYPE I error. A TYPE I error is when a true null hypothesis is rejected. The tradition in econometrics is to use 5% or 10% for the critical level. Let's use 5%.

5%

To demonstrate the difference between TYPE I and TYPE II errors, consider the judicial system in the United States. Any defendant is considered innocent until proven guilty. That is, the null hypothesis is that the defendant is not guilty.

Ho: Defendant is not guilty  Ha: Defendant is guilty

Suppose the defendant is in truth not guilty and the jury finds her guilty. This is a TYPE I error since a true null is rejected. If a guilty defendant is found not guilty by the jury, this is a TYPE II error. Here, a false null hypothesis is not being rejected.

| In Truth → | Defendant Is Guilty | Defendant Is Not Guilty |
|---|---|---|
| Jury Finds ↓ | | |
| Defendant guilty | **Proper verdict** | **TYPE I error** |
| Defendant not guilty | **TYPE II error** | **Proper verdict** |

Econometricians, like jurists, abhor TYPE I errors. The American judicial process has all sorts of mechanisms to ensure that an innocent defendant will be found not guilty. Miranda rights and the right to an attorney are two examples of these mechanisms.

Econometricians prevent against TYPE I errors by setting very low critical levels for hypothesis tests. A 5% chance of committing a TYPE I error is the norm and 10% is typically the highest most econometricians are willing to risk in hypothesis testing.

Unfortunately, there is only one way to ensure that no TYPE I errors will occur: do not reject any null hypotheses. Declare every defendant not guilty. But then we would make the maximum number of TYPE II errors. There is an inverse relationship between the probability of TYPE I and TYPE II errors.

In econometrics the critical level of hypothesis tests is set at 5% to protect against the possibility of making TYPE I errors. This means more TYPE II errors are made than if the critical level was higher. However, like jurists who are unsure in a trial, econometricians would rather let a guilty defendant go free than convict an innocent person.

(3) State the decision rule

The decision rule is used to test the hypothesis. After performing a few tests it will become apparent which rules should be used in which circumstances. For a test of significance, the decision rule is:

$$\text{If } |t - \text{ratio}| > t^c, \text{ then reject Ho}$$

The t-ratio, or t-statistic, is defined as:

$$t - \text{ratio} = \frac{\hat{\beta}_1 - \beta_{Ho}}{\text{SE}(\hat{\beta}_1)}; \text{ where } \beta_{Ho} \text{ is the value of } \beta_1$$

stated in the hull hypothesis.

$t^c$ is the critical t-ratio found in a t-table such as the one in the back of this book. To look up $t^c$, three pieces of information are needed:

(1) The degrees of freedom of the test = n – k = 30 – 2 = 28
    n is the number of observations used in the regression
    k is the number of structural parameters in the regression. There are two: $\hat{\beta}_0$ and $\hat{\beta}_1$
(2) The critical level of the test = 5%
(3) The fact that a test of significance is two-sided

Tests of significance are two-sided because the alternate hypothesis is $\beta_1 \neq 0$. $\beta_1$ may differ from zero in two ways—by being greater than zero or by being less than zero. The ability to distinguish between one-sided and two-sided tests will become apparent with more experience.

(4) Get the numbers

Here the t-ratio is calculated and $t^c$ is found.

$$GPA_i = 2.87 - 0.02 \ ST_i + e_i$$
$$\quad\quad\quad (0.21) \ (0.06) \ \leftarrow \text{standard errors}$$
$$SER = 0.45 \ \ |\overline{GPA}| = 2.81 \ \ r^2 = 0.004 \ \ n = 30$$

$$t - ratio = \frac{\hat{\beta}_1 - \beta_{Ho}}{SE(\hat{\beta}_1)}$$

$$= \frac{-0.02 - 0}{0.06}$$

$$= -0.33$$

$GPA_i$ is grade point average of the ith student

$ST_i$ is average daily study time of the ith student

All three numbers plugged into the formula for the t-ratio are found in the regression results.

From the table in the back of the book, $t^c = 2.048$. Critical values for the t-distribution and other distributions are available online as well. To look up $t^c$, one needs to know n, k, and the fact that the test is two-tailed. Most econometric packages show t-ratios for tests of significance as part of the regression results

(5) Reject or do not reject the null hypothesis

In this example $|\text{t-ratio}| < t^c$. Therefore, the test results in "do not reject Ho." This implies that $\beta_1$ is not likely to be different from zero.

Do Not Reject Ho: $\beta_1$ is not likely to be different from zero

Think about that for a second. If $\beta_1 = 0$, then no matter how much study time (ST) increases, GPA will not be affected. In other words, study time is an insignificant factor in determining a student's GPA. Do you trust this result? Why or why not?

Here is the summary of the entire five-step procedure for this particular test of significance.

## Test of significance

(1) Ho: $\beta_1 = 0$  Ha: $\beta_1 \neq 0$
(2) 5%

(3) If | t-ratio| > t$^c$, then reject Ho
(4) 0.33 < 2.048 (d.f. = n – k = 30 – 2 = 28)
(5) Do Not Reject Ho; $\beta_1$ is not likely to be different from zero.

Let's take a deeper dive into hypothesis tests to understand what they truly imply. Consider the population regression function: WHY$_i$ = $\beta_0$ + $\beta_1$EX$_i$ +u$_i$ and suppose $\beta_1$ = 0. Now draw random samples of n = 30 from this population and run the regression WHY$_i$ = $\hat{\beta}_0$ + $\hat{\beta}_1$EX$_i$ + e$_i$. Do this 100,000 times with fresh data from the same population each time. On occasion, $\hat{\beta}_1$ will be positive and on other occasions $\hat{\beta}_1$ will be negative. It may even equal zero once or twice.

Most of the regressions will result in a t-ratio for $\hat{\beta}_1$ that lies between –2.048 and positive 2.048. A t-ratio in this range will occur in about 95,000 of the 100,000 regressions. However, in 2,500 (or 2.5%) of the regressions, the t-ratio will be greater than 2.048. This is because the sample drawn was not representative of the entire population in those cases. In another 2,500 regressions, the t-ratio will be less than –2.048. Again, this is because the sample was strange compared to the population. Thus, we end up erroneously rejecting Ho in a test of significance 5% of the time. The probability of committing a TYPE I error is 5% because the critical level of the test was set at 5%.

Graphically, this situation is depicted by showing the probability density function of the t-ratio for n = 30 and k = 2 when Ho is true.

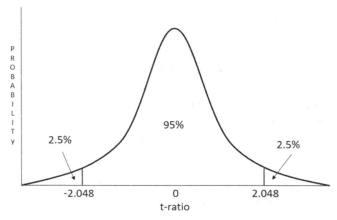

**Figure 4.1** A probability density function for a t-ratio.

The probability of obtaining a t-ratio greater than 2.048 is 2.5%. This is represented by the area under the t-distribution to the right of t-ratio = 2.048. Similarly, the probability of obtaining a t-ratio less than –2.048 is 2.5%. Overall, there is 5% chance we will be rejecting a true null hypothesis since Ho is rejected when |t-ratio| > 2.048. That is to say, there is a 5% chance we will make a TYPE I error. This is what it means to set the critical level of a hypothesis test at 5%.

## CONFIDENCE INTERVALS

Rather than an exact estimate of $\beta_1$, a confidence interval provides a range of values within which $\beta_1$ is likely to fall. To form a 95% confidence for $\beta_1$:

95% CI for $\beta_1$:

$$\hat{\beta}_1 + /-SE(\hat{\beta}_1)(t^c)$$

$$-0.02 + /-0.06(2.048)$$

$$\rightarrow \quad -0.14 \text{ to } 0.10$$

---

$GPA_i = 2.87 - 0.02 \ ST_i + e_i$

$\quad$ (0.21) (0.06) $\quad \leftarrow$ standard errors

$SER = 0.45 \ |\overline{GPA}| = 2.81 \ r^2 = 0.004 \ n = 30$

$GPA_i$ is grade point average of the ith student

$ST_i$ is average daily study time of the ith student

---

The numbers for $\hat{\beta}_1$ and $SE(\hat{\beta}_1)$ are found in the regression results. $t^c$ is found using the degrees of freedom for the interval: d.f. = n – k = 30 – 2 = 28. All confidence intervals are two-tailed. Since this interval is at 95%, $t^c$ is taken from the 5% critical level (100 – 95 = 5). To summarize, look up $t^c$ using d.f. = 28 for a two-tailed test at the 5% critical level.

If an infinite number of such intervals are constructed, 95% of them will contain the true $\beta_1$. Notice that the interval spans zero. This corresponds with the test of significance at the 5% critical level that indicated that $\hat{\beta}_1$ is not statistically different from zero.

A 90% confidence interval is similarly constructed:

90% CI for $\hat{\beta}_1$: $\quad -0.02 + /-0.06(1.701) \quad \rightarrow \quad -0.12 \text{ to } 0.08$

The only difference is $t^c$ = 1.701 in this case because d.f. = 28 for a two-tailed test at the 10% critical level.

If an infinite number of such intervals are constructed, 90% of them will contain the true $\beta_1$. Notice that the 90% confidence interval is smaller than the 95% confidence interval. This makes sense. To be more confident, a wider interval is needed. A 100% confidence interval is very wide. It would run from negative infinity to positive infinity.

## POSITIVE SIGN TEST

A positive sign test is different from a test of significance in that it is not interested in the estimator being different from zero, but greater than zero. $\hat{\beta}_0 = 2.87$ in our example. Let's test if this is significantly greater than zero. Here is the five-step procedure:

(1) Ho: $\beta_0 = 0$ Ha: $\beta_0 > 0$

(2) 5%

(3) If t-ratio > $t^c$, then reject Ho

(4) 13.67 > 1.701 (d.f. = n – k = 30 – 2 = 28)

(5) Reject Ho; $\beta_0$ is likely to be positive

$GPA_i = 2.87 - 0.02 \ ST_i + e_i$
$\quad (0.21) \quad (0.06) \quad \leftarrow$ standard errors
$SER = 0.45 \ |\overline{GPA}| = 2.81 \ r^2 = 0.004 \ n = 30$

$GPA_i$ is grade point average of the ith student

$ST_i$ is average daily study time of the ith student

Notice the differences between this test and the test of significance:

(1) Ha is now $\beta_0 > 0$, not $\beta_0 \neq 0$.
(2) The decision rule is "If t-ratio > $t^c$, then reject Ho," not "If | t-ratio | > $t^c$, then reject Ho." Nevertheless, the t-ratio is calculated with the same formula.
(3) The degrees of freedom are the same as in a test of significance. However, this is a one-tailed test, so there is a different $t^c$. The test is one-tailed because it only checks if $\beta_0$ is greater than zero, not greater than or less than zero.

The rejection of Ho implies $\beta_0$ is very likely positive.

## NEGATIVE SIGN TEST

A negative sign test is different from a test of significance in that it is solely concerned with the estimator being less than zero. A negative sign test is more specific in that Ha is $\beta_1 < 0$, not $\beta_1 \neq 0$. $\hat{\beta}_1 = -0.02$ in our example. Let's test if this is significantly less than zero.

(1) Ho: $\beta_1 = 0$ Ha:
    $\beta_1 < 0$
(2) 5%
(3) If t-ratio < $-t^c$, then reject Ho
(4) $-0.33 > -1.701$ (d.f. = n $-$ k = 30 $-$ 2 = 28)
(5) Do not reject Ho; $\beta_1$ is not likely to be negative

$$GPA_i = 2.87 - 0.02 \; ST_i + e_i$$
$$\quad\;\; (0.21) \; (0.06) \;\; \leftarrow \text{standard errors}$$
$$SER = 0.45 \quad |\overline{GPA}| = 2.81 \quad r^2 = 0.004 \quad n = 30$$

$GPA_i$ is grade point average of the ith student

$ST_i$ is average daily study time of the ith student

Notice the differences between this test and the test of significance:

(1) Ha is now $\beta_1 < 0$, not $\beta_1 \neq 0$.
(2) The decision rule is "If t-ratio < $-t^c$, then reject Ho," not "If |t-ratio| > tc, then reject Ho." Nevertheless, the t-ratio is calculated with the same formula.
(3) The degrees of freedom are the same as in a test of significance. However, this is a one-tailed test, so there is a different $t^c$. The test is one-tailed because it only checks if $\beta_1$ is less than zero, not less than or greater than zero.

The conclusion of this negative sign test is that $\beta_1$ is unlikely to be negative.

## A REVIEW OF THE DECISION RULES

So far there are three decision rules. It is easy to remember which decision rule to use in each instance because the rules are aligned with the alternate hypotheses. If Ha has an inequality, then the decision rule is "if |t-ratio| > $t^c$, reject Ho." If Ha has a greater than sign, then the decision rule is "if t-ratio > $t^c$, reject Ho." If Ha has a less than sign, then the decision rule is "if t-ratio < $-t^c$, reject Ho."

**Review of decision rules**

If Ha has a $\neq$: if $|$t-ratio$| > t^c$, reject Ho
If Ha has a $>$: if t-ratio $> t^c$, reject Ho
If Ha has a $<$: if t-ratio $< -t^c$, reject Ho

(The latter two tests are one-tailed tests.)

## SPECIFIC VALUE TEST

A specific value test is used to determine if an estimator equals some pre-specified value, not zero. Specific value tests can be one or two-tailed. It depends on how they are set up. For instance, we might ask if $\beta_0$, which is estimated by $\hat{\beta}_0 = 2.87$ in our example, is significantly less than 3. This is a one-tailed test since the alternate hypothesis is Ha: $\beta_0 < 3$.
    Be careful in calculating the t-ratio since $\beta_{Ho} \neq 0$ in this test:

$$t - \text{ratio} = \frac{\hat{\beta}_0 - \beta_{Ho}}{SE(\hat{\beta}_0)}$$

$$= \frac{2.87 - 3}{0.21}$$

$$= -0.62$$

Here is the entire test:

$GPA_i = 2.87 - 0.02\ ST_i + e_i$
      (0.21)  (0.06)  $\leftarrow$ standard errors
    $SER = 0.45\ |\overline{GPA}| = 2.81\ r^2 = 0.004\ n = 30$

$GPA_i$ is grade point average of the ith student
$ST_i$ is average daily study time of the ith student

(1) Ho: $\beta_0 = 3$ Ha: $\beta_0 < 3$
(2) 5%
(3) If t-ratio $< -t^c$, then
     reject Ho
(4) $-0.62 > -1.701$ (d.f. = n − k = 30 − 2 = 28)
(5) Do Not Reject Ho; $\beta_0$ is not likely to be less than 3

The result is do not reject Ho, implying $\beta_0$ is not significantly less than 3. Had the test asked, "is $\beta_0$ likely to be equal to 3, or different from 3," then a two-tailed test is warranted:

(1) Ho: $\beta_0 = 3$ Ha: $\beta_0 \neq 3$
(2) 5%

(3) If $|\text{t-ratio}| > t^c$, then reject Ho

(4) $0.62 < 2.048$ (d.f. $= n - k = 30 - 2 = 28$)

(5) Do Not Reject Ho; $\beta_0$ is not likely to be different from 3

## TEST FOR $R^2 = 0$

If the coefficient of determination ($r^2$) equals zero, it implies that the explanatory variable explains none of the variation in the dependent variable. In our example, $r^2 = 0.004$. Is this close enough to suggest the true $r^2$ equals zero?

For this hypothesis test, the test statistic follows an F-distribution. F-statistics can only be positive so they are always one-sided. Here is the five-step procedure:

(1) Ho: $r^2 = 0$ Ha: $r^2 > 0$

(2) 5%

(3) If $F > F^c$, then reject Ho

(4) $0.104 < 4.20$ (d.f. $= k - 1$ in the numerator and $n - k$ in the denominator)

(5) Do Not Reject Ho; $r^2$ is not statistically greater than zero.

The F is calculated with the formulas below:

$$F = \frac{\Sigma(Y_i - \bar{Y})^2/(k - 1)}{\Sigma e_i^2/(n - k)}$$

$F^c$ is found in a table such as in the back of this book. To look up $F^c$, find where the degrees of freedom in the numerator ($k - 1 = 1$) intersect with the degrees of freedom in the denominator ($n - k = 30 - 2 = 28$) for test at the 5% critical level. $F^c$ also can be found online.

In this example we do not reject Ho: $r^2$ is not statistically greater than zero. Study time does not account for any of the variation in GPA according to this econometric model.

## PROBABILITY VALUES

Probability values can be found for any of the hypothesis tests presented in this chapter. Once the t-ratio or F-statistic for a hypothesis test is determined, it is possible to deduce what critical level is required in step 2 to result in "Reject Ho" in step 5.

A probability value is the lowest level of significance that can be used in a hypothesis test while still rejecting Ho. As such, p-values (as they are commonly known) provide a quick method for determining the results of a hypothesis test: If the p-value is less than 0.05, then the result of the hypothesis test will be to reject Ho at the 5% critical level.

Consider the GPA regression used throughout this chapter.

---

$$GPA_i = 2.87 - 0.02 \ ST_i + e_i$$
$$\qquad\quad (0.01) \quad (0.73) \quad \leftarrow p - values$$

$$SER = 0.45 \quad |\overline{GPA}| = 2.81 \quad r^2 = 0.004 \quad n = 30$$

$GPA_i$ is grade point average of the ith student.
$ST_i$ is average daily study time of the ith student.

---

In the results above, the standard errors have been replaced with p-values. The p-value on the coefficient on ST is 0.73. Since this is greater than the critical level of the test (0.05), the test of significance will result in "do not reject Ho." Ho is $\beta_1 = 0$. Therefore, ST is insignificant at the 5% critical level since the p-value is greater than 0.05.

Even if the critical level of this test of significance is set at 72% the result is still "do not reject Ho." Only when the critical level surpasses 73% would the test result in "reject Ho" and conclude that ST is significant. However, critical levels above 10% are not generally acceptable in econometrics.

It can be tricky to calculate p-values. The t-ratio, degrees of freedom, and whether the test is one- or two-tailed are involved. Fortunately, p-value calculators can be found online and most econometric software reports them.

## TERMS

Confidence interval—A range of values within which the true value of an estimated parameter is likely to fall.

Critical level (level of significance)—The probability of making a TYPE I error in a hypothesis test.

F-ratio (F-statistic)—Any statistic that follows the F-distribution.

Probability value—The lowest level of significance that can be used in a hypothesis test while still rejecting Ho.

t-ratio (t-statistic)—Any statistic that follows the t-distribution.

TYPE I error—When a true null hypothesis is rejected.

TYPE II error—When a false null hypothesis is not rejected.

## CHAPTER 4 PROBLEMS

(1) Given the following regression results:

---

$CORUPT_i = 5.47 - 0.05\ MIL_i + e_i$

       (0.49)  (0.05)   $\leftarrow$ standard errors

       (0.00)  (0.34)   $\leftarrow$ p $-$ values

$SER = 2.35\ |\overline{CORUPT}| = 5.14\ \ r^2 = 0.02\ \ n = 48$

                 (F $-$ statistic for $r^2 = 0.95$)

$CORUPT_i$ is the corruption level of the country
(1 is low; 10 is high)
$MIL_i$ is military presence in the country
(military personnel per 1,000 citizens)

---

(A) Do a test of significance on the coefficient on MIL. Show the five-step procedure.

(B) Would the results of your test turn out differently if the critical level of the test was 40% instead of 5%? Explain.

(C) Is the constant term significant at the 1% critical level? Explain your response without resorting to a test of significance.

(D) Form a 90% confidence interval around the coefficient on MIL.

(E) Determine if $r^2 = 0$ for this regression. Show the five-step procedure.

(F) Would your results for E be different if the critical level of the test was 33%? Explain. (p-Value for this test is 0.34.)

(G) Do a test to determine if the coefficient on MIL equals zero or if it is greater than zero. Show the five-step procedure.

(H) Do a test to determine if the coefficient on MIL equals $-0.1$ or not. Show the five-step procedure.

(2) Given the following regression results:

---

$CORUPT_i = 7.54 - 0.25\ OVER\ 65_i + e_i$

       (0.62)  (0.06)   $\leftarrow$ standard errors

       (0.00)  (0.00)   $\leftarrow$ p $-$ values

$SER = 1.99\ \ |\overline{CORUPT}| = 5.14\ \ r^2 = 0.29\ \ n = 32$

                 (F $-$ statistic for $r^2 = 12.25$)

$CORUPT_i$ is the corruption level of the country
(1 is low; 10 is high)
$OVER65_i$ is percentage of the population 65 or older

---

(A) Do a test of significance on the coefficient on OVER65. Show the five-step procedure.

(B) Would the results of your test turn out differently if the critical level of the test was 1% instead of 5%? Explain your response without resorting to a test of significance.

(C) Is the constant term significant at the 1% critical level? Explain your response without resorting to a test of significance.

(D) Form a 90% confidence interval around the coefficient on OVER65.

(E) Determine if $r^2 = 0$ for this regression. Show the five-step procedure.

(F) Would your results for E be different if the critical level of the test was 3%? Explain. (p-Value for this test is 0.01.)

(G) Do a test to determine if the coefficient on OVER65 equals zero or if it is greater than zero. Show the five-step procedure.

(H) Do a test to determine if the coefficient on OVER65 equals −1.00 or not. Show the five-step procedure.

(3) Mark the following statements TRUE or FALSE

(A) A 95% confidence interval will be smaller than a 90% confidence interval.

(B) A positive sign test is one-tailed.

(C) A negative sign test is two-tailed.

(D) A test of significance is two-tailed.

(E) k = 2 in $WHY_i = \hat{\beta}_0 + \hat{\beta}_1 EX_i + e_i$.

(F) The higher the critical level of the test, the less chance there is that the test will result in a TYPE II error.

(G) A coefficient that is significant at the 1% critical level may not be significant at the 2% critical level.

(H) If the critical level of a hypothesis test is 5%, then the probability of committing a Type II error is 95%.

(I) If the p-value is less than 0.05, then the hypothesis test will reject Ho at the 5% critical level.

(J) If a test of significance results in "Reject Ho," then the p-value for the test must be greater than 0.05.

# 5 Multivariate Regression

## PARAMETER ESTIMATION IN MULTIVARIATE REGRESSION

In a multivariate regression there are two or more explanatory variables. Consider the case of two explanatory variables (X1 and X2):

$$Y_i = \hat{\beta}_0 + \hat{\beta}_1 X1_i + \hat{\beta}_2 X2_i + e_i$$

Here there are three structural parameters: $\hat{\beta}_0$, $\hat{\beta}_1$, and $\hat{\beta}_2$. Ordinary least squares (OLS) is the technique for finding these values. This technique yields the unique set of values for $\hat{\beta}_0$, $\hat{\beta}_1$, and $\hat{\beta}_2$ that minimize $\Sigma e_i^2$. Rearranging terms from the previous equation:

$$e_i = Y_i - \hat{\beta}_0 - \hat{\beta}_1 X1_i - \hat{\beta}_2 X2_i$$

OLS finds the unique set of values for these three estimators that minimizes:

$$\Sigma e_i^2 = \Sigma(Y_i - \hat{\beta}_0 - \hat{\beta}_1 X1_i - \hat{\beta}_2 X2_i)^2$$

That requires taking three partial derivatives and setting the resulting equations equal to zero. The three normal equations can then be solved for $\hat{\beta}_0$, $\hat{\beta}_1$, and $\hat{\beta}_2$. The formula for $\hat{\beta}_1$ is:

DOI: 10.4324/9781003213758-5

$$\hat{\beta}_1 = \frac{\begin{array}{c}(\Sigma(Y_i - \bar{Y})(X1_i - \overline{X1}))(\Sigma X2_i - \overline{X2})^2 \\ - (\Sigma(Y_i - \bar{Y})(X2_i - \overline{X2}))(\Sigma(X1_i - \overline{X1})(X2_i - \overline{X2}))\end{array}}{(\Sigma X1_i - \overline{X1})^2(\Sigma X2_i - \overline{X2})^2 - (\Sigma(X1_i - \overline{X1})(X2_i - \overline{X2}))^2}$$

The formula for $\hat{\beta}_2$ is of similar length. The derivations of these formulas are shown in an appendix at the end of this chapter.

Adding explanatory variables to an econometric model dramatically lengthens the formula for each structural parameter. In the 1970s the field of econometrics was revolutionized by the availability of computers programmed to perform these cumbersome calculations.

## THE INTUITION OF MULTIVARIATE REGRESSION

A regression with one explanatory variable, sometimes referred to as simple regression, can be depicted by fitting a line between observations in two-dimensional space.

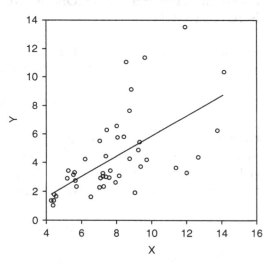

Figure 5.1 A simple regression is a line.

A regression with two explanatory variables is akin to fitting a plane in three-dimensional space.

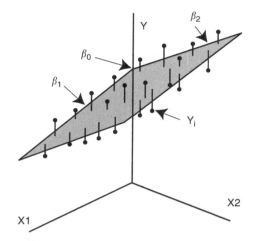

**Figure 5.2** A regression with two X-variables is a plane.

A regression with three explanatory variables would be fitting a three-dimensional object into observations in four-dimensional space. A regression with four explanatory variables would be fitting a four-dimensional object into observations in five-dimensional space, and so on.

## THE VARIANCE AND STANDARD ERRORS OF THE ESTIMATORS

Going to multivariate regression from simple regression, the formulas for the variances and standard errors of the structural parameters are changed. These formulas are shown for the case of two explanatory variables. The formulas become more complex as the number of explanatory variables increases.

$$\operatorname{var}(\hat{\beta}_0) = \left[ \frac{1}{n} + \frac{\overline{X1}^2 \Sigma x_{2i}^2 + \overline{X2}^2 \Sigma x_{1i}^2 - 2\overline{X1}\,\overline{X2}\Sigma x_{1i}x_{2i}}{(\Sigma x_{1i}^2)(\Sigma x_{2i}^2) - (\Sigma x_{1i}x_{2i})^2} \right] \bullet \hat{\sigma}^2;$$

where $x_{1i} = X1_i - \overline{X1}$; $x_{2i} = X2_i - \overline{X2}$

$$\operatorname{SE}(\hat{\beta}_0) = \sqrt{\operatorname{var}(\hat{\beta}_0)}$$

$$\text{var}(\hat{\beta}_1) = \frac{\Sigma x_{2i}^2}{(\Sigma x_{1i}^2)(\Sigma x_{2i}^2) - (\Sigma x_{1i} x_{2i})^2} \cdot \hat{\sigma}^2;$$

where $x_{1i} = X1_i - \overline{X1}$; $x_{2i} = X2_i - \overline{X2}$

$$SE(\hat{\beta}_1) = \sqrt{\text{var}(\hat{\beta}_1)}$$

$$\text{var}(\hat{\beta}_2) = \frac{\Sigma x_{1i}^2}{(\Sigma x_{1i}^2)(\Sigma x_{2i}^2) - (\Sigma x_{1i} x_{2i})^2} \cdot \hat{\sigma}^2;$$

where $x_{1i} = X1i - \overline{X1}$; $x_{2i} = X2i - \overline{X2}$

$$SE(\hat{\beta}_2) = \sqrt{\text{var}(\hat{\beta}_2)}$$

The interpretation of these standard errors has not changed. If $SE(\hat{\beta}_2) = 1.23$ it means that $\hat{\beta}_2$ is expected to vary by 1.23 on average in repeated sampling.

## GOODNESS-OF-FIT IN MULTIVARIATE REGRESSION

The measures of goodness-of-fit for simple regressions are slightly altered when moving to multivariate regressions. The SER is still interpreted and (almost) calculated the same way. For a simple regression the SER is:

$$\hat{\sigma} = \sqrt{\frac{\Sigma e_i^2}{n - 2}}$$

However, for multivariate regressions the 2 becomes a k:

$$\hat{\sigma} = \sqrt{\frac{\Sigma e_i^2}{n - k}}; \text{ where k is the number of structural parameters.}$$

The value of k comes up frequently going forward so it is best to have a clear understanding of it. A simple regression has one explanatory variable (X1) and two structural parameters ($\hat{\beta}_0$ and $\hat{\beta}_1$):

$$Y_i = \hat{\beta}_0 + \hat{\beta}_1 X1_i + e_i$$

In this case k = 2, the number of structural parameters.

A multivariate regression has more than one explanatory variable. Here there are three explanatory variables (X1, X2, and X3), and four structural parameters ($\hat{\beta}_0$, $\hat{\beta}_1$, $\hat{\beta}_2$ and $\hat{\beta}_3$):

$$Y_i = \hat{\beta}_0 + \hat{\beta}_1 X1_i + \hat{\beta}_2 X2_i + \hat{\beta}_3 X3_i + e_i$$

In this case k = 4. Take care, some econometrics textbooks define k to be the number of explanatory variables, which is usually one less than the way k is defined in this and other textbooks.

The interpretation of the SER is not changed. If $\hat{\sigma}^2 = 0.48$, then the typical distance of an observation from the population regression is estimated to be 0.487.

Another measure of goodness-of-fit is the coefficient of determination, denoted with $r^2$. In regressions with one X-variable, the coefficient of determination ($r^2$) is equal to the square of the correlation coefficient (r) between the Y-variable and the X-variable. Moving to multivariate regressions, this is no longer true because there is more than one X-variable. Therefore, $r^2$ is denoted with $R^2$ in multivariate regressions. There is no change at all in the formula for calculating the coefficient of determination:

$$R^2 = 1 - \frac{\Sigma e_i^2}{\Sigma (Y_i - \bar{Y})^2}$$

The interpretation of $R^2$ is not changed from when it was symbolized by $r^2$ in simple regressions. If $R^2 = 0.18$, then 18% of the variation in Y is explained by the X-variables.

$R^2$ is monotonically increasing with respect to k. That means $R^2$ cannot decrease even when a completely irrelevant variable is added to a regression. Hence, it is inappropriate to compare $R^2$'s from regressions that have a different number of explanatory variables. The regression with more explanatory variables has an advantage.

If the dependent variable of two regressions is the same, but the number of explanatory variables is different, use adjusted $R^2$ ($\bar{R}^2$) to compare which regression fits best:

$$\bar{R}^2 = 1 - \frac{\Sigma e_i^2/(n - k)}{\Sigma (Y_i - \bar{Y})^2/(n - 1)}$$

$\bar{R}^2$ will decrease if an additional explanatory variable has little or no impact on the dependent variable.

Two other measures of goodness-of-fit can be used as alternatives to, or in conjunction with, $\bar{R}^2$. These are the Akaike information criterion (AIC) and the Schwarz (SC) criterion. Like $\bar{R}^2$, the purpose of these measures is to compare the fit of regressions that have the same dependent variable but not the same number of explanatory variables. Unlike $\bar{R}^2$, lower is better with these two statistics.

Akaike Information Criterion: $\text{AIC} = -2[(-n/2)(1 + \log(2\pi) + \log(\hat{\sigma}^2/n))]/n + 2k/n$

Schwarz Criterion: $\text{SC} = -2[(-n/2)(1 + \log(2\pi) + \log(\hat{\sigma}^2/n))]/n + (k \log n)/n$

Consider the regressions below:

| | |
|---|---|
| $Y_i = 433.18 - 1.23X1_i + e_i$ <br> $\bar{R}^2 = 0.20$   AIC = 12.97   SC = 13.8 | $Y_i = 369.70 - 1.25X1_i + 0.05X2_i + e_i$ <br> $\bar{R}^2 = 0.19$   AIC = 12.99   SC = 13.16 |

All three measures of goodness-of-fit agree. The simple regression fits better. It has a higher $\bar{R}^2$, a lower AIC, and a lower SC. Notice both regressions have the same dependent variable. This is critical because comparing these measures of goodness-of-fit is valid only when the dependent variable is exactly the same.

## AN ILLUSTRATIVE EXAMPLE WITH HYPOTHESIS TESTING

Let's consider a classic econometric study as an example of multivariate regression (Andersen and Jordan 1969). In this study, Andersen and Jordan hypothesized that changes in nominal GDP would depend on changes in monetary and fiscal policy. They measured monetary and fiscal policy in a variety of ways using quarterly data from the first quarter of 1952 through the second quarter of 1968. Here the study is replicated using annual data from 1964.

$$\text{NGDP}_t = 127.35 + 1.06 \ \text{M2}_{t-1} - 0.29 \ \text{FP}_{t-1} + e_t$$
$$\quad \ \ (3.75) \quad (5.55) \quad \quad (-0.71) \quad \leftarrow \text{t-ratios}$$
$$\text{SER} = 132.65 \quad \overline{\text{NGDP}} = 282.42 \quad R^2 = 0.47 \quad n = 42$$

NGDP is the change in nominal GDP
M2 is the change in the M2 money supply
FP is the change in standardized federal budget

Notice that the subscript "t" appears instead of the usual "i." This is because the data used to estimate the econometric model are time-series rather than cross-sectional. M2 and FP are lagged one period (t–1). Changes in the money supply or fiscal policy actions take a year to impact the economy. This replication confirms Andersen and Jordan's original results—monetary policy has an impact on nominal GDP but fiscal policy is statistically insignificant.

Changes in the money supply (M2) have a significant and positive effect on changes in nominal GDP (NGDP). The t-ratio on M2 is 5.55 and significant at the 5% critical level. Changes in fiscal policy (FP) are not significant.

Before doing any hypothesis testing, let's interpret the regression results noticing how the interpretations differ from those in a simple regression.

## Interpretations

$\hat{\beta}_0$ = 127.35: If $\text{M2}_{t-1}$ and $\text{FP}_{t-1}$ = 0, then $\text{NGDP}_t$ = 127.35.

$\hat{\beta}_1$ = 1.06: If $\text{M2}_{t-1}$ increases 1 unit, then NGDP increases 1.06 units, holding $\text{FP}_{t-1}$ constant.

$\hat{\beta}_2$ = −0.29: $\text{FP}_{t-1}$ increases 1 unit, then NGDP decreases 0.29 units, holding $\text{M2}_{t-1}$ constant.

$R^2$ = 0.47: 47% of the variation in NGDP is explained by $\text{M2}_{t-1}$ and $\text{FP}_{t-1}$.

SER = 132.65: The typical absolute error is estimated to be 132.65.

Consider the interpretation of $\hat{\beta}_1$: If $\text{M2}_{t-1}$ increases 1 unit, then NGDP increases 1.06 units, holding $\text{FP}_{t-1}$ constant. In other words, $\hat{\beta}_1$ shows the impact of $\text{M2}_{t-1}$ on NGDP, *holding the other independent variables in the regression constant.*

This seemingly mundane addition to the interpretation of $\hat{\beta}_1$ is remarkable. Economic theorists often use the term "ceteris paribus," Latin for *holding other things constant*. Regression analysis can accommodate and test theories that involve ceteris paribus assumptions.

The Andersen–Jordan study is interested in assessing the impact of monetary and fiscal policy on nominal GDP. Using data from the real-world economy, it may seem like the separate effects of monetary and fiscal policy are impossible to untangle. The money supply and the federal budget both change constantly. If nominal GDP increases, was it because of the change in the money supply or the change in the federal budget?

The Andersen–Jordan study shows the impact of a change in $M2_{t-1}$ on $NGDP_t$ holding $FP_{t-1}$ constant, even though both $M2_{t-1}$ and $FP_{t-1}$ were changing simultaneously.

Data for biometric studies are frequently taken from scientific experiments. The biologist testing the effects of caffeine on cognition can control for the other factors that might affect cognition: sleep time, diet, distractions, and more are held constant among the subjects of the experiment. Econometricians seldom have the advantage of experimental data. Andersen and Jordan could not change the money supply in the United States, keep the federal budget constant, and then note the effect on nominal GDP. Their data were simply drawn from the past history of the US economy. Everything was changing simultaneously and nothing was controlled for.

Multivariate regression allows for the use of non-experimental data. When conditions are right, multivariate regression gives the impact of one independent variable while holding the other independent variables constant.

## HYPOTHESIS TESTING

Notice that the coefficient on $FP_{t-1}$ has the correct sign: an increase in the standardized federal budget is expected to contract the economy and decrease nominal GDP. As the federal budget tends toward surplus, nominal GDP decreases. However, the coefficient is not statistically different from zero.

Test of Significance for $\beta_2$
(1) Ho: $\beta_2 = 0$ Ha: $\beta_2 \neq 0$
(2) 5%

(3) If |t-ratio| > $t^c$, then reject Ho
(4) 0.71 < 2.023 (d.f. = n - k = 42 - 3 = 39)
(5) Do Not Reject Ho; $\beta_2$ is not likely to be significant

Changes in the money supply, however, have a positive impact on nominal GDP according to a positive sign test:

**Positive Sign Test for $\beta_1$**
(1) Ho: $\beta_1 = 0$ Ha: $\beta_1 > 0$
(2) 5%
(3) If t-ratio > $t^c$, then reject Ho
(4) 5.55 > 1.685 (d.f. = n - k = 42 - 3 = 39)
(5) Reject Ho; $\beta_1$ is likely to be positive

These results suggest that monetary policy is effective while fiscal policy is not. The Andersen–Jordan study had quite an impact on macroeconomics when it was released. Keynesians had to defend their views in light of this evidence against the efficacy of fiscal policy. Monetarist ideas, on the other hand, were supported.

There is one small change in the hypothesis tests conducted earlier. Since the Andersen–Jordan study is multivariate, k is no longer two in the determination of the degrees of freedom. There are three structural parameters in their regression and therefore k = 3 in these hypothesis tests.

For those interested, an appendix to this chapter explains degrees of freedom.

## MODEL SPECIFICATION

Whether or not to include a particular variable in a regression can be a complex decision. It is inappropriate, and unethical, to run regression after regression, slightly altering the set of explanatory variables each time, stopping when the results conform to intuition. Hypothesis testing in this situation is invalid since the researcher actively worked to ensure the results would support preconceived notions.

The proper approach to model specification is to research which explanatory variables belong in a particular regression. Theory is the best guide. A literature review of the theory being tested is vital.

It is crucial to include every explanatory variable that has a nontrivial impact on the dependent variable. Economic theory may not specify the entire list of variables that should be included. In that case, experimenting with different variables becomes necessary. Again, it is invalid and un-ethical to hunt for preconceived results.

Econometrics is testing theories with data. A related field is data mining. Data mining is scouring the data to develop useful theories. It is the converse of econometrics. The two fields become confounded when theory does not specify the complete list of explanatory variables to be included in an econometric test. This situation arises often. In practice, econometricians delve into the field of data mining to determine which explanatory variables belong in the regression.

In these cases, it is important to continue mining even after pre-conceived notions are attained. Once a regression is settled on and the theory is put to the test, it is important to determine the "fragility" of that regression. That means further testing to see if the results change substantially when another variable is added or the variables are mea-sured in different ways. Fragile results mean the underlying regression would yield different results if a minor alteration were made. Fragile results cannot be trusted.

Suppose the theory being tested is that X affects Y but the complete list of explanatory variables to be included in the regression is unclear. Twenty regressions using various combinations of explanatory variables are tried. Only 2 of the 20 regressions show X to be significant. Then it is unethical to present those two regressions as evidence that X affects Y. The preponderance of the evidence indicates that X does not affect Y. The research project is not a failure in this case. In fact, an import con-clusion can be made: the most plausible regressions suggest X does not affect Y. This is a valid and useful result.

When theory does not indicate whether a particular variable should be included in a model, there are some statistical indicators that can help.

- Correct sign—Sometimes it is possible to suggest reasons why an independent variable could have a positive coefficient or a negative coefficient. On the other hand, if the expected sign on a coefficient is unambiguous and the regression results in the wrong sign, it implies there is something amiss. The regression may have inap-propriate independent variables or this particular variable does not belong in the regression.
- Significance—Explanatory variables with anemic t-ratios (<2 in absolute value) or high p-values (>0.10) are candidates for exclu-sion from the model. Such variables will not pass a test of significance at normal levels.
- Goodness-of-fit—If adjusted $R^2$ decreases with the addition of an explanatory variable, it is an indication that the variable does not

belong. Similarly, if the Akaike and Schwarz criteria increase, then it is an indication that the variable does not belong in the regression.

- Altered coefficients—When an independent variable is added to a regression model and the coefficients on the other independent variables hardly change, it is an indication that the added variable does not belong.

In their paper, Andersen and Jordan developed a theory that concluded monetary and fiscal policy were the only theoretically justified variables for explaining changes in nominal GDP. In this way, their regressions were a test of that theory. The result that fiscal policy is insignificant could be challenged by arguing that their theory was based on incorrect assumptions.

Moreover, Andersen and Jordan were unsure about how to measure the variables in their study. They tried a variety of measures for monetary policy (including changes in M1 and changes in the monetary base) and several fiscal policy variables. They understood that running a bank of regressions could cause skepticism about their results so they reported all their viable regression results and almost all the results pointed in the same direction: monetary policy affects nominal GDP but fiscal policy does not.

## UNDERSPECIFICATION

Underspecification is when an important explanatory variable is excluded from a regression. Let's omit monetary policy $(M2_{t-1})$ from the Andersen–Jordan model and see what happens:

Correctly Specified Andersen–Jordan Equation

---

$NGDP_t = 127.35 + 1.06\ M2_{t-1} - 0.29\ FP_{t-1} + e_t$
$\quad\quad (3.75)\quad (5.55)\quad\quad (-0.71)\ \leftarrow$ t-ratios
$SER = 132.65\ \overline{NGDP} = 282.42\ R^2 = 0.47\ n = 42$
Adjusted $R^2 = 0.45$ Akaike = 12.68 Schwarz = 12.81

Underspecified Andersen–Jordan Equation

---

$$NGDP_t = 276.91 - 0.81\ FP_{t-1} + e_t$$
$$(10.15)\ (-1.56) \leftarrow \text{t-ratios}$$
$$SER = 175.26 \quad \overline{NGDP} = 282.42 \quad r^2 = 0.06 \quad n = 42$$
$$\text{Adjusted } R^2 = 0.03 \quad \text{Akaike} = 13.22 \quad \text{Schwarz} = 13.30$$

---

Notice that adjusted $R^2$ has plummeted indicating that the fit of the underspecified regression is much worse. The Akaike and the Schwarz statistics are higher, also suggesting a worse fit. Notice how different the estimators are in both regressions. The constant term went from 127.35 to 276.91 and the coefficient on $FP_{t-1}$ went from −0.29 to −0.81. Such dramatic differences imply that the omitted variable belongs in the regression.

All indications are that the regression without the monetary policy variable is underspecified. The consequence of leaving a relevant explanatory variable out of a regression is severe—biased parameter estimates and residual statistics. Biased estimators do not average out to their true values in repeated sampling. In layman's terms, biased results cannot be trusted. In econometric terms, the estimates of $\hat{\beta}_0$ and $\hat{\beta}_1$ tend to miss their true marks: $\beta_0$ and $\beta_1$. Therefore, the estimates of the residual statistics—SER, $SE(\hat{\beta}_1)$, $SE(\hat{\beta}_2)$, t-ratios, and p-values—cannot be trusted.

## OVERSPECIFICATION

In this section, the original Andersen–Jordan model is intentionally overspecified. A variable that certainly does not belong in the model is added. $RAND_t$ is a series of random numbers.

Correctly Specified Andersen–Jordan Equation

---

$$NGDP_t = 127.35 + 1.06\ M2_{t-1} - 0.29\ FP_{t-1} + e_t$$
$$(3.75)\quad (5.55)\qquad (-0.71)\ \leftarrow \text{t-ratios}$$
$$SER = 132.65 \quad \overline{NGDP} = 282.42 \quad R^2 = 0.47 \quad n = 42$$
$$\text{Adjusted } R^2 = 0.45 \quad \text{Akaike} = 12.68 \quad \text{Schwarz} = 12.81$$

---

Overspecified Andersen–Jordan Equation

$$NGDP_t = 152.46 + 1.05 \ M2_{t-1} - 0.23 \ FP_{t-1} - 8.42 \ RAND_t + e_t$$
$$\quad\quad (3.75) \quad (5.55) \quad\quad (-0.71) \quad\quad\quad (-0.93) \leftarrow \text{t-ratios}$$
$$SER = 132.87 \quad \overline{NGDP} = 282.42 \quad R^2 = 0.49 \quad n = 42$$
$$\text{Adjusted } R^2 = 0.44 \ \text{Akaike} = 12.71 \ \text{Schwarz} = 12.87$$

Adjusted $R^2$ is lower in the overspecified model, while the Akaike and Schwarz statistics are higher. All three statistics thereby suggest that the fit is worse in the overspecified regression and that RAND does not belong in the model. Notice that the estimators have hardly changed with the addition of RAND. The coefficient on $FP_{t-1}$ went from 1.06 to 1.05. This also implies that RAND is extraneous.

The consequence of including an irrelevant explanatory variable in a regression is inefficient (not best) estimators. An inefficient, or not best, estimator will vary more in repeated sampling than the efficient estimator. The standard errors of the estimators are larger than would be the case with a properly specified model.

With an overspecified model, hypothesis tests should be conducted with caution. The t-ratios used in those tests will be derived from bloated standard errors. Type II errors will become more likely.

An overspecified regression has unbiased estimators but they jump around more in repeated sampling. Maybe the regression in hand is one where the estimators have jumped rather far from their true targets. Thus, overspecification should be avoided. However, overspecified regressions are not as flawed as underspecified regressions. Inefficient estimators are more useful than biased estimators.

## UNBIASED AND BEST ESTIMATORS

It is important to have a firm grasp of the concepts of unbiased and best estimators. If the $\hat{\beta}$'s of $Y_i = \hat{\beta}_0 + \hat{\beta}_1 X1_i + \hat{\beta}_2 X2_i + e_i$ are estimated with OLS, then they have some desirable statistical attributes. The estimated set of $\hat{\beta}$'s is unique. These estimators minimize $\Sigma e_i^2$. No other set of estimators will result in a lower or equivalent minimum. The residuals from the OLS regression will sum to zero. And under ideal conditions, the $\hat{\beta}$'s are unbiased and best.

If an econometric model is appropriately specified, then the estimators are unbiased and best. Underspecified models result in biased estimators. Overspecified models result in estimators that are not best (inefficient).

A biased estimator is like a thermometer that tends to overestimate temperature. Sometimes this faulty thermometer reads too high, sometimes too low, and sometimes it is exactly accurate. But on average it reads too high. A thermometer that tends to underestimate is biased downward.

An unbiased thermometer sometimes reads too high, sometimes too low, and sometimes is exactly accurate. However, it reads too high just as often as it reads too low. It is impossible to guess if its current reading is too high or too low.

An unbiased $\hat{\beta}$ could be too high or too low, but there is no tendency for it to be either. It is probably not equal to $\beta$, but it could be. What makes an estimator unbiased is there is no tendency to over- or underestimate the true value.

An estimator is best if it varies less than others. Imagine two thermometers on a day where the temperature is a constant for hours on end. The thermometer whose readings jump around the least as the hours go by is best in the statistical sense of the word.

Cheap thermometers can be biased and inefficient. Their readings tend to be too high (or low) and they give widely divergent readings even though the temperature is the same.

## AN EXAMPLE OF SEARCHING FOR AN APPROPRIATE ECONOMETRIC MODEL

Suppose a gun-rights group claims that gun ownership prevents crime in an area. The following cross-sectional data are available to test this claim:

The dependent variable is VCRIME—the violent crime rate in each state of the United States.

Possible independent variables are:

GUNSPC—gun ownership per capita in the state
INCRATE—the incarceration rate of the state
MEDAGE—the median age in the state
PCGSP—per capita gross state product
POPDEN—population density of the state
UNEM—the unemployment rate in the state

Here is a portion of the data set:

| STATE | VCRIME | GUNSPC | INCRATE | MEDAGE | PCGSP | POPDEN | UNEM |
|---|---|---|---|---|---|---|---|
| Alabama | 524.2 | 33.150 | 946 | 38.9 | 40,279 | 97 | 3.8 |
| Alaska | 829.0 | 21.380 | 691 | 34.5 | 70,936 | 1 | 6.5 |
| Arizona | 508.0 | 25.610 | 877 | 37.7 | 43,096 | 63 | 4.9 |
| Arkansas | 554.9 | 26.570 | 900 | 38.1 | 38,467 | 58 | 3.6 |
| California | 449.3 | 8.710 | 581 | 36.5 | 67,698 | 254 | 4.3 |
| Colorado | 368.1 | 16.480 | 635 | 36.8 | 59,057 | 55 | 3.4 |
| Connecticut | 228.0 | 22.960 | 468 | 40.9 | 67,784 | 738 | 3.8 |
| Delaware | 453.4 | 5.040 | 756 | 40.1 | 66,023 | 496 | 3.2 |
| District of Columbia | 1,004.9 | 68.050 | 1,153 | 34.0 | NA | 11,516 | 5.6 |
| Florida | 408.0 | 16.350 | 833 | 42.0 | 43,052 | 397 | 3.4 |
| ⋮ | ⋮ | ⋮ | ⋮ | ⋮ | ⋮ | ⋮ | ⋮ |

A simple regression of VCRIME on GUNSPC is likely to be under-specified. Nevertheless, it is interesting to see if gun ownership rates by themselves have a negative effect on violent crime as hypothesized.

$$\text{VCRIME}_i = 2.87 - 0.02 \ \text{GUNSPC}_i + e_i$$
$$\quad\quad\quad (29.91) \quad (0.77) \quad \leftarrow \text{standard errors}$$
$$\text{SER} = 173.00 \quad \overline{\text{VCRIME}} = 389.43 \quad r^2 = 0.004 \quad n = 51$$
$$\text{Adjusted } R^2 = -0.02 \ \text{Akaike} = 13.18 \ \text{Schwarz} = 13.26$$

The coefficient on GUNSPC is negative but not significant, suggesting gun ownership rates have no effect on violent crime rates across states. But these results are likely to be biased due to underspecification. The regression excludes independent variables that impact VCRIME. Notice that adjusted $R^2$ can be negative. This occurs when $R^2$—or $r^2$ in this case—is near zero.

A review of the literature on this topic indicates there is no consensus on what factors are important in determining the violent crime rate. There are many possible factors that should be held constant when isolating the effect of gun ownership rates on VCRIME.

There are six possible independent variables in the data set so it is possible to run the 63 regressions that encompass every possible combination of independent variables. Then the regression with the highest adjusted $R^2$ could be used to test the theory that gun ownership prevents crime. There are computer programs that will do this.

Such an unconsidered research technique is not endorsed by econometricians. The results of each regression have to be considered with respect to several criteria, not just which fits best. Do any estimators have obviously incorrect signs? Overspecified regressions are inferior. Do the results change markedly when a variable is removed? Most importantly, this heedless technique could result in a fragile regression. Fit is only one consideration when searching for an appropriate econometric model.

Here is a model that adds POPDEN to the simple regression:

$$VCRIME_i = 369.70 - 0.09\ GUNSPC_i + 0.05\ POPDEN_i + e_i$$

$$(26.77)\quad (0.69)\qquad\qquad (0.0005) \leftarrow \text{standard errors}$$

$$SER = 153.71\quad \overline{VCRIME} = 389.43\quad r^2 = 0.23\quad n = 51$$

$$\text{Adjusted } R^2 = 0.20\ \text{Akaike} = 12.97\ \text{Schwarz} = 13.08$$

The coefficient on GUNSPC is negative but once again fails a test of significance. POPDEN is significant and the positive coefficient makes sense: more densely populated states have more violent crime per capita. Crowding people together leads to more conflict and violent crime. This regression, however, appears to be overspecified. GUNSPC is not close to being significant. Perhaps in combination with other independent variables GUNSPC will be significant.

Regression results can be reported in a more efficient manner. The table below shows four regressions from the scores run to find the best model to explain VCRIME.

Dependent Variable is VCRIME n = 51

|  | Model A | Model B | Model C | Model D |
|---|---|---|---|---|
| Constant | 2.87*** | 369.70*** | −108.61 | −109.92 |
|  | (29.91) | (26.77) | (83.17) | (83.60) |
| GUNSPC | −0.02 | −0.09 | −0.66 |  |
|  | (0.77) | (0.69) | (0.54) |  |
| POPDEN |  | 0.05*** | 0.03*** | 0.03*** |
|  |  | (0.0005) | (0.01) | (0.01) |
| INCRATE |  |  | 0.34*** | 0.31*** |
|  |  |  | (0.09) | (0.09) |
| UNEM |  |  | 72.56*** | 73.76*** |
|  |  |  | (21.37) | (21.46) |
| Adjusted $R^2$ | −0.02 | 0.20 | 0.54 | 0.54 |

Standard errors in parentheses: *significant at 10%; **significant at 5%; ***significant at 1%

At the top of the table, the dependent variable for all the regressions is reported as is the number of observations used to estimate the models.

Model A in the table portrays the first regression:

$$VCRIME_i = 2.87 - 0.02\ GUNSPC_i + e_i$$
$$\quad\ (29.91)\ (0.77)\quad \leftarrow \text{standard errors}$$

Model B is the second regression:

$$VCRIME_i = 369.70 - 0.09\ GUNSPC_i + 0.05\ POPDEN_i + e_i$$
$$\quad\ (26.77)\quad (0.69)\qquad\qquad (0.0005)\quad \leftarrow \text{standard errors}$$

Model C includes a constant term and the independent variables GUNSPC, POPDEN, INCRATE, and UNEM.

Model D is the same as C but excludes GUNSPC. Models C and D fit equally well according to adjusted $R^2$. However, Model C appears to include an extraneous variable: GUNSPC. Once that variable is removed, the fit does not get worse and the coefficients on the remaining variables hardly change. These are indications that an extraneous variable was removed. The four regressions in the table show that GUNSPC is not an important determinant of VCRIME. Econometric analysis of this data set rejects the notion that gun ownership prevents, or promotes, violent crime.

Notice the star * system for indicating which variables are significant at three different critical levels. The star system and the presentation of regression tables such as this one are ubiquitous in econometrics.

The table features four informative and representative models from dozens that were considered. The results do not support the hypothesis that gun ownership deters violent crime. None of the models throughout the process could produce a significant GUNSPC. This shows that the results are not fragile.

Searching for an appropriate econometric model when theory does not provide enough guidance is a craft. There are mechanized procedures for uncovering good models, but craft cannot be programmed. Indeed, analyzing scores of regressions one at a time gives the researcher a true sense of what the data say about the theory being tested.

## TERMS

Adjusted $R^2 (\bar{R}^2)$—A statistic that tends to decrease when an irrelevant explanatory variable is added to a regression.

Akaike information criterion (AIC)—A statistic that tends to increase when an irrelevant explanatory variable is added to a regression.

Biased estimator—In repeated sampling, the average of the estimates will not equal the true value.

Data Mining—Using trial and error to allow the data to determine the variables that belong in a model.

Inefficient estimator—An estimator that varies more in repeated sampling than the efficient estimator.

Multivariate regression—A regression that includes more than one explanatory variable.

Overspecification—When a regression includes one or more irrelevant explanatory variables.

Schwarz criterion (SC)—A statistic that tends to increase when an irrelevant explanatory variable is added to a regression.

Simple regression—A regression with one explanatory variable.

Underspecification—When an important explanatory variable is excluded from a regression.

## CHAPTER 5 PROBLEMS

(1) Use the data in SDATA.XLS and statistical software to run the following regression:

$$GPA_i = \hat{\beta}_0 + \hat{\beta}_1 ST_i + e_i$$

where GPA = grade point average and ST = study time per day

(A) Interpret the value you obtained for $\hat{\beta}_0$.

(B) Interpret the value you obtained for $\hat{\beta}_1$.

(C) How much does $\hat{\beta}_1$ typically vary in repeated sampling?

(D) Perform a test of significance on $\hat{\beta}_1$. Show the five-step procedure.

(E) What percent of the variation in GPA is explained by study time?

(F) Perform a test to determine if $r^2 = 0$. Show the five-step procedure.

(G) According to these results, how many hours per day would study time have to increase in order to raise GPA by 0.1?

(H) Plot the scattergram between GPA and ST with the estimated regression line drawn in.

(I) What is the average distance of an observation from the regression line?

(J) Will you cut back on your study time now that you have seen these results? Explain why or why not.

(2) Use the data in SDATA.XLS and statistical software to run the following regression:

$$GPA_i = \hat{\beta}_0 + \hat{\beta}_1 \; ST_i + \hat{\beta}_2 SAT_i + e_i$$

where GPA = grade point average.
  ST = study time per day
  SAT = SAT score

(A) Interpret the value you obtained for $\hat{\beta}_0$.

(B) Interpret the value you obtained for $\hat{\beta}_1$.

(C) Perform a positive sign test on $\hat{\beta}_1$. Show the five-step procedure.

(D) Interpret the value you obtained for $\hat{\beta}_2$.

(E) Perform a test to determine if $\hat{\beta}_0 < 1$. Show the five-step procedure.

(F) Interpret the value you obtained for $R^2$.

(G) Which regression fits the data better, this one or the one in question 1? On what do you base your response?

(H) The typical student in the survey studies about 3.0 hours per day and had an SAT score of 1,125.
  What would you expect the average student's GPA to be given your research into this matter?

(3) Use the data in CONSUMP.XLS and statistical software to run the following regression:

$$RCONPC_t = \hat{\beta}_0 + \hat{\beta}_1 \; REALYDPC_t + \hat{\beta}_2 \; REALR_t + e_t$$

where RCONPC = real consumer spending in the USA per capita
  REALYDPC = real disposable income per capita
  REALR = real interest rate on one-year Treasury Bonds

(A) Do all the explanatory variables attain their expected signs?

(B) What explanatory variables might be missing from this regression?

(4) Use the data in MBAPAY.XLS and statistical software to run the following regression:

$$\text{MBAPAY}_i = \hat{\beta}_0 + \hat{\beta}_1 \text{ AVGMAT}_i + \hat{\beta}_2 \text{ ACRATE}_i + e_i$$

where MBAPAY$_i$ = average starting salary of MBA students from
                school i
      AVGMAT$_i$ = average GMAT score at school i
      ACRATE$_i$ = acceptance rate at school i
      CC = University of Michigan Index of Consumer Confidence

(A) Do all the explanatory variables attain their expected signs?
(B) What explanatory variables might be missing from this regression?

(5) Use the data in CONSUMP.XLS and statistical software to run the following regression:

$$\text{RCONPC}_t = \hat{\beta}_0 + \hat{\beta}_1 \text{ REALYDPC}_t + \hat{\beta}_2 \text{ REALR}_t + \hat{\beta}_3 \text{ CC}_t + e_t$$

where RCONPC = real consumer spending in the USA per capita
      REALYDPC = real disposable income per capita
      REALR = real interest rate on one-year Treasury Bonds
      CC = University of Michigan Index of Consumer Confidence

(A) Does CC attain its expected sign? Explain.
(B) Does a test of significance on CC justify its presence in the regression?
(C) Does CC belong in the regression according to Adjusted $R^2$? Explain.
(D) Does CC belong in the regression according to the Akaike information criterion? Explain.
(E) Does CC belong in the regression according to the Schwarz criterion? Explain.
(F) Does this regression fit better than the regression from question 3 above? Explain.
(G) Do you think the estimators in
    $\text{RCONPC}_t = \hat{\beta}_0 + \hat{\beta}_1 \text{ REALYDPC}_t + \hat{\beta}_2 \text{ REALR}_t + e_t$ are
    biased? Inefficient? Neither? Explain.
(H) Do you think the estimators in
    $\text{RCONPC}_t = \hat{\beta}_0 + \hat{\beta}_1 \text{ REALYDPC}_t + \hat{\beta}_2 \text{ REALR}_t + \hat{\beta}_3 \text{CC}_t + e_t$ are
    biased? Inefficient? Neither? Explain.

(6) Use the data in MBAPAY.XLS and statistical software to run the following regression:

$$\text{MBAPAY}_i = \hat{\beta}_0 + \hat{\beta}_1 \text{ AVGMAT}_i + \hat{\beta}_2 \text{ ACRATE}_i + \hat{\beta}_3 \text{AVGPA}_i + e_i$$

where RCONPC = real consumer spending in the USA per capita
REALYDPC = real disposable income per capita
REALR = real interest rate on one-year Treasury Bonds
CC = University of Michigan Index of Consumer Confidence

(A) Does AVGPA attain its expected sign? Explain.
(B) Does a test of significance on AVGPA justify its presence in the regression?
(C) Does AVGPA belong in the regression according to Adjusted $R^2$? Explain.
(D) Does AVGPA belong in the regression according to the Akaike information criterion? Explain.
(E) Does AVGPA belong in the regression according to the Schwarz criterion? Explain.
(F) Does this regression fit better than the regression from question 4 above? Explain.
(G) Do you think the estimators in
$\text{MBAPAY}_i = \hat{\beta}_0 + \hat{\beta}_1 \text{ AVGMAT}_i + \hat{\beta}_2 \text{ ACRATE}_i + e_i$ are biased? Inefficient? Neither? Explain.
(H) Do you think the estimators in
$\text{MBAPAY}_i = \hat{\beta}_0 + \hat{\beta}_1 \text{ AVGMAT}_i + \hat{\beta}_2 \text{ ACRATE}_i + \hat{\beta}_3 \text{AVGPA}_i + e_i$ are biased? Inefficient? Neither? Explain.

## APPENDIX TO CHAPTER 5

## DERIVING THE ORDINARY LEAST SQUARES ESTIMATORS WITH TWO EXPLANATORY VARIABLES

Consider: $Y_i = \hat{\beta}_0 + \hat{\beta}_1 X1_i + \hat{\beta}_2 X2_i + e_i$

Re-write terms to isolate $e_i$:

$$e_i = Y_i - \hat{\beta}_0 - \hat{\beta}_1 X1_i - \hat{\beta}_2 X2_i$$

Find the values of $\hat{\beta}_0$, $\hat{\beta}_1$, and $\hat{\beta}_2$ that minimize $\Sigma e_i^2 = \Sigma (Y_i - \hat{\beta}_0 - \hat{\beta}_1 X1_i - \hat{\beta}_2 X2_i)^2$.

Start by taking the partial derivative of $\Sigma e_i^2$ with respect to $\hat{\beta}_0$:

$$\frac{\partial \Sigma (Y_i - \hat{\beta}_0 - \hat{\beta}_1 X1_i - \hat{\beta}_2 X2_i)^2}{\partial \hat{\beta}_0} = 2\Sigma (Y_i - \hat{\beta}_0 - \hat{\beta}_1 X1_i - \hat{\beta}_2 X2_i)(-1) = 0$$

Divide both sides of the above by −2 and distribute the sum sign:

$$\Sigma Y_i - n\hat{\beta}_0 - \hat{\beta}_1 \Sigma X1_i - \hat{\beta}_2 \Sigma X2_i = 0$$

Move the negative terms to the right side of the equation:

$$\Sigma Y_i = n\hat{\beta}_0 + \hat{\beta}_1 \Sigma X1_i + \hat{\beta}_2 \Sigma X2_i \text{ (normal equation)}$$

Solve for $\hat{\beta}_0$:

$$\hat{\beta}_0 = \frac{\Sigma Y_i - \hat{\beta}_1 \Sigma X1_i - \hat{\beta}_2 \Sigma X2_i}{n} = \bar{Y} - \hat{\beta}_1 \bar{X}1_i - \hat{\beta}_2 \bar{X}2_i$$

----------------------------------------------------------------------

Next take the partial derivative of $\Sigma e_i^2 = \Sigma (Y_i - \hat{\beta}_0 - \hat{\beta}_1 X1_i - \hat{\beta}_2 X2_i)^2$ with respect to $\hat{\beta}_1$:

$$\frac{\partial \Sigma (Y_i - \hat{\beta}_0 - \hat{\beta}_1 X1_i - \hat{\beta}_2 X2_i)^2}{\partial \hat{\beta}_1} = 2\Sigma (Y_i - \hat{\beta}_0 - \hat{\beta}_1 X1_i - \hat{\beta}_2 X2_i)(-X1_i) = 0$$

Divide both sides of the above by −2 and distribute the sum sign:

$$\Sigma Y_i X1_i - \hat{\beta}_0 \Sigma X1_i - \hat{\beta}_1 \Sigma X1_i X1_i - \hat{\beta}_2 \Sigma X2_i X1_i = 0$$

Move the negative terms to the right side of the equation and solve for $\hat{\beta}_1$:

$$\Sigma Y_i X1_i = \hat{\beta}_0 \Sigma X1_i + \hat{\beta}_1 \Sigma X1_i X1_i + \hat{\beta}_2 \Sigma X2_i X1_i \text{ (normal equation)}$$

$$\vdots$$

$$\hat{\beta}_1 = \frac{(\Sigma y_i x_{1i})(\Sigma x_{2i}^2) - (\Sigma y_i x_{2i})(\Sigma x_{1i} x_{2i})}{(\Sigma x_{1i}^2)(\Sigma x_{2i}^2) - (\Sigma x_{1i} x_{2i})^2};$$

where $x_{1i} = X1_i - \overline{X1}$; $x_{2i} = X2_i - \overline{X2}$; $y_i = Y - \bar{Y}$

----------------------------------------------------------------------

Next take the partial derivative of $\Sigma e_i^2 = \Sigma(Y_i - \hat{\beta}_0 - \hat{\beta}_1 X1_i - \hat{\beta}_2 X2_i)^2$ with respect to $\hat{\beta}_2$:

$$\frac{\partial \Sigma(Y_i - \hat{\beta}_0 - \hat{\beta}_1 X1_i - \hat{\beta}_2 X2_i)^2}{\partial \hat{\beta}2} = 2\Sigma(Y_i - \hat{\beta}_0 - \hat{\beta}_1 X1_i - \hat{\beta}_2 X2_i)(-X2_i) = 0$$

Divide both sides of the above by $-2$ and distribute the sum sign:

$$\Sigma Y_i X2_i - \hat{\beta}_0 \Sigma X2_i - \hat{\beta}_1 \Sigma X1_i X2_i - \hat{\beta}_2 \Sigma X2_i X2_i = 0$$

Move the negative terms to the right side of the equation and solve for $\hat{\beta}_2$:

$$\Sigma Y_i X2_i = \hat{\beta}_0 \Sigma X2_i + \hat{\beta}_1 \Sigma X1_i X2_i + \hat{\beta}_2 \Sigma X2_i X2_i \quad \text{(normal equation)}$$

$$\vdots$$

$$\hat{\beta}_2 = \frac{(\Sigma y_i x_{2i})(\Sigma x_{2i}^2) - (\Sigma y_i x_{1i})(\Sigma x_{1i} x_{2i})}{(\Sigma x_{1i}^2)(\Sigma x_{2i}^2) - (\Sigma x_{1i} x_{2i})^2};$$

$$\text{where } x_{1i} = X1_i - \overline{X1}; \ x_{2i} = X2_i - \overline{X2}; \ y_i = Y - \overline{Y}$$

## DEGREES OF FREEDOM

$\hat{\beta}_1$ is a more reliable estimator of $\beta_1$ when n (the number of observations in the data set) is larger. If n = 4, it is more likely that these few observations will not provide a representative sample of the population under consideration. Even if n = 52, there is some likelihood that the sample will not properly represent a population of, say, 2,000. However, it is more likely that the population will be well represented when n = 52 compared to when n = 4.

The increased confidence in estimators derived from larger samples is evident in hypothesis testing. Consider the following regression:

$$Y_i = 4.56 + 1.23 X_i + e_i$$
$$(3.33) \leftarrow \text{t-ratio}$$

Here is a test of significance for $\beta_1$ when n = 4:

(1) Ho: $\beta_1$ = 0 Ha: $\beta_1 \neq 0$
(2) 5%
(3) If |t-ratio| > $t^c$, then reject Ho
(4) 3.33 < 4.304 (d.f. = n – k = 4 – 2 = 2)
(5) Do Not Reject Ho; $\beta_1$ is not likely to be significant

The test indicates that $\beta_1$ may very well be equal to zero. Here is a test of significance for $\beta_1$ had the same results been obtained when n = 52:

(1) Ho: $\beta_1$ = 0 Ha: $\beta_1 \neq 0$
(2) 5%
(3) If |t-ratio| > $t^c$, then reject Ho
(4) 3.33 > 2.009 (d.f. = n – k = 52 – 2 = 50)
(5) Reject Ho; $\beta_1$ is likely to be significant

Unlike the test when n = 4, the test of significance with the larger sample concludes that $\beta_1$ is likely to be different from zero. The only difference between the two tests is n and that alters $t^c$, the critical t-statistic. The additional data points make a difference and that is why the t-statistics in the critical values table decrease as n increases.

In this example, $\hat{\beta}_0$ = 4.56 and $\hat{\beta}_1$ = 1.23. Given those values and 50 of the 52 observations on Y and X, the last two observations on Y and X can be mathematically deduced. That is to say, the last two observations on Y and the last two observations on X are not free to be any values once the values of $\hat{\beta}_0$ and $\hat{\beta}_1$ are determined. Therefore we cannot count them as part of the sample when hypothesis testing. The degrees of freedom in this hypothesis test are not 52, but 52 – 2 = 50.

In a multivariate regression, suppose there are three explanatory variables and therefore four structural parameters: $\hat{\beta}_0$, $\hat{\beta}_1$, $\hat{\beta}_2$, and $\hat{\beta}_3$. So k = 4. If n = 52, then the degrees of freedom for a test of significance are n – k = 52 – 4 = 48. This is because once the values of the four structural parameters are determined and 48 observations on Y, X1, X2, and X3 are given, the remaining four observation on Y, X1, X2, and X3 can be determined mathematically.

Thus the degrees of freedom in hypotheses tests depend on n and k (the number of structural parameters).

# 6 Alternate Functional Forms

## REGRESSION THROUGH THE ORIGIN

A regression line can be forced through the origin (0,0) by suppressing the intercept term:

$$Y_i = \hat{\beta}_1 X_i + e_i$$

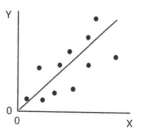

**Figure 6.1** Regression through the origin.

$\hat{\beta}_0$ is forced to equal zero by excluding it from the regression. As always, ordinary least squares finds the values of the structural parameters such that $\Sigma e_i^2$ is minimized. In this case, there is only one structural parameter, $\hat{\beta}_1$. The value of $\hat{\beta}_1$ that minimizes $\Sigma e_i^2$ is:

$$\hat{\beta}_1 = \frac{\Sigma X_i Y_i}{\Sigma X_i^2}$$

> The derivation of this formula is shown in an appendix to this chapter.

There should be strong theoretical reasons for excluding the constant term. The structural parameters and the residual statistics will be biased

DOI: 10.4324/9781003213758-6

if the intercept is inappropriately suppressed. In addition, $R^2$ and adjusted $R^2$ are invalid in regressions through the origin.

As an example of regression through the origin, consider Okun's Law (Okun 1962). In the early 1960s, Okun posited a linear relationship between unemployment and economic growth. He theorized that increases in the unemployment lower production in the economy. Specifically, each 1% increase in the unemployment rate was expected to widen the gap between potential and real GDP by 2–3%.

To test Okun's Law regress the gap between potential and real GDP growth on the change in the unemployment rate using annual data on the US economy from 1959.

---

$$GDPGAP_t = -0.08 - 1.87 \ CHGUN_t + e_t$$
$$(-0.05) \ (-10.31) \quad \leftarrow \text{t–ratios}$$
$$SER = 1.11 \quad |\overline{GDPGAP}| = 1.55 \quad R^2 = 0.70 \quad n = 47$$

where GDPGAP is the real GDP growth minus potential GDP growth; CHGUN is the change in the unemployment rate.

---

The coefficient on CHGUN implies that a 1% increase in the unemployment rate will widen the GDPGAP by 1.87%, not quite the 2–3% Okun hypothesized.

The constant term is not statistically different from zero in this regression and theoretically it should be equal to zero: if the change in the unemployment rate from one year to the next is zero, then the change in the GDPGAP should be zero as well.

Therefore, Okun's law may be tested with a regression through the origin.

---

$$GDPGAP_t = -1.87 \ CHGUN_t + e_t$$
$$(-10.39) \quad \leftarrow \text{t–ratio}$$
$$SER = 1.10 \quad |\overline{GDPGAP}| = 1.55 \quad n = 47$$

where GDPGAP is the real GDP growth minus potential GDP growth; CHGUN is the change in the unemployment rate.

---

The coefficient on CHGUN hardly changes when the constant term is omitted, just as expected when something extraneous is excluded. $R^2$ and adjusted $R^2$ are not reported since they are invalid in this case, as are Akaike and Schwarz. The SER indicates an inadequate fit.

Even if theory suggests the intercept term should be suppressed, researchers often include one because measures of goodness-of-fit ($R^2$, adjusted $R^2$, Akaike, and Schwarz) will be valid. Moreover, forcing the regression line through the origin, even when theory suggests it is appropriate, can worsen the fit of a regression.

# UNITS OF MEASUREMENT AND ESTIMATES

Regression estimates will be affected by changes in the units of measurement, but the substance of the regression results will be unaffected. Consider the case where nominal personal consumption expenditures (PCON) are regressed on nominal disposable personal income (DPI). Here are the raw data and the regression results:

| Year | PCON | DPI |
|------|------|-----|
| 1959 | 317.7 | 350.1 |
| 1960 | 331.8 | 365.2 |
| 1961 | 342.2 | 381.6 |
| ⋮ | ⋮ | ⋮ |
| | (billions of $) | (billions of $) |

$$PCON_t = -68.55 + 0.93\ DPI_t + e_t$$
$$\quad\quad (-4.42)\quad (322.25)\quad \leftarrow \text{t-ratios}$$
$$SER = 73.64 \quad \overline{PCON} = 3715.54$$
$$r^2 = 0.99 \quad n = 53$$

The interpretation here is that a 1-unit increase in income (DPI) causes a 0.93-unit increase in spending (PCON). In other words, the marginal propensity to consume is estimated to be 0.93. The data are measured in billions of dollars. It would be strange if the results changed simply because PCON and DPI were measured in millions, rather than billions, of dollars. Here are the regression results when the data are in millions of dollars:

| Year | PCON | DPI |
|------|------|-----|
| 1959 | 317,700 | 350,100 |
| 1960 | 331,800 | 365,200 |
| 1961 | 342,200 | 381,600 |
| ⋮ | ⋮ | ⋮ |
| | (millions of $) | (millions of $) |

$$PCON_t = -68,550 + 0.93\ DPI_t + e_t$$
$$\quad\quad (-4.42)\quad (322.25)\quad \leftarrow \text{t-ratios}$$
$$SER = 73,640 \quad \overline{PCON} = 3,715,540$$
$$r^2 = 0.99 \quad n = 53$$

The new results still peg the marginal propensity to consume at 0.93. The interpretation is still if DPI increases 1 unit, then PCON is expected to increase 0.93 units. The only difference is the units are now millions, not billions, of dollars.

The constant term, the SER, and the mean of the dependent variable have changed. They have been multiplied by 1,000. But nothing has changed in essence. The constant term is interpreted to mean that if DPI = 0, then PCON = –68,550 million dollars; whereas before the constant term was interpreted to mean when DPI = 0, then PCON = –68.55 billion dollars. There is no difference in meaning. The SER is larger, but not proportionally as it is compared to a larger mean of PCON.

Changing the units of measurement can result in the coefficient on DPI changing decimal places as well. Watch what happens if PCON is measured in millions and DPI is measured in billions of dollars.

| Year | PCON | DPI |
|------|------|-----|
| 1959 | 317,700 | 350.1 |
| 1960 | 331,800 | 365.2 |
| 1961 | 342,200 | 381.6 |
| ⋮ | ⋮ | ⋮ |
| | (millions of \$) | (billions of \$) |

$PCON_t = -68{,}550 + 930\ DPI_t + e_t$
$\quad(-4.42)\ (322.25) \leftarrow \text{t–ratios}$
$SER = 73{,}640 \quad \overline{PCON} = 3{,}715{,}540$
$r^2 = 0.99 \quad n = 53$

The coefficient on DPI is now 930, but the estimate of the marginal propensity to consume is unaffected because the interpretation is if DPI increases by 1 unit (1 billion dollars), then PCON is expected to increase 930 units (930 million dollars). In other words, PCON is expected to increase 93 cents when DPI increases by \$1.

There is an important lesson to take away from this exercise: the magnitude of a coefficient says nothing about its significance. Coefficients can be made larger or smaller simply by changing the units measuring the variables. However, t-ratios and p-values are invariant with respect to changes in the units of measurement. And most importantly, the analysis of the final results is not affected.

To determine if an X-variable has a significant impact, use the corresponding t-ratio or p-value. The magnitude of the coefficient attached to the X-variable can be deceiving.

## THE DOUBLE-LOG MODEL

Ordinary least squares fits straight lines between observations on a scattergram. However, it is possible to fit curvilinear lines using a technique that transforms the data into different units of measurement, fits a straight line, and then returns the fitted line to its original units.

The result is a curved line. The technique is called "alternate functional forms." The most prevalent alternate functional forms are presented in this chapter. The first and most popular is the double-log model.

Consider the annual demand for milk in the United States since 1959.

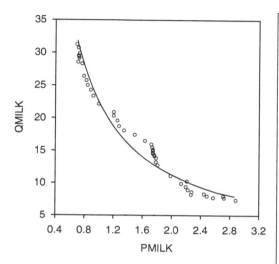

**Figure 6.2** The demand for milk in the United States.

QMILK—milk consumption (gal-
    lons per person per year)
PMILK—price of milk (dollars per
    gallon)

Astute readers may notice that unlike most demand curves, this one has the price on the horizontal axis. Placing the independent variable, PMILK, on the X-axis is mathematically correct. Therefore, the demand curves drawn in economics textbooks and classrooms are incorrect in the mathematical sense. It has been suggested that the tradition of placing the price on the Y-axis is in homage to Alfred Marshall, who thusly drew demand curves in his 1890 text *Principles of Economics.*

It appears as if a bowed line, convex to the origin, fits the data better than a straight line. This can be accomplished by transforming the data, in this case by taking natural logarithms.

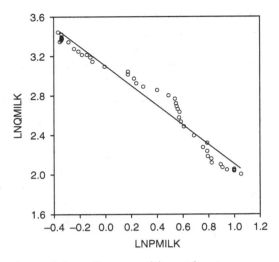

**Figure 6.3** The demand for milk (natural logarithms).

LNQMILK—the natural log of QMILK
LNPMILK—the natural log of PMILK

A straight line is fit to the natural logs of the observations. When the axes of this diagram are put back into the original (non-logged) scale the straight line bends to give the curved line in the original diagram.

It is easy to apply this technique. Given data on PMILK and QMILK, take the natural logarithms of those data (LNPMILK and LNQMILK).

| obs | PMILK | QMILK | LNPMILK | LNQMILK |
|-----|-------|-------|---------|---------|
| 1959 | 0.690000 | 31.29000 | −0.371064 | 3.443299 |
| 1960 | 0.710000 | 30.69000 | −0.342490 | 3.423937 |
| 1961 | 0.710000 | 29.72000 | −0.342490 | 3.391820 |
| 1962 | 0.710000 | 29.35000 | −0.342490 | 3.379293 |
| ⋮ | ⋮ | ⋮ | ⋮ | ⋮ |

Now regress LNQMILK on LNPMILK:

$$\text{LNQMILK}_t = 3.09 - 0.99 \ \text{LNPMILK}_t + e_t$$

This is akin to fitting the straight line to the scattergram of LNQMILK and LNPMILK. Let's interpret these results carefully:

$\hat{\beta}_0 = 3.09 \rightarrow$ If PMILK = 1,   then LNQMILK = 3.09 (QMILK = 21.98)

$\hat{\beta}_1 = -0.99 \rightarrow$ If PMILK increases 1%,   then QMILK $\downarrow$ 0.99%

The interpretation of $\hat{\beta}_0$ begins "If PMILK = 1" because if PMILK = 1, then LNPMILK = 0. Plugging LNPMILK = 0 into the regression leaves LNQMILK = 3.09. Taking the anti-log of 3.09 gives QMILK = 21.98.

Because of the natural-log transformation, a 1-unit increase in LNPMILK can be interpreted as a 1% increase in PMILK. Thus, a 1% increase in PMILK causes 0.99% reduction in QMILK.

These results suggest the elasticity of the demand for milk is nearly unitary. If the price goes up 1%, the quantity demanded falls by 0.99%. The interpretation of $\hat{\beta}_1$ as an elasticity is why this particular alternate functional form is sometimes called the "constant elasticity model." It also goes by the names "log-log model" or "double-log model."

The double-log form is popular with econometricians for several reasons:

(1) The value of $\beta_1$ can be interpreted as an elasticity. (If X increases 1%, then Y is expected to change by $\beta_1$ percent.)
(2) The natural logs of many economic time series are normally distributed.
(3) The double-log form can yield a wide variety of shapes determined by the data itself.

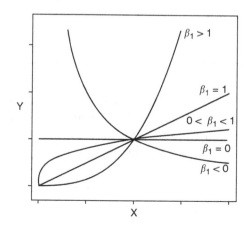

**Figure 6.4** The double-log model at various values of $\beta_1$.

The results and interpretations of the double-log model are compared with the linear model in the boxes here:

| Linear:<br>$QMILK_t = 35.17 - 11.27$<br>$\quad PMILK_t + e_t \; R^2 = 0.94$<br>If PMILK = 0, then<br>$\quad QMILK = 35.17$<br>If PMILK ↑ 1 unit, then<br>$\quad QMILK \downarrow 11.27$ units | Double-log:<br>$LNQMILK_t = 3.09 - 0.99$<br>$\quad LNPMILK_t + e_t \; R^2 = 0.96$<br>If PMILK = 1, then<br>$\quad LNQMILK = 3.09$<br>$\quad (QMILK = 21.98)$<br>If PMILK ↑ 1%, then<br>$\quad QMILK \downarrow 0.99\%$ |

The $R^2$'s for both models indicate good fit. However, it is incorrect to say that the double-log model has a better fit than the linear model. The $R^2$'s are not comparable since the dependent variables are not the same for both models. Adjusted $R^2$, Akaike, Schwarz, and SER are not comparable as well.

The double-log model relies on transforming the data by taking natural logs. Taking logarithms to any other base will not do because the resulting estimators would not have the salutary interpretations.

The double-log model can only be applied when all of the data are positive values. The natural logarithm of a nonpositive number is undefined. Therefore, it is not possible to transform any data that have zero or negative values. Other alternate functional forms can be applied in these situations.

## THE LOG-LIN MODEL

Another alternate functional form is the semi-log, or log-lin, model. In this model the natural log of the dependent variable is taken, but not that of the independent variable. This model gives percentage changes in the dependent variable for unit changes in the independent variable.

$$LNQMILK_t = 3.84 - 0.70 \; PMILK_t + e_t$$

$\hat{\beta}_0 = 3.84 \rightarrow$ If PMILK = 0, then LNQMILK = 3.84 (QMILK = 46.53)

$\hat{\beta}_1 = -0.70 \rightarrow$ If PMILK increases 1 unit, then QMILK decreases 70%

Notice the difference between the interpretations of the double-log model and the log-lin model:

| Log-Lin: | Double-Log: |
|---|---|
| $LNQMILK_t = 3.84 - 0.70$ $PMILK_t + e_t$  $R^2 = 0.98$ | $LNQMILK_t = 3.09 - 0.99$ $LNPMILK_t + e_t$  $R^2 = 0.96$ |
| If PMILK = 0, then | If PMILK = 1, then |
| LNQMILK = 3.84 | LNQMILK = 3.09 |
| (QMILK = 46.53) | (QMILK = 21.98) |
| If PMILK ↑ 1 unit, then | If PMILK ↑ 1%, then |
| QMILK ↓ 70% | QMILK ↓ 0.99% |

Notice that the decimal point moves two places to the right when interpreting the coefficient on PMILK. This is not the case in the double-log model.

The log-lin model can be used when it is not possible to take the natural logarithm of the independent variable. If any of the observations on a variable are zero or negative, then taking the natural logarithm is not possible. The natural log of a nonpositive number is undefined.

The log-lin model has an interesting interpretation in regressions with a trend variable. A trend variable increases one unit each time period. The table here shows real GDP in the United States and a trend variable.

| obs | RGDP | TREND |
|---|---|---|
| 1948 | 18,520 | 1 |
| 1949 | 1,843.1 | 2 |
| 1950 | 2,004.2 | 3 |
| 1951 | 2,159.3 | 4 |
| ⋮ | ⋮ | ⋮ |

Now estimate the log-lin model: $LNRGDP_t = 7.58 + 0.032\ TREND_t + e_t$

Interpret the coefficient on TREND: If TREND increases 1 unit, then RGDP increases 3.2%. In other words, each year real GDP is expected to increase 3.2%. The log-lin model gives average growth rates when the independent variable is a trend.

## THE LIN-LOG MODEL

The lin-log model is appropriate when the dependent variable changes an absolute amount for a given percentage change in the independent variable. Here it is applied to the milk data.

$$QMILK_t = 23.18 - 16.52 \ LNPMILK_t + e_t$$

$\hat{\beta}_0 = 23.18 \rightarrow$ If PMILK = 1, then QMILK = 23.18

$\hat{\beta}_1 = -16.52 \rightarrow$ If PMILK increases 1%, then QMILK decreases 0.1652 units

Again, a curvilinear line will be fit to the scattergram. The $R^2$ of this regression can be compared to that of the linear regression since both have QMILK as the dependent variable. Adjusted R2 can be used as well, however, there is no need to resort to $\overline{R}^2$ since the number of explanatory variables is the same in both regressions. Also, the Akaike and Schwarz criteria can be compared. The lin-log model fits better with an $R^2$ of 0.99 compared to 0.94 in the linear model. This suggests that curving a line through the scattergram is fitting better than a using a straight line.

Notice that the decimal point moves two places to the left when interpreting the coefficient on PMILK in the lin-log model. In the double-log

| Linear:<br>$QMILK_t = 35.17 - 11.27$<br>　$PMILK_t + e_t, R^2 = 0.94$<br>If PMILK = 0, then<br>　QMILK = 35.17<br>If PMILK ↑ 1 unit, then<br>　QMILK ↓ 11.27 units | Lin-Log:<br>$QMILK_t = 23.18 - 16.52$<br>　$LNPMILK_t + e_t, R^2 = 0.99$<br>If PMILK = 1, then<br>　QMILK = 23.18<br>If PMILK ↑ 1%, then<br>　QMILK ↓ 0.1652 units |
| --- | --- |

model the decimal place does not move when $\hat{\beta}_1$ is interpreted. In the log-lin model the decimal point moves two places to the right. This is because the double-log model posits that a percentage change in the X-variable causes a percentage change in the Y-variable. In the log-lin and lin-log models, percentage changes in one variable are related to unit changes in the other variable. Thus, the decimal place must be adjusted to account for that.

# THE RECIPROCAL MODEL

The reciprocal model uses the reciprocal of the independent variable.

$$QMILK_t = 1.34 + 20.37(1/PMILK)_t + e_t$$

Often this model is used to estimate asymptotic relationships because of the unique interpretation of the intercept term.

$\hat{\beta}_0 = 1.34 \rightarrow$ As PMILK approaches infinity, QMILK $\rightarrow$ 1.34

$\hat{\beta}_1 = 20.37 \rightarrow$ If PMILK increases, then QMILK decreases

The interpretation of $\hat{\beta}_1$ is an interpretation of its sign only. Positive 20.37 means that if PMILK increases, then QMILK is expected to decrease. This is because an increase in PMILK reduces the value of the independent variable, 1/PMILK.

The reciprocal model fits better than the linear model:

| | |
|---|---|
| Reciprocal: $QMILK_t = 1.34 + 20.37$ $(1/PMILK)_t + e_t$ $R^2 = 0.97$ As PMILK $\rightarrow \infty$, QMILK $\rightarrow 1.34$ If PMILK $\uparrow$, then QMILK $\downarrow$ | Linear: $QMILK_t = 35.17 - 11.27$ $PMILK_t + e_t$ $R^2 = 0.94$ If PMILK = 0, then QMILK = 35.17 If PMILK $\uparrow$ 1 unit, then QMILK $\downarrow$ 11.27 units |

Once again, $R^2$, $\overline{R}^2$, Akaike, and Schwarz can be used to compare fits since the dependent variables of both regressions match as does k = 2. The superior fit of the reciprocal form suggests that a curvilinear line fits better than a straight line.

# THE POLYNOMIAL MODEL

The polynomial form is used to model parabolic or semi-parabolic relationships. If the regression line sloped downward at an increasing or decreasing rate, the polynomial form would capture that.

$$\text{QMILK}_t = 44.07 - 24.54 \ \text{PMILK}_t + 4.07 \ \text{PMILK}_t^2 + e_t$$

$$\hat{\beta}_0 = 44.07 \ \rightarrow \ \text{If PMILK} = 0, \quad \text{then QMILK} = 44.07$$

$\hat{\beta}_1 = -24.54$ and $\hat{\beta}_2 = 4.07 \rightarrow$ as PMILK increases, QMILK decreases at a decreasing rate.

Notice that $\hat{\beta}_1$ and $\hat{\beta}_2$ are interpreted in tandem. The magnitude of these coefficients has no straightforward interpretation. However, when the coefficient on PMILK is negative and the coefficient on $PMILK^2$ is positive, it suggests a parabola that decreases at a decreasing rate. The positive/negative pattern on the coefficients of $\hat{\beta}_1$ and $\hat{\beta}_2$ are interpreted as follows:

$$Y_t = \hat{\beta}_0 + \hat{\beta}_1 X_t + \hat{\beta}_2 X_t^2 + e_t$$

If $\hat{\beta}_1 > 0$ and $\hat{\beta}_2 > 0$, then as X increases, Y increases at an increasing rate.
If $\hat{\beta}_1 < 0$ and $\hat{\beta}_2 < 0$, then as X increases, Y decreases at an increasing rate.
If $\hat{\beta}_1 > 0$ and $\hat{\beta}_2 < 0$, then as X increases, Y increases at a decreasing rate.
If $\hat{\beta}_1 < 0$ and $\hat{\beta}_2 > 0$, then as X increases, Y decreases at a decreasing rate.

---

Polynomial:

$$\text{QMILK}_t = 44.07 - 24.54 \ \text{PMILK}_t + 4.07 \ \text{PMILK}_t^2 + e_t$$

If PMILK = 0, then QMILK = 44.07

Since $\hat{\beta}_1 < 0$ and $\hat{\beta}_2 > 0$, then as PMILK ↑, QMILK ↓ up to a point and then QMILK ↑ (the relationship is U-shaped)

---

In this case $\hat{\beta}_1 < 0$ and $\hat{\beta}_2 > 0$, so the interpretation is as PMILK increases, QMILK will decrease at a decreasing rate:

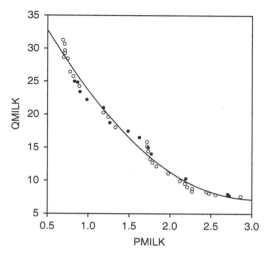

**Figure 6.5** The polynomial functional form.

If the scattergram suggests a U-shaped curve, or an inverted U-shape, the polynomial functional form is appropriate. In this example the data suggest a curve that slopes downward at a decreasing rate. It never turns up because the data do not. Indeed, it makes no sense for a demand curve to be U-shaped. However, in another example where the observed data had a U-shape, the polynomial regression line would eventually turn upward.

## MIXING AND MATCHING ALTERNATE FORMS

It is legitimate to mix and match alternate functional forms as in the multiple regression here. Each coefficient is interpreted individually, holding the others constant.

---

Mix and Match:

$$QMILK_t = 22.59 - 15.82 \ LNPMILK_t + 3.58 (1/PCOOKIE)_t + e_t$$

(where PCOOKIE is the price of cookies)

If PMILK = 1 and as PCOOKIE → ∞, QMILK → 22.59

If PMILK ↑ 1%, then QMILK ↓ 0.1582 units, holding PCOOKIE constant

If PCOOKIE ↑, then QMILK ↓, holding PMILK constant

---

Hopefully there are good theoretical reasons for choosing such a peculiar alternate functional form.

Note that there is rarely a good reason to use the square of a variable but not the variable itself, as in:

$$QMILK_t = \hat{\beta}_0 + \hat{\beta}_1 PMILK_t{}^2 + e_t$$

## FINDING THE CORRECT FUNCTIONAL FORM

It is critical that regressions are run in the appropriate functional form. If the relationship between X and Y is curvilinear and the regression is run in the linear form, the results will be biased. Therefore, it is just as important to specify the correct functional form as it is to include all the relevant independent variables.

Theory is the best guide for determining the appropriate functional form. If a particular relationship is likely to be asymptotic, then the reciprocal form should be used. It is often instructive to see which functional form other researchers used on a given topic.

Unfortunately, theory and previous work are not always specific about the functional form of a statistical relationship. The second-best solution is to let the data suggest the appropriate functional form. For instance, one functional form may fit much better than the others.

Not all of the various functional forms can be compared directly for fit. The $R^2$, $\overline{R}^2$, Akaike, and Schwarz criteria for regressions that do not have the same dependent variable are not comparable. In some alternate functional forms the dependent variable is logged and in others it is not. Still, one can discern if a linear specification is appropriate because the fit of a linear regression can be compared to the lin-log, reciprocal, and polynomial specifications.

Finally, just looking at a scattergram of the relationship can be useful. We saw that the scattergram for the demand for milk suggested an alternate functional form.

## TERMS

Alternate functional form—A regression where at least one of the variables is transformed into different units such as natural logarithms or raised to some exponential power.

Regression through the origin—A regression where the constant term is suppressed.

Trend variable—An explanatory variable that takes on integer values that increase by one each period.

## CHAPTER 6 PROBLEMS

(1) Given the scattergram below, is regression through the origin a good idea in this case? Explain why or why not.

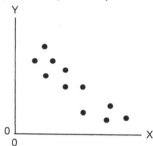

(2) Use the data in OKUNUK.XLS and statistical software to run the following regression:

$$GDPGAP_t = \hat{\beta}_0 + \hat{\beta}_1 CHGUN_t + e_t$$

where GDPGAP = real GDP growth minus potential GDP growth in the UK

CHGUN = change in the unemployment rate in the UK

(A) According to a test of significance, does $\hat{\beta}_0$ belong in the regression?

(B) According to economic reasoning, does $\hat{\beta}_0$ belong in the regression?

(C) Re-run the regression excluding $\hat{\beta}_0$. Does $\hat{\beta}_1$ change much from the prior regression?

(D) Which regression of the two fits best? On what do you base your response?

(3) In the regression below, what would be the new values of $\hat{\beta}_0$, $\hat{\beta}_1$, their t-ratios, SER, $r^2$, and the mean of WEIGHT if WEIGHT was measured in ounces instead of pounds?

$$\text{WEIGHT}_i = 51.12 + 1.85 \ \text{HEIGHT}_i + e_i$$
$$\phantom{\text{WEIGHT}_i = }(4.72) \quad (9.85) \quad \leftarrow t - \text{ratios}$$
$$\text{SER} = 20.38 \quad \overline{\text{WEIGHT}} = 156.78$$

$$r^2 = 0.49 \quad n = 4800$$

(4) In the regression below, what would be the new values of $\hat{\beta}_0, \hat{\beta}_1$, their t-ratios, SER, $r^2$, and the mean of HEIGHT if AGE was measured in months instead of years and height was measured in inches instead of feet?

$$\text{HEIGHT}_i = 1.68 + 0.35 \ \text{AGE}_i + e_i$$
$$\phantom{\text{HEIGHT}_i = }(7.723) \quad (2.11) \quad \leftarrow t - \text{ratios}$$
$$\text{SER} = 12.45 \quad \overline{\text{HEIGHT}} = 5.54$$

$$r^2 = 0.38 \quad n = 120$$

(5) Use the data in EGG.XLS and statistical software to do the following problems:

Run the following regression: $\text{QEGG}_t = \hat{\beta}_0 + \hat{\beta}_1 \ \text{PEGG}_t + e_t$

where QEGG is per capita egg consumption each year 1973–1997
PEGG is the average price of a dozen eggs in the USA
(A)  (i) Interpret the value you obtained for $\hat{\beta}_0$.
     (ii) Interpret the value you obtained for $\hat{\beta}_1$.
     (iii) If the price of eggs goes up \$1 per dozen, what is the expected change in egg consumption according to this regression?
(B)  Run the regression in the double-log form.
     (i) Interpret the value you obtained for $\hat{\beta}_0$.

(ii) Interpret the value you obtained for $\hat{\beta}_1$.

(iii) If the price of eggs goes up 1%, what is the expected percentage change in egg consumption according to this regression?

(C) Run the regression in the semi-log form (where the natural log of PEGG is taken).

    (i) Interpret the value you obtained for $\hat{\beta}_0$.

    (ii) Interpret the value you obtained for $\hat{\beta}_1$.

    (iii) If the price of eggs goes up 1%, what is the expected change in egg consumption according to this regression?

(D) Run the regression in the semi-log form (where the natural log of QEGG is taken).

    (i) Interpret the value you obtained for $\hat{\beta}_0$.

    (ii) Interpret the value you obtained for $\hat{\beta}_1$.

    (iii) If the price of eggs goes up $1 per dozen, what is the expected percentage change in egg consumption according to this regression?

(E) Run the regression in the reciprocal form.

    (i) Interpret the value you obtained for $\hat{\beta}_0$.

    (ii) Interpret the value you obtained for $\hat{\beta}_1$.

    (iii) If the price of eggs goes up $1 per dozen, will egg consumption increase or decrease according to this regression?

(F) Run the regression in the polynomial form.

    (i) Interpret the value you obtained for $\hat{\beta}_0$.

    (ii) Interpret the values you obtained for $\hat{\beta}_1$ and $\hat{\beta}_2$.

(G) (i) Do the data in this study require an alternate functional form or is the linear form satisfactory? Explain.

    (ii) Which of the six regressions fits the data best? Explain.

(6) Use the data in MATISSE.XLS and statistical software to do the following problems:

Does the size of a master's painting have an effect on its price? To shed light on this issue run the following regression:

$$PRICE_i = \hat{\beta}_0 + \hat{\beta}_1 \ SIZE_i + e_i$$

where PRICE is the price of paintings by Matisse sold at auction in dollars

SIZE is the size of the paintings in square inches

(A)   (i) Interpret the value you obtained for $\hat{\beta}_0$.
     (ii) Interpret the value you obtained for $\hat{\beta}_1$.
    (iii) If one Matisse canvas is 60 square inches larger than another, will it cost more? Exactly how much more (or less)?
    (iv) According to this regression, what would a 1,500-square-inch Matisse sell for at auction?

(B) Run the regression in the double-log form.
    (i) Interpret the value you obtained for $\hat{\beta}_0$.
    (ii) Interpret the value you obtained for $\hat{\beta}_1$.
    (iii) If one Matisse canvas is 5% larger than another, will it cost more? Exactly how much more (or less) in percentage terms?
    (iv) According to this regression, what would a 1,500-square-inch Matisse sell for at auction?

(C) Run the regression in the semi-log form (where the natural log of price is taken).
    (i) Interpret the value you obtained for $\hat{\beta}_0$.
    (ii) Interpret the value you obtained for $\hat{\beta}_1$.
    (iii) If one Matisse canvas is 60 square inches larger than another, will it cost more? Exactly how much more (or less) in percentage terms?
    (iv) According to this regression, what would a 1,500-square-inch Matisse sell for at auction?

(D) Run the regression in the semi-log form (where the natural log of size is taken).
    (i) Interpret the value you obtained for $\hat{\beta}_0$.
    (ii) Interpret the value you obtained for $\hat{\beta}_1$.
    (iii) If one Matisse canvas is 5% larger than another, will it cost more? Exactly how much more (or less)?
    (iv) According to this regression, what would a 1,500-square-inch Matisse sell for at auction?

(E) Run the regression in the reciprocal form.
    (i) Interpret the value you obtained for $\hat{\beta}_0$.
    (ii) Interpret the value you obtained for $\hat{\beta}_1$.
    (iii) If one Matisse canvas is 60 square inches larger than another, will it cost more? Exactly how much more (or less)?
    (iv) According to this regression, what would a 1,500-square-inch Matisse sell for at auction?

(F) Run the regression in the polynomial form.
  (i) Interpret the value you obtained for $\hat{\beta}_0$.
  (ii) Interpret the values you obtained for $\hat{\beta}_1$ and $\hat{\beta}_2$.
  (iii) If one Matisse canvas is 60 square inches larger than another, will it cost more? Exactly how much more (or less)?
  (iv) According to this regression, what would a 1,500-square-inch Matisse sell for at auction?
(G)  (i) Do the data in this study require an alternate functional form or is the linear form satisfactory? Explain.
  (ii) Which of the six regressions fits the data best? Explain.
(7) Use the data in SDATA.XLS and statistical software to do the following problem:
  Which functional form do you think is appropriate for the regression:

$$GPA_i = \hat{\beta}_0 + \hat{\beta}_1 ST_i + e_i \quad \text{Explain your response.}$$

(8) Use the data in EKC.XLS and statistical software to test the environmental Kuznets's theory. This theory posits an inverted–U shaped relationship between pollution and economic development (Dasgupta et al. 2002).

$$PART = \hat{\beta}_0 + \hat{\beta}_1\ GDPCAP_i + \hat{\beta}_2\ GDPCAP_i^2 + e_i$$

where PART is suspended particulates in the largest city of the nation
(A) Run the following polynomial regression and discuss its implications for the Kuznets's curve:

$$CO2CAP_i = \hat{\beta}_0 + \hat{\beta}_1\ GDPCAP_i + \hat{\beta}_2\ GDPCAP_i^2 + e_i$$

where CO2CAP is per capita carbon dioxide emissions in 48 nations
  GDPCAP is per capita GDP in these nations
(B) Run the following regression and discuss its implications for the Kuznets's curve:

$$SO2CAP_i = \hat{\beta}_0 + \hat{\beta}_1\ GDPCAP_i + \hat{\beta}_2\ GDPCAP_i^2 + e_i$$

where SO2CAP is per capita sulfur dioxide emissions in 48 nations
(C) Run the following regression and discuss its implications for the Kuznets's curve:

(9) Interpret every structural parameter in each of the following regressions considering:
   (A) $LNWAGES_i = 2.1 + 1.3 EXP_i + e_i$
   (B) $WAGES_i = 2.1 + 1.3 EXP_i - 2.3 EXPSQ_i + e_i$
   (C) $WAGES_i = 2.5 - 0.1 (1/EXP)_i + e_i$

> WAGES = pay per hour of work
> LNWAGES = natural log of WAGES
> EXP = years of experience
> EXPSQ = EXP squared

(10) In the spaces below draw the following regression results:
   (A) $LNWAGES = 2.1 + 1.3 EXP$

   (B) $WAGES = 2.1 + 1.3 EXP - 2.3 EXPSQ$

   (C) $WAGES = 2.5 - 0.1 (1/EXP)$

## APPENDIX TO CHAPTER 6

## DERIVATION OF $\hat{\beta}_1$ WITH REGRESSION THROUGH THE ORIGIN

Given: $Y_i = \hat{\beta}_1 X_i + e_i$, find the value of $\hat{\beta}_1$ that minimizes $\Sigma e_i^2$

Substitute $e_i = Y_i - \hat{\beta}_1 X_i$ into $\Sigma e_i^2$: $\Sigma (Y_i - \hat{\beta}_1 X_i)^2$

Take the derivative with respect to $\hat{\beta}_1$ and set it equal to zero:

$$\frac{d\Sigma(Y_i - \hat{\beta}_1 X_i)^2}{d\hat{\beta}_1} = 2\Sigma(Y_i - \hat{\beta}_1 X_i)(-X_i) = 0$$

Divide both sides of this equation by $-2$ leaving: $\Sigma(Y_i - \hat{\beta}_1 X_i)(X_i) = 0$

Distribute the summation sign: $\Sigma Y_i X_i - \hat{\beta}_1 \Sigma X_i^2 = 0$

Move the second term to the other side gives: $\Sigma Y_i X_i = \hat{\beta}_1 \Sigma X_i^2$ This is known as a "normal equation."

Rearrange terms and divide through by $\Sigma X_i^2$ to get:

$$\hat{\beta}_1 = \frac{\Sigma X_i Y_i}{\Sigma X_i^2}$$

# 7 Dichotomous Variables

## DICHOTOMOUS VARIABLES

Dichotomous variables take on the values of zero or one only. They are more commonly called "dummy" variables and they may be referred to as qualitative variables since they are used to distinguish between different classes, categories, or types.

In this example, MALE is a dummy variable.

$$DRINKS_i = 18.31 - 3.75\ GPA_i + 4.74\ MALE_i + e_i$$
$$(8.56)\ (-6.23)\qquad (7.55)\quad \leftarrow t - ratios$$
$$SER = 8.62 \quad \overline{DRINKS} = 7.59 \quad R^2 = 0.13 \quad n = 695$$

where DRINKS—an undergraduate's number of alcoholic drinks
        per week
      GPA—the student's GPA
      MALE—1 if the student is male; 0 otherwise

Here are the first few observations in the data set:

| OBS | DRINKS | GPA | MALE |
|-----|--------|-----|------|
| 1 | 3 | 3.7 | 0 |
| 2 | 30 | 3.3 | 0 |
| 3 | 4 | 3 | 1 |
| 4 | 0 | 3 | 0 |
| 5 | 0 | 4 | 1 |
| ⋮ | ⋮ | ⋮ | ⋮ |

DOI: 10.4324/9781003213758-7

The formulas for estimating the structural parameters and the residual statistics are unaffected by the presence of a dummy variable. However, the interpretations are somewhat different.

$\hat{\beta}_0$ = 18.31 → A nonmale with 0 GPA is expected to have 18.31 alcoholic drinks per week.

$\hat{\beta}_1$ = −3.75 → If GPA increases 1 unit, DRINKS (males and nonmales) decreases 3.75 units.

$\hat{\beta}_2$ = 4.74 → A male has 4.74 more drinks than a nonmale with the same GPA.

Graphing the interpretations indicates that the dummy variable allows for different intercepts for males and nonmales. However, the slopes of the two regression lines are parallel.

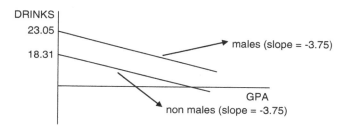

**Figure 7.1** A dichotomous variable allows for different intercepts.

The regression line for nonmales starts at 18.31. The interpretation of the intercept term makes this apparent. The nonmale regression line slopes downward at a rate of 3.75 drinks for each unit increase in GPA. This is gleaned from the interpretation of the coefficient on GPA.

The regression line for males also has a slope of −3.75. The coefficient on GPA applies to both groups. The coefficient attached to the dummy variable indicates that the regression line for males begins 4.74 units higher than that for nonmales. (18.31 + 4.74 = 23.05).

It does not matter if the dummy variable is defined to be "1 if the student is male; 0 otherwise" or in the converse manner "1 if the student is nonmale; 0 otherwise." The regression results will mean the same thing either way; however, some of the coefficients will be altered. Using the converse definition of the dummy variable yields the following regression:

$$\text{DRINKS}_i = 23.05 - 3.75 \ \text{GPA}_i - 4.74 \ \text{MALE}_i + e_i$$

$\hat{\beta}_0$ = 23.05 → A male with 0 GPA is expected to have 23.05 alcoholic drinks per week.

$\hat{\beta}_1 = -3.75 \rightarrow$ If GPA increases 1 unit, DRINKS (males and nonmales) decreases 3.75 units.

$\hat{\beta}_2 = -4.74 \rightarrow$ A nonmale has 4.74 fewer drinks than a male with the same GPA.

Graphing the interpretations gives exactly the same diagram as previously. The boxes here compare the original regression results with those when the dummy variable is defined conversely.

Male = 1 if the respondent is male; 0 otherwise

$$DRINKS_i = 18.31 - 3.75\ GPA_i + 4.74\ MALE_i + e_i$$
$$(8.56)\ (-6.23) \qquad (7.55) \quad \leftarrow t - \text{ratios}$$
$$SER = 8.62 \quad \overline{DRINKS} = 7.59 \quad R^2 = 0.13 \quad n = 695$$

Male = 1 if the respondent is **nonmale**; 0 otherwise

$$DRINKS_i = 23.\ 05 - 3.75\ GPA_i - 4.\ 74\ MALE_i + e_i$$
$$(8.56)\ (-6.23) \qquad (7.55)\ \leftarrow t - \text{ratios}$$
$$SER = 8.62 \quad \overline{DRINKS} = 7.59 \quad R^2 = 0.13 \quad n = 695$$

There is a pattern to how the coefficients change when the dummy variable is defined in the opposite manner. The new constant term is the combination of the initial constant term with the coefficient on the dummy variable. The coefficient on GPA is unaffected. The coefficient on MALE changes sign.

## INTERACTIVE TERMS

Interactive terms interact with dummy variables to allow for different slopes for different categories. To form an interactive variable, multiply the dummy variable by one of the continuous variables. Going back to the regression from the previous section, an interactive term has been added: MALE*GPA:

$DRINKS_i = 11.66-1.86\ GPA_i + 17.67\ MALE_i-3.75\ MALE * GPA_i + e_i$

   (3.93) (−2.20)  (4.33)    (−3.21)  ← t − ratios

  SER = 8.56  $\overline{DRINKS}$ = 7.59  $R^2$ = 0.15  n = 695

DRINKS—an undergraduate's number of alcoholic drinks
    per week
GPA—the student's GPA
MALE—1 if the student is male; 0 otherwise
MALE * GPA—MALE × GPA

$\hat{\beta}_0$ = 11.66 → A nonmale with 0 GPA is expected to have 11.66 alcoholic drinks per week.

$\hat{\beta}_1$ = −1.86 → If GPA increases 1 unit, DRINKS for nonmales decreases 1.86 units.

$\hat{\beta}_2$ = 17.67 → A male with zero GPA drinks 17.67 units more than a nonmale with zero GPA.

$\hat{\beta}_3$ = −3.75 → If GPA increases 1 unit then DRINKS for a male will decrease 3.75 units over and above the 1.86 units for a nonmale.

The interpretations can be used to make a graphical depiction of the regression lines.

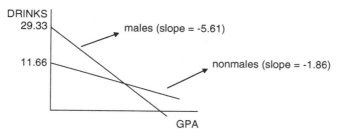

Figure 7.2 An interactive variable allows for different slopes.

The interpretation of the constant term makes it apparent that the regression line for nonmales starts at 11.66. To find the intercept for males, add 17.67 to 11.66. The interpretation of −1.86 indicates that it is the slope for nonmales. To find the slope for males, subtract 3.75 from −1.86.

How would the regression results change if the dummy was defined in the opposite manner: Male—1 if the respondent is **not** male; 0 otherwise? Again, the regression results would be altered, but so would the interpretations. The diagram above would be unchanged.

---

DRINKS$_i$ = 29.33 − 5.61 GPA$_i$ − 17.67 MALE$_i$ + 3.75 MALE * GPA$_i$ + e$_i$

      (3.93) (−2.20)    (4.33)        (3.21)  ← t − ratios

SER = 8.56  $\overline{\text{DRINKS}}$ = 7.59  $R^2$ = 0.15  n = 695

DRINKS—an undergraduate's number of alcoholic drinks
      per week
GPA—the student's GPA
MALE—0 if male; 1 otherwise
MALE*GPA—MALE × GPA

---

$\hat{\beta}_0$ = 29.33 → A male with zero GPA is expected to have 29.33 alcoholic drinks per week.

$\hat{\beta}_1$ = −5.61 → If GPA increases 1 unit, DRINKS for males decreases 5.61 units.

$\hat{\beta}_2$ = −17.67 → A nonmale with zero GPA drinks 17.67 units less than a male with zero GPA.

$\hat{\beta}_3$ = 3.75 → If GPA increases 1 unit then DRINKS for a nonmale will decrease 3.75 units less than the −5.61 units for a male.

The boxes compare the original regression results with those when the dummy variable is flip-flopped.

Male = 1 if the respondent is male; 0 otherwise

---

DRINKS$_i$ = 11.66 − 1.86 GPA$_i$ + 17.67 MALE$_i$ − 3.75 MALE * GPA$_i$ + e$_i$

      (3.93) (−2.20)    (4.33)        (3.21)  ← t − ratios

SER = 8.56  $\overline{\text{DRINKS}}$ = 7.59  $R^2$ = 0.15  n = 695

Male = 1 if the respondent is **not** male; 0 otherwise

$$DRINKS_i = 29.33 - 5.61 \ GPA_i - 17.67 \ MALE_i + 3.75 \ MALE * GPA_i + e_i$$
$$(3.93) \ (-2.20) \qquad (4.33) \qquad\qquad (3.21) \quad \leftarrow t-ratios$$
$$SER = 8.56 \quad \overline{DRINKS} = 7.59 \quad R^2 = 0.15 \quad n = 695$$

There is a pattern to how the coefficients change when the dummy variable is defined in the opposite manner. The new coefficient on GPA is a combination of the initial coefficient with the coefficient on the interactive term. The new constant term is the combination of the initial constant term with the coefficient on the dummy variable. The coefficients on MALE and MALE*GPA change sign.

## LINEAR PROBABILITY MODELS

Up to this point, dummy variables served as independent variables. Dichotomous variables can be dependent variables as well. If ordinary least squares is used to estimate a regression with a dummy dependent variable, then it is known as a linear probability model.

Spector and Mazzeo (1980) used a linear probability model to investigate the factors affecting final letter grades in macroeconomics. The dependent variable in their study was AMACRO, a dichotomous variable.

AMACRO—1 if final grade in macroeconomics is an A; 0 otherwise

The independent variables were:

GPA—GPA of student at the beginning of macroeconomics
TUCE—score on the TUCE exam prior to macroeconomics (the TUCE is a 33 multiple-choice exam that Tests Understanding of College Economics)
PSI—1 if student received personalized instruction (tutoring); 0 otherwise

$$AMACRO_i = -1.4980 + .4639 \ GPA_i + .0111 \ TUCE_i + .3786 \ PSI_i + e_i$$
$$(2.86) \qquad (0.54) \qquad\quad (2.72) \quad \leftarrow t-ratios$$

### *Interpretations*

If GPA, TUCE, and PSI = 0, then the probability of obtaining an A in macroeconomics = –149.80%.

If GPA increases 1 unit then the probability of obtaining an A in macroeconomics increases 46.39%, holding TUCE constant, regardless of PSI.

If TUCE increases 1 unit then the probability of obtaining an A in macroeconomics Increases 1.11%, holding GPA constant, regardless of PSI.

If PSI = 1 then the student receives personalized instruction and increases their odds of obtaining an A in macroeconomics by 37.86%, holding GPA and TUCE constant.

An attractive feature of this model is that the coefficients are interpreted as probabilities. Yet, all linear probability models suffer from some drawbacks. First, the standard measures of fit are invalid in these models. Determining if the model fits well involves checking its accuracy at predicting A-students.

A more disconcerting drawback of linear probability models is their predictions can be out of bounds (greater than 1 or less than 0). Consider a student with a 3.5 GPA, a score of 28 on the TUCE exam, and who received personalized instruction:

$$\overline{AMACRO}i = -1.4980 + .4639 \ GPA_i + .0111 \ TUCE_i + .3786 \ PSI_i$$
$$.815 = -1.4980 + .4639 \ (3.5) + .0111 \ (28) \quad + .3786 \ (1)$$

This student has an 81.5% chance of receiving an A in macroeconomics. However, a student with a GPA of 3.9, a 33 on the TUCE exam, and who received personalized instruction has a 106% chance of obtaining an A:

$$\overline{AMACRO}i = -1.4980 + .4639 \ GPA_i + .0111 \ TUCE_i + .3786 \ PSI_i$$
$$1.06 = -1.4980 + .4639 \ (3.9) + .0111 \ (33) \quad + .3786 \ (1)$$

This is A prediction that is out of bounds. Only the gods know for certain whether this student will receive an A in the course. And even they are only 100% sure.

Another out-of-bounds prediction occurs with this next student as well:

$$\overline{AMACRO}i = -1.4980 + .4639 \ GPA_i + .0111 \ TUCE_i + .3786 \ PSI_i$$
$$- 0.26 = -1.4980 + .4639 \ (2.2) + .0111 \ (20) \quad + .3786 \ (0)$$

A student with a GPA of 2.2, a TUCE score of 20, and who did not receive personalized instruction has a negative 0.26 chance of getting an A according to the linear probability model. Negative probabilities are nonsense. The diagram below depicts what is happening.

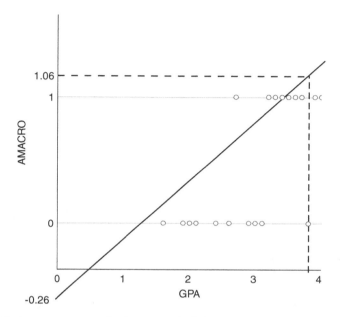

**Figure 7.3** A scattergram of a linear probability model.

AMACRO takes on the values of 0 or 1 only. Therefore, the observations on the scattergram will lie on these values. Here, AMACRO is plotted against GPA. High GPAs will be associated with AMACRO = 1, while low GPA students are more likely to have AMACRO = 0. A linear probability model fits a straight line through the observations using the ordinary least squares formulas. A student with a 3.9 GPA has a 106% chance of obtaining an A when the ordinary least squares line is used to make the prediction.

## LOGISTIC MODELS

Logistic models are based on the logistic equation. These models fit an S-shaped curve to scattergrams with dichotomous dependent variables. Logistic models give predictions that are less than one and greater than zero in all instances and thus avoid the problem associated with linear probability models.

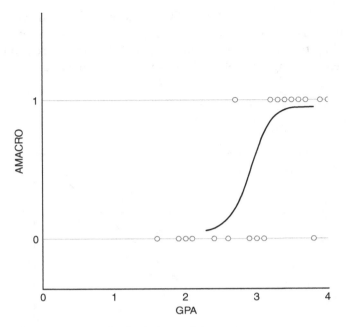

**Figure 7.4** A scattergram of a logistic model.

The logistic specification of Spector and Mazzeo's model for A's in macroanalysis is:

$$AMACRO_i = \frac{1}{1 + e^{-(\hat{\beta}_0 + \hat{\beta}_1\, GPA_i + \hat{\beta}_2\, TUCE_i + \hat{\beta}_3\, PSI_i + e_i)}}$$

With a little algebra, this specification can be re-written as:

$$\ln\left(\frac{AMACRO_i}{1 - AMACRO_i}\right) = \hat{\beta}_0 + \hat{\beta}_1\ GPA_i + \hat{\beta}_2 TUCE_i + \hat{\beta}_3 PSI_i + e_i$$

There is an estimation problem with the logistic model. If $AMACRO_i =$ 0 or 1, then $\ln\left(\frac{AMACRO_i}{1 - AMACRO_i}\right)$ is undefined and $AMACRO$ only equals 0 or 1. The maximum likelihood procedure overcomes this problem and is typically used to estimate the structural parameters of logistic models.

The maximum likelihood procedure is an algorithm that begins with in-itial values for the estimators and adjusts them based on the residuals ($e_i$'s).

The adjusted values of the estimators result in new $e_i$'s and the algorithm decides how to adjust the estimates again given these new $e_i$'s. This iterative process continues until sequential estimates of the estimators do not vary much.

Applying the maximum likelihood procedure to Spector and Mazzeo's data gives:

$$\ln\left(\frac{AMACRO_i}{1 - AMACRO_i}\right) = -13.0 + 2.8 \ GPA_i + 0.1 \ TUCE_i + 2.4 \ PSI_i + ei$$

$$(2.24) \qquad (0.72) \qquad (2.23) \leftarrow t - ratios$$

## Interpretations

The estimators in logistic models do not have intuitive interpretations so only two of them are interpreted here as examples:

-13.0—If GPA, TUCE, and PSI = 0, then the natural log of the odds ratio = -13.0.

2.8—If GPA increases 1 unit, then the natural log of the odds ratio increases 2.8 units, holding TUCE constant, regardless of PSI status.

## Predicting with Logistic Models

The predictions generated by logistic models are always between zero and one. Even the students with out-of-bounds predictions in the linear probability model are within bounds here.

It takes some effort to obtain these predictions. The students' GPA, TUCE, and PSI are plugged into the results from the logistic model:

$$\ln\left(\frac{AMACRO}{1 - AMACRO}\right) = -13.0 + 2.8 \ GPA_i + 0.1 \ TUCE_i + 2.4 \ PSI_i + e_i$$

$$1.909 = -13.0 + 2.8 \ (3.5) + 0.1(28) + 2.4 \ (1)$$

$$3.620 = -13.0 + 2.8(3.9) + 0.1(33) + 2.4 \ (1)$$

$$-4.904 = -13.0 + 2.8(2.2) + 0.1 \ (20) + 2.4 \ (0)$$

These results are converted into probabilities. Starting with the student with GPA = 3.5, TUCE = 28, and PSI = 1:

$$\ln\left(\frac{AMACRO}{1-AMACRO}\right) = -13.0 + 2.8(3.5) + 0.1(28) + 2.4(1) = 1.909$$

Take the anti-log of 1.909:

$$\left(\frac{AMACRO}{1-AMACRO}\right) = 6.746$$

Solve for AMACRO. Start by cross multiplying the equation above:

$$AMACRO = (1-AMACRO)\,(6.746)$$

Distribute the 6.746:

$$AMACRO = 6.746 - 6.746\ AMACRO$$

Move –6.746 AMACRO to the left side of the equality sign:

$$AMACRO + 6.746\ AMACRO = 6.746$$

Factor the two terms on the left of the equality sign:

$$AMACRO(1 + 6.746) = 6.746$$

Divide both sides by (1 + 6.746):

$$AMACRO = \frac{6.746}{1 + 6.746} = \frac{6.746}{7.746} = .87$$

The student with an 81.5% chance of obtaining an A according to the linear probability model has an 87% chance according to the logistic model.

The student with a 106% chance of obtaining an A according to the linear probability model has a 97% chance here.

$$\ln\left(\frac{AMACRO}{1-AMACRO}\right) = 3.620$$

Take the anti-log of 3.620:

$$\left(\frac{AMACRO}{1-AMACRO}\right) = 37.34$$

Solve for AMACRO:

$$AMACRO = (1-AMACRO)\ (37.34)$$

$$AMACRO = 37.34 - 37.34\ AMACRO$$

$$AMACRO + 37.34\ AMACRO = 37.34$$

$$AMACRO\ (1 + 37.34) = 37.34$$

$$AMACRO = \frac{37.34}{1 + 37.34} = \frac{37.34}{38.34} = .97$$

Finally, the student who had a negative 26% chance of obtaining an A has a 0.7% chance according to the logistic model.

$$\ln\left(\frac{AMACRO}{1-AMACRO}\right) = -4.904$$

Take the anti-log of −4.904:

$$\left(\frac{AMACRO}{1-AMACRO}\right) = 0.007$$

Solve for AMACRO:

$$AMACRO = (1-AMACRO)\ (0.007)$$

$$AMACRO = 0.007 - 0.007\ AMACRO$$

$$AMACRO + 0.007\ AMACRO = 0.007$$

$$AMACRO\ (1 + 0.007) = 0.007$$

$$AMACRO = \frac{0.007}{1 + 0.007} = \frac{0.007}{1.007} = 0.007$$

The usual measures of goodness-of-fit are not appropriate for logistic models. Instead, econometricians consider the model's ability to forecast correctly. For example, when the AMACRO model predicts a student's probability of getting an A is greater than 50%, then it is as if the model predicted that the student would get an A. Less than 50%, then the model is indicating the student will not get an A.

These predictions can be compared to how the students in the sample actually performed. If the model is not predicting many of the students' grades correctly, then it does not fit well.

## TERMS

Dummy variable (Dichotomous variable)—Independent or dependent variables that take on the values of zero or one only.

Interactive term—A dummy variable combined with another independent variable.

Linear probability model—A regression with a dichotomous dependent variable that is estimated with ordinary least squares.

Logistic model—An alternate function form that fits an S-shape to regressions with dichotomous dependent variables.

Maximum likelihood procedure—A technique for estimating the structural parameters of a non-linear econometric model, such as a logistic model.

## CHAPTER 7 PROBLEMS

(1) (A) Interpret every structural parameter in the following regression:

$$PROFSAL_i = 17.969 + 1.3707\ EXP_i + 3.3336\ DUM_i + e_i$$

where PROFSAL is the professor's salary;
      EXP is the professor's experience in years;
      DUM = 1 if the professor is male; 0 otherwise.

(B) Draw a diagram reflecting the regression results with PROFSAL on the vertical axis and EXP on the horizontal axis.

(C) A male professor with 10 years of experience is expected to make how much in salary?

(D) A nonmale professor with 10 years' experience is expected to make how much in salary?

(E) What would be the new values of the structural parameters if the dummy was defined as 1 if the professor is nonmale; 0 otherwise?

(F) Using the redefined dummy variable regression, how much would a male professor with 10 years of experience make in salary?

(2) Use the data in SDATA.XLS and statistical software to run the following regression:

$$GPA_i = \hat{\beta}_0 + \hat{\beta}_1 ST_i + \hat{\beta}_2 SAT_i + \hat{\beta}_3 MALE_i + e_i$$

where GPA = grade point average
      ST = study time per day
     SAT = SAT score
     MALE = 1 if the student is male; 0 otherwise

(A) Interpret the coefficient on SAT.

(B) Interpret the coefficient on the dummy variable.

(C) Would a male or a nonmale student with the same SAT scores and study time be expected to have a higher GPA? By exactly how much?

(D) What would be the values of the four structural coefficients if the dummy variable had been defined as 1 = nonmale; 0 otherwise?

(3) (A) Interpret every structural parameter in the following regression:

$$PROFSAL_i = 16.1718 + 1.2016 \ EXP_i + 3.2245 \ DUM_i$$
$$- 1.0001 \ DUM * EXP_i + e_i$$

where PROFSAL is the professor's salary;
     EXP is the professor's experience in years;
     DUM = 1 if the professor is male; 0 otherwise.

(B) Draw a diagram reflecting the regression results with PROFSAL on the vertical axis and EXP on the horizontal axis.

(C) What would be the new values of the structural parameters if the dummy was defined as 1 if the professor is nonmale; 0 otherwise?

(4) Use the data in SDATA.XLS and statistical software run the following regression:

$$GPA_i = \hat{\beta}_0 + \hat{\beta}_1 \, ST_i + \hat{\beta}_2 \, MALE_i + \hat{\beta}_3 \, INTER_i + e_i$$

where INTER is MALE × ST

(A) Interpret all four structural parameters.
(B) Who benefits more from an extra unit of ST, males or nonmales? Exactly how much more.
(C) What would be the new values for the structural parameters if the dummy for gender was defined: 1 = nonmale; 0 otherwise?
(D) Graph your regression results labeling all intercepts and slopes.

(5) (A) Interpret every structural parameter in the following regression:

$$GPA_i = 0.37 + 0.81 \, HSGPA_i + 0.00001 \, SAT_i - 0.38 \, GREEK_i + e_i$$

where GPA is grade point average in college;
       HSGPS is high school GPA;
       SAT is SAT score.
       GREEK equals 1 if the student is a member of a sorority or fraternity; 0 otherwise.

(B) Draw a diagram reflecting the regression results with GPA on the vertical axis and SAT on the horizontal axis.

(6) (A) Interpret every structural parameter in the following regression:

$$PERSAV_t = 41.8081 + 0.0321 \, INC_t - 19.7655 \, DUM_t$$
$$- 0.0021 \, DUM * INC_t + e_t$$

where PERSAV is personal savings in the USA;
       INC is disposable personal income in the USA;
       DUM = 1 if 1982 or later; 0 otherwise.

(B) Draw a diagram reflecting the regression results with PERSAV on the vertical axis and INC on the horizontal axis.
(C) What would be the new values of the structural parameters if the dummy was flip-flopped?

(7) Use the data in WAGES.XLS and statistical software run to run a regression where wages are explained by a constant term, education, experience, and a dummy variable for gender.

| Name | Variable |
|------|----------|
| WAGES | Wages |
| LNWAGES | The natural logarithm of wages |
| ED | Education in years |
| NONWH | 1 If nonwhite; 0 otherwise |
| FEM | 1 If nonmale; 0 otherwise |
| MARRIED | 1 If married; 0 otherwise |
| EXPER | Experience in years |
| EXPSQ | Experience squared |
| UNION | 1 If union member; 0 otherwise |
| PRO | 1 If employed in a profession; 0 otherwise |

(A) Interpret the coefficient on education.

(B) Interpret the coefficient on the dummy variable.

(8) Use the data in WAGES.XLS and statistical software to run a regression where wages are explained by a constant term, education, a dummy variable for gender, and an interactive term.

(A) Interpret all four structural parameters.

(B) Draw the regression results labeling the values of all intercepts and slopes.

(C) What would be the values of the structural parameters if the gender dummy was defined to be 1 if male; 0 otherwise?

(9) Use the data in WAGES.XLS and statistical software to run a regression where the natural logarithm of wages is explained by a constant term, education, experience, and dummy variables for marital status, gender, race, union membership, and professional status.

(A) Interpret the coefficient on education.

(B) Interpret the coefficient on marital status.

(C) Interpret the coefficient on union membership.

(D) Does this regression provide evidence of racial and gender discrimination? Explain.

(10) Use the data in WAGES.XLS and statistical software to run a regression where MARRIED is explained by a constant term, WAGES, ED, and PRO.

(A) Interpret all four structural parameters.

(B) What is the probability that a college grad (ED = 16) in a profession with WAGES = 9.0 is married?

(11) Use the data in EXTRAMARITAL.XLS and statistical software to estimate a linear probability model where EXTRA is explained by a constant term, AGE, HPPYM, RELIG, and YRSMAR.

EXTRA = 1 if person participated in an extramarital affair in the past year; 0 otherwise

AGE = the age of the person

HPPYM = person's perception of their marital happiness (1 = very unhappy; 5 = very happy)

RELIG = person's perception of their religiousness (1 = very unreligious; 5 = very religious)

YRSMAR = years married

(A) Interpret all 5 structural parameters.

(B) What is the probability that a 52-year-old person married for 27 years had an extramarital affair last year? Assume the person's RELIG = 2 and HAPPYM = 3.

(12) Use the data in EXTRAMARITAL.XLS and statistical software to estimate a logistic model where EXTRA is explained by a constant term, AGE, HPPYM, RELIG, and YRSMAR. What is the probability that a 52-year-old person married for 27 years had an extramarital affair last year? Assume the person's RELIG = 2 and HAPPYM = 3.

(13) Label each statement below TRUE or FALSE.

(A) R-squared is not a good measure of fit for a linear probability model.

(B) A logistic model can yield a predicted value for the dependent variable that is equal to one, but never greater than one.

(C) A linear probability model can yield a predicted value for the dependent variable that is equal to one, but never greater than one.

(D) R-squared is not valid in regressions including dummy independent variables.

(E) R-squared is invalid in regressions including dummy dependent variables.

# 8 The Classical Linear Regression Model

## THE ORDINARY LEAST SQUARES ESTIMATORS ARE BLUE

Although many choices are available when faced with calculating the structural parameters of $Y_i = \hat{\beta}_0 + \hat{\beta}_1 X_i + e_i$, the most popular technique is ordinary least squares (OLS). When $\hat{\beta}_0$ and $\hat{\beta}_1$ are calculated so that $\Sigma e_i^2$ is minimized, the estimates have some very desirable statistical qualities. These qualities are captured in the acronym BLUE—best, linear, unbiased estimators.

However, the OLS estimators are BLUE only under certain conditions. These conditions and the analysis of the statistical properties that follow from them are known as the classical linear regression model (CLRM).

## LINEAR

The ordinary least squares estimators are linear under certain conditions. Linear in this case means that the formulas for $\hat{\beta}_0$ and $\hat{\beta}_1$ are linear—their formulas do not contain any nonlinearities such as exponents, reciprocals, or logarithms. This is certainly true of our formula for $\hat{\beta}_0 = \bar{Y} - \hat{\beta}_1 \bar{X}$. Every term in this formula is a constant value ($\hat{\beta}_0$ and $\hat{\beta}_1$) or given ($\bar{Y}$ and $\bar{X}$). Thus, the formula for $\hat{\beta}_0$ is linear.

However, the formula for $\hat{\beta}_1$ has a quotient and an exponent:

$$\hat{\beta}_1 = \frac{\Sigma(X_i - \bar{X})Y_i}{\Sigma(X_i - \bar{X})^2}$$

DOI: 10.4324/9781003213758-8

These nonlinearities can be removed by writing the formula as

$$\hat{\beta}_1 = \Sigma w_i Y_i \quad \text{where} \quad w_i = \frac{(X_i - \bar{X})}{\Sigma(X_i - \bar{X})^2}$$

This does not get rid of the nonlinearities. It only masks them in the term $w_i$. However, the $w_i$'s are constants if the $X_i$'s, that form them, are predetermined. In other words, the $w_i$'s are comprised only of $X_i$'s which are given, so the $w_i$'s are constant values despite the non-linearities. The formula $\hat{\beta}_1 = \Sigma w_i Y_i$ is comprised of constants ($w_i$'s) and given values ($Y_i$'s).

Unfortunately, in econometrics it is rarely the case that the $X_i$'s are predetermined or fixed. Consider the following regression:

$$\text{GPA}_i = \hat{\beta}_0 + \hat{\beta}_1 \, \text{ST}_i + e_i \qquad \text{where GPA}_i \text{ is grade point average of}$$

the ith student

$\text{ST}_i$ is average daily study time of the ith

student

The variable ST is predetermined if prior to collecting any data from students, it is decided that ST should equal 0.5 h, 1.0 h, 1.5 h, 2.0 h, and 2.5 h. Then a randomly selected group of students is tasked with studying 0.5 h a day for an academic year. At the end of the year their GPA's are recorded. Next a randomly selected group of students is required to study 1.0 h a day. After the semester, their GPAs are recorded. Continue in this manner through ST = 3.0 h.

Typically data are not collected this way. Instead, randomly selected students are asked for their ST and GPA. If a student reports ST = 0.75, that student is not excluded from the study. In other words, the variable ST is stochastic, not predetermined, given, or fixed. In this situation, $\hat{\beta}_1$ is nonlinear.

A nonlinear $\hat{\beta}_1$ is not an immediate problem and in no way makes $\hat{\beta}_1$ less desirable. However, some upcoming proofs will be more conveniently accomplished with a linear $\hat{\beta}_1$. In addition, it can be shown that $\hat{\beta}_1$ is linear even if the $X_i$'s are not predetermined so long as the $X_i$'s are not correlated with the true error terms ($u_i$'s) from the regression.

The first assumption of the CLRM is that the independent variables are predetermined or at least not correlated with the error term: $E[u_i X_i] = 0$.

Concisely stated, $\hat{\beta}_0$ and $\hat{\beta}_1$ are linear if the $X_i$'s are predetermined or if the $X_i$'s are not correlated with the error terms from the regression. Linearity is not a highly desirable statistical attribute, but it will make some upcoming proofs easier.

## UNBIASED

Unbiased results are desirable in any scientific study. This is true of regression analysis as well. However, the term "unbiased" has a particular meaning in regard to statistical estimators. An estimator is unbiased if its expected value (average in repeated sampling) is equal to the true value of the parameter: $E[\hat{\beta}_1] = \beta_1$. The expected value of $\hat{\beta}_1$ is equal to $\beta_1$. A biased method of calculating $\hat{\beta}_1$ would result in the average in repeated sampling being higher (overestimate) or lower (underestimate) than $\beta_1$: $E[\hat{\beta}_1] \neq \beta_1$. The expected value of $\hat{\beta}_1$ is not equal to $\beta_1$.

It is highly unlikely that any particular sample regression will yield the true value of $\beta_1$. However, an estimate is unbiased if the regression is run 100,000 times, drawing fresh data from the same population each time, and the average $\hat{\beta}_1$ of those regressions equals the true value, $\beta_1$.

How can it be determined that the OLS estimators are unbiased since $\beta_1$ is unknown? First, there is a mathematical proof that $E[\hat{\beta}_1] = \beta_1$ under certain assumptions. That proof is provided in an appendix to this chapter. Second, the proof that the ordinary least squares estimators are unbiased has been verified with Monte Carlo studies. A Monte Carlo study draws repeated samples from a known population and then analyzes the characteristics of the sample regressions.

Monte Carlo studies allow econometricians to know the true values of $\beta_0$ and $\beta_1$ by assuming a regression with, say, 5,000 observations, encompases the entire, error-free population of observations. The structural parameters of a regression line through these 5,000 observations are the true $\beta_0$ and $\beta_1$, and the error terms are the true $u_i$'s.

Now take a random sample of 40 observations from the 5,000 and run a sample regression. A computer could run 100,000 of these regressions, drawing a fresh sample of 40 observations each time, in a matter of seconds. For an unbiased estimator, the average $\hat{\beta}_0$ and $\hat{\beta}_1$ from the 100,000 regressions will be equal to the true $\beta_0$ and $\beta_1$ from the population regression with 5,000 observations.

Monte Carlo studies show that $\hat{\beta}_0$ and $\hat{\beta}_1$ are unbiased under certain conditions. Those conditions come to light in the mathematical proof that $\hat{\beta}_0$ and $\hat{\beta}_1$ are unbiased. It is impossible to complete the proof that $\hat{\beta}_1$ is unbiased without assuming the expected value of each error term is zero for any given value of X: $E[u_i|X_i] = 0$. This means that the best guess of the distance of an observation from the regression line is zero regardless of the value of the independent variable.

In notational form, there is a subtle difference between the assumption required for linearity ($E[u_i\,X_i] = 0$) and the assumption required for unbiasedness ($E[u_i|X_i] = 0$). That vertical line between $u_i$ and $X_i$ makes all the difference. The assumption for linearity states that the expected value of $u_i$ *times* $X_i$ is zero. Since the product of $u_i$ and $X_i$ is zero they are uncorrelated.

The assumption for unbiasedness states that expected value of $u_i$ *given* $X_i$ is zero. In other words, it does not matter if $X_i$ is a large value or small value or in the middle, $u_i$ is expected to be zero.

Regressions in the wrong functional form will yield biased estimates of the structural parameters. In such a regression, $E[u_i|X_i] \neq 0$, which is a direct violation of the assumption needed to prove unbiased parameter

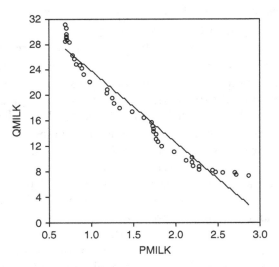

**Figure 8.1** The demand for milk with a regression line.

estimates. To see this, consider the example of the demand for milk. Here a straight line is fit to the data when an alternate functional form is appropriate. In this situation $E[u_i|X_i] \neq 0$. To see this, notice that when the value of X (PMILK) is low, $u_i$ is likely to be positive (the observations are above the regression line), not 0. Similarly, when the value of

X (PMILK) > 2.5, $u_i$ is likely to be positive. When $1.0 <$ PMILK $< 2.5$, the $u_i$'s are likely to be negative. Thus, $E[u_i]$ (the expected value of $u_i$) depends on $X_i$ and is not always expected to equal to zero.

Another violation of the assumption required for unbiased estimators occurs when a regression is in the correct functional form but excludes an important explanatory variable. Again, this is because $E[u_i|X_i] \neq 0$. Consider this example where X2, an important explanatory variable, is left out of a regression.

Correctly specified regression: $Y_i = \beta_0 + \beta_1 X1_i + \beta_2 X2_i + u_i$
Underspecified regression: $Y_i = \hat{\beta}_0 + \hat{\beta}_1 X1_i + e_i$

In this case, $e_i = \beta_2 X2_i + u_i$. The error term, $e_i$, is composed of the $u_i$'s plus the omitted variable, X2, times its coefficient, $\beta_2$. The value of the $e_i$'s depends on the $X_i$'s, so $E[u_i|X_i] \neq 0$.

To summarize, the second assumption of the CLRM is that the expected value of each error term is zero for any given value of X: $E[u_i|X_i] = 0$. This assumption is violated when regressions are in the wrong functional form or when important explanatory variables are omitted. The estimates of the structural parameters and all the residual statistics are biased in these cases.

## BEST

Under certain conditions the ordinary least squares estimators are best. It sounds as if OLS estimates are unbeatable, but the term "best" has a very particular meaning in this context. An estimator is best if it varies the least of all possible estimators in repeated sampling.

Consider once again the Monte Carlo experiment where 5,000 observations on Y and X are assumed to be the entire population of observations. Running 100,000 regressions of Y on X with randomly drawn samples of 40 from this population will yield 100,000 separate estimates of $\beta_0$ and $\beta_1$. If the 100,000 estimates of $\beta_1$ average to the true $\beta_1$, then the OLS estimator is unbiased. If the 100,000 estimates of $\beta_1$ have a smaller standard error than any other linear and unbiased estimator, then the OLS estimator is best.

More concisely, the best estimator has minimum variance in its class. In this case, the class is all possible linear estimators of $\beta_0$ and $\beta_1$. The term "best estimator" is synonymous with "efficient estimator."

Monte Carlo experiments can be used to show one estimator is more efficient than another. But it can be proved that the OLS estimators are best. This is the proof of the famous Gauss–Markov theorem: the OLS estimators are best in the class of all linear, unbiased estimators.

The Gauss–Markov proof is shown in an appendix to this chapter. Suffice it to say here that it is impossible to get through the proof without making two further assumptions:

(1) $E[u_i u_j] = 0$ for all $i \neq j$, which means the error terms are not related to each other. Autocorrelation, or serial correlation, is when the error terms are related to one another. Therefore, the assumption is that the error terms are not serially correlated.

(2) $E[u_i^2] = E[u_j^2] = \sigma^2$, which means that all the error terms have the same variance. When the error terms do not all have the same variance it is called heteroskedasticity. The assumption is that the error terms all have the same variance.

A Monte Carlo Study on Unbiased and Best Estimators

Obtain 5,000 observations on X and Y and assume this is the entire population.

| Observation | Y | X |
|---|---|---|
| 1 | 12.56 | −0.14 |
| 2 | 35.82 | 0.52 |
| 3 | 47.31 | 0.27 |
| ⋮ | ⋮ | ⋮ |
| 5,000 | 65.82 | 0.05 |

Estimate $Y_i = \beta_0 + \beta_1 X_i + u_i$

$\beta_0 = 14.56$ and $\beta_1 = 89.76$

Now draw a random sample of 40 observations from the population of 5,000.

Estimate $Y_i = \hat{\beta}_0 + \hat{\beta}_1 X_i + e_i$

$\hat{\beta}_0 = 11.87$ and $\hat{\beta}_1 = 73.55$

Return the 40 observations back into the population of 5,000. Draw another random sample of 40 observations on X and Y.

$$\text{Estimate } Y_i = \hat{\beta}_0 + \hat{\beta}_1 X_i + e_i$$

$$\hat{\beta}_0 = 17.26 \text{ and } \hat{\beta}_1 = 71.89$$

Return the 40 observations back into the population of 5,000. Continue taking samples of 40 observations and estimating $Y_i = \hat{\beta}_0 + \hat{\beta}_1 X_i + e_i$.

After 100,000 iterations of this process, there will be 100,000 estimates of $\beta_0$ and $\beta_1$.

| Sample | $\hat{\beta}_0$ | $\hat{\beta}_1$ |
|--------|------|------|
| 1 | 11.87 | 73.55 |
| 2 | 17.26 | 71.89 |
| ⋮ | ⋮ | ⋮ |
| 100,000 | 15.52 | 88.43 |

Take the average of the column of $\hat{\beta}_0$'s and the average the column of $\hat{\beta}_1$'s. The two averages should be very close to $\beta_0 = 14.56$ and $\beta_1 = 89.76$ if $\hat{\beta}_0$ and $\hat{\beta}_1$ are unbiased estimators.

Take the variance of the column of $\hat{\beta}_0$'s and the variance the column of $\hat{\beta}_1$'s. If these variances are smaller than the variance of any other method of estimating $\beta_0$ and $\beta_1$, then $\hat{\beta}_0$ and $\hat{\beta}_1$ are best, or what is the same thing—efficient.

# THE CLASSICAL LINEAR REGRESSION MODEL

OLS fits a straight line between observations on X and Y such that $\Sigma e_i^2$ is minimized. This line will be best, linear, and unbiased if four assumptions are met.

The Assumptions of the Classical Linear Regression Model

---

(1) The independent variables are predetermined or at least not correlated with the error term: $E[u_i \, X_i] = 0$

(2) The expected value of the error terms is zero: $E[u_i \mid X_i] = 0$

(3) The error terms are not related to one another: $E[u_i \, u_j] = 0$ for all $i \neq j$

(4) The error terms all have the same variance: $E[u_i^2] = E[u_j^2] = \sigma^2$ for all $i \neq j$

---

Underspecified econometric models violate assumption 2. If assumption 2 does not hold, then the proof that the OLS estimators are unbiased cannot be completed. Indeed, underspecified regressions yield biased parameter estimates.

Overspecified econometric models are inefficient. The estimators vary more in repeated sampling than if the model were correctly specified.

Regressions in the incorrect functional form will yield biased results. This is because such regressions violate assumption 2.

If assumption 3 does not hold, then the error terms are said to be autocorrelated. Assumption 3 is necessary to complete the Gauss–Markov proof. Hence, regressions that violate assumption 3 will yield inefficient (not best) estimators.

If assumption 4 is violated, then the error terms are said to be heteroskedastic. Assumption 4 is necessary to complete the Gauss–Markov proof. Therefore, regressions that violate assumption 4 will yield inefficient (not best) estimators.

Notice that the assumptions of the CLRM concern the $u_i$'s, not the $e_i$'s. There is no need to assume anything about the $e_i$'s. They are available and can be checked to see if they violate any CLRM assumptions. Indeed, in later chapters the $e_i$'s will be inspected because they could mimic the $u_i$'s and give indications of whether or not the $u_i$'s are meeting the CLRM assumptions.

Hypothesis testing was introduced in Chapter 4. In order to conduct hypothesis tests it is necessary to make an additional assumption about the regression model: the error terms are normally distributed. If the error terms are normally distributed, then $\hat{\beta}_0$ and $\hat{\beta}_1$ will be normally distributed since they are linear functions of the error terms. $\hat{\beta}_1$ is indeed a linear function of the $u_i$'s:

$$\hat{\beta}_1 = \Sigma w_i Y_i = \Sigma w_i (\beta_0 + \beta_1 X_i + u_i).$$

And $\hat{\beta}_0$ is a linear function of $\hat{\beta}_1$:

$$\hat{\beta}_0 = \bar{Y} - \hat{\beta}_1 \bar{X}.$$

When $\hat{\beta}_0$ and $\hat{\beta}_1$ are normally distributed, hypothesis tests can be carried out based on known distributions. The t-table and F-table for critical values are only applicable if the error terms, and thus $\hat{\beta}_0$ and $\hat{\beta}_1$, are normally distributed.

Econometricians often want to quickly state that the error terms meet all the assumptions of the CLRM. For instance, an econometric research paper may state the error terms are "white noise" or "well-behaved." The implication is that the results presented in the paper are BLUE—best, linear, unbiased estimators.

Casual Ways of Stating the CLRM Assumptions Are Met

(1) The error terms are white noise
(2) The error terms are well-behaved
(3) The error terms are i.i.d. (independently and identically distributed) with a mean of zero

Some textbooks list only three assumptions of the CLRM. This textbook has four. The first assumption assures that $\hat{\beta}_0$ and $\hat{\beta}_1$ are linear. Linearity is not a desirable characteristic except that it makes the proofs shown in the appendices simpler. More advanced textbooks can accomplish the same proofs without assuming linearity. Thus the need for only three assumptions.

Other textbooks list as many as ten assumptions of the CLRM. They include assumptions that most others take for granted. For instance, any regression must have $n \geq k$, the number of observations must be greater than or equal to the number of structural parameters. If this assumption is not met $\hat{\beta}_0$ and $\hat{\beta}_1$ are undefined and cannot be calculated Similarly, if any independent variables are an exact linear combination of each other (for instance, $X1 = 10 + 2.5\ X2$), then $\hat{\beta}_0$ and $\hat{\beta}_1$ are undefined and cannot be calculated. The box below lists these and other implicit assumptions.

Implicit Assumptions of the CLRM

---

The data are from a random sample.

There is no measurement error in the variables.

n must be $\geq k$.

In a multiple regression, no explanatory variable can be an exact linear combination of the others.

---

Data analysis can take many forms. OLS is a popular option because the analysis yields estimators that are BLUE. However, these desirable statistical qualities prevail only when certain assumptions are met. These are the assumptions of the CLRM.

In addition to the assumptions of the CLRM, if the error terms are normally distributed, then hypothesis testing is possible. When the error terms are normally distributed the distributions of the OLS estimators and residual statistics are known. Because of the central limit theorem, it is highly likely that the error terms of a properly specified regression will be normally distributed so long as n is greater than 30.

## TERMS

Autocorrelation—When the error terms of a regression are related to one another: $E[u_i u_j] \neq 0$ for all $i \neq j$.

Best estimator (efficient estimator)—The estimator that varies the least out of all possible estimators in repeated sampling.

BLUE—An acronym for best, linear, unbiased estimator.

Fixed variable (predetermined variable)—An independent variable with values determined before the data are collected.

Gauss–Markov proof—The proof that $\hat{\beta}_0$ and $\hat{\beta}_1$ are best.

Heteroskedasticity—The error terms of a regression do not all have the same variance: $E[u_j^2] = \sigma^2$.

Linear estimator—An estimator whose formula is linear.

Monte Carlo study—An econometric study that draws repeated samples from a known population and then analyzes the characteristics of the sample regressions.

Unbiased estimator—An estimator whose expected value is equal to the true value of the parameter: $E[\hat{\beta}_1] = \beta_1$.

# CHAPTER 8 PROBLEMS

(1) Mark the following statements TRUE or FALSE:
  (A) $\hat{\beta}_1$ is BLUE in the presence of serial correlation.
  (B) In order to show that $\hat{\beta}_1$ is best, it must be assumed that the $e_i$'s are not correlated with each other.
  (C) In order to show that $\hat{\beta}_1$ is unbiased, it must be assumed that the true error terms are not correlated with each other.
  (D) One of the conditions necessary for hypothesis testing is that the $u_i$'s are normally distributed.
  (E) One of the conditions necessary to prove that the OLS estimators are BLUE is that the $u_i$'s are normally distributed.
  (F) The estimators from a regression where the $u_i$'s do not all have the same variance are biased.
  (G) The estimators from a regression where the $u_i$'s do not all have the same variance are inefficient.
  (H) The estimators from a regression where the $u_i$'s are not normally distributed are not best.
  (I) The estimators from a regression where the $u_i$'s are serially correlated are biased.
  (J) The OLS estimators are undefined if n < k.
  (K) An econometric model in the wrong functional form is biased.
  (L) An underspecified econometric model is biased.
  (M) An overspecified econometric model is biased.
  (N) An econometric model is biased if $E[\hat{\beta}_1] \neq \beta_1$.
  (O) An econometric model is best if $E[\hat{\beta}_1] = \beta_1$.
(2) Given: Stalk Height$_i$ = 2.0 + 3.0 Rainfall$_i$ + 4.0 Fertilizer$_i$ + $e_i$

  where Stalk Height is the average height of corn stalks in a field
  Rainfall is average rainfall per week on the field
  Fertilizer is the amount of fertilizer applied to the field

  (A) Interpret the value of the intercept.
  (B) Interpret the value of the coefficient on Rainfall.
  (C) Suppose you were told that the true value of the coefficient on Rainfall is 3.1. Does this mean the estimate above is biased? Explain.
  (D) Suppose you were told that the equation does not meet assumption 2 of the CLRM (The error term has a zero population mean.) Does this mean that the coefficient on Rainfall is definitely not 3.0? Explain.

(E) When the data for this regression were gathered, Fertilizer was carefully applied to the various plots of corn so that each plot received exactly 2 lbs/acre of fertilizer more than the previous plot. Rainfall was measured using "dip canisters" in the standard meteorological way. Which of these explanatory variables is fixed? Explain.

(F) Since one of the explanatory variables is not predetermined, why is it still possible that the estimators of this regression are linear?

## APPENDIX TO CHAPTER 8

## PROOF THAT $\hat{\beta}_1$ IS UNBIASED

Assume $\hat{\beta}_1$ is a linear estimator of $\beta_1$.

$$\hat{\beta}_1 = \frac{\Sigma(X_i - \bar{X})Y_i}{\Sigma(X_i - \bar{X})^2} = \Sigma w_i Y_i; \quad \text{where } w_i = \frac{(X_i - \bar{X})}{\Sigma(X_i - \bar{X})^2}$$

$$\hat{\beta}_1 = \Sigma w_i Y_i = \Sigma w_i(\beta_0 + \beta_1 X_i + u_i) = \beta_0 \Sigma w_i + \beta_1 \Sigma w_i X_i + \Sigma w_i u_i$$

$\hat{\beta}_1 = \beta_1 + \Sigma w_i u_i$ since $\Sigma w_i = 0$ and $\Sigma w_i X_i = 1$ (These two assertions are proved below.)

Then $E[\hat{\beta}_1] = E[\beta_1 + \Sigma w_i u_i] = \beta_1$ only if $E[\Sigma w_i u_i] = 0$

For $\hat{\beta}_1$ to be unbiased it must be the case that $E[\Sigma w_i u_i] = 0$. This will hold if $E[u_i|X_i] = 0$, since the $w_i$'s are comprised only of $X_i$'s. Thus we must assume that the expected value of the error terms is zero for each value of $X_i$ in order to prove that $\hat{\beta}_1$ is an unbiased estimator of $\beta_1$.

Now to prove the two assertions made in the middle of the proof:

$\Sigma w_i = 0$

$$\Sigma w_i = \frac{\Sigma(X_i - \bar{X})}{\Sigma(X_i - \bar{X})^2} = \frac{\Sigma X_i - n\bar{X}}{\Sigma(X_i - \bar{X})^2} = \frac{0}{\Sigma(X_i - \bar{X})^2}$$

$\Sigma w_i X_i = 1$

$$\Sigma w_i X_i = \frac{\Sigma(X_i - \bar{X})X_i}{\Sigma(X_i - \bar{X})^2} = \frac{\Sigma X_i^2 - \bar{X}\Sigma X_i}{\Sigma X_i^2 - \bar{X}\Sigma X_i} = 1$$

## PROOF THAT $\hat{\beta}_0$ IS UNBIASED

It is straightforward to show that $\hat{\beta}_0$ $(= \bar{Y} - \hat{\beta}_1 \bar{X})$ is an unbiased estimator of $\beta_0$. Since $\bar{Y}$, $\bar{X}$, and $\hat{\beta}_1$ are unbiased estimators of the true $\bar{Y}$, $\bar{X}$, and $\beta_1$, then $\hat{\beta}_0$ will be an unbiased estimator of $\beta_0$. This is because $\hat{\beta}_0$ is a linear combination of these three unbiased estimators.

## PROOF THAT $\hat{\beta}_1$ IS BEST

Assume $\hat{\beta}_1$ is a linear and unbiased estimator of $\beta_1$.

$$\hat{\beta}_1 = \frac{\Sigma(X_i - \bar{X})Y_i}{\Sigma(X_i - \bar{X})^2} = \Sigma w_i Y_i; \quad \text{where } w_i = \frac{(X_i - \bar{X})}{\Sigma(X_i - \bar{X})^2}$$

$$\text{VAR}(\hat{\beta}_1) = E[(\hat{\beta}_1 - \beta_1)^2] = E[(\beta_1 + \Sigma w_i u_i - \beta_1)^2] = \sigma^2 \Sigma w_i^2$$

Now consider another arbitrary estimator:

$$\tilde{\beta}_1 = \Sigma c_i Y_i; \quad \text{where } c_i = w_i + d_i$$

$$\tilde{\beta}_1 = \Sigma c_i(\beta_0 + \beta_1 X_i + u_i) = \beta_0 \Sigma c_i + \beta_1 \Sigma c_i X_i + \Sigma c_i u_i$$

$\tilde{\beta}_1$ is unbiased if and only if $\Sigma c_i = 0$ and $\Sigma c_i X_i = 1$, the $c_i$ are fixed and $\Sigma u_i = 0$. We can deduce that $\Sigma di = 0$ since $\Sigma c_i = \Sigma w_i + \Sigma d_i$ and $\Sigma c_i = 0$ and $\Sigma w_i = 0$. Also, $\Sigma d_i X_i = 0$ since $\Sigma c_i X_i = \Sigma w_i X_i + \Sigma d_i X_i$ and $\Sigma c_i X_i = 1$ and $\Sigma w_i X_i = 1$.

$$\text{VAR}(\tilde{\beta}_1) = E[(\tilde{\beta}_1 - \beta_1)^2] = E[(\beta_1 + \Sigma c_i u_i - \beta_1)^2] = \sigma^2 \Sigma c_i^2$$

$$\Sigma c_i^2 = \Sigma w_i^2 + \Sigma d_i^2 + 2 \Sigma w_i d_i = \Sigma w_i^2 + \Sigma d_i^2 \text{ since } \Sigma w_i d_i = 0$$

$$(\text{using } \Sigma di = 0 \text{ and } \Sigma d_i X_i = 0)$$

So that:

$$\text{VAR}(\tilde{\beta}_1) = \sigma^2(\Sigma w_i^2 + \Sigma d_i^2) = \sigma^2 \Sigma w_i^2 + \sigma^2 \Sigma d_i^2 =$$

$$\text{VAR}(\hat{\beta}_1) + \sigma^2 \Sigma d_i^2$$

If $\Sigma d_i^2 \neq 0$, then $\text{VAR}(\tilde{\beta}_1) > \text{VAR}(\hat{\beta}_1)$; If $\Sigma d_i^2 = 0$, then $\text{VAR}(\tilde{\beta}_1) = \text{VAR}(\hat{\beta}_1)$
Q.E.D.

The most difficult step of this proof is in the third line:

$\text{VAR}(\hat{\beta}_1) = E[(\hat{\beta}_1 - \beta_1)^2] = E[(\beta_1 + \Sigma w_i u_i - \beta_1)^2] = \sigma^2 \Sigma w_i^2$ It is not easy to see that

$E[(\beta_1 + \Sigma w_i u_i - \beta_1)^2] = \sigma^2 \Sigma w_i^2$. The positive $\beta_1$ cancels with the negative $\beta_1$ leaving:

$E[(\Sigma w_i u_i)^2] = \sigma^2 \Sigma w_i^2$. Expanding the left side:

$$E[(\Sigma w_i u_i)^2] = E[(w_1 u_1 + w_2 u_2 + \ldots + w_n u_n)(w_1 u_1 + w_2 u_2 + \ldots + w_n u_n)] =$$

$$E[w_1^2 u_1^2 + w_2^2 u_2^2 + \ldots + w_n^2 u_n^2 + 2w_1 u_1 w_2 u_2 + 2w_1 u_1 w_3 u_3 + \ldots$$
$$+ 2w_2 u_2 w_3 u_3 + 2w_2 u_2 w_4 u_4 + \ldots + 2w_{n-1} u_{n-1} w_n u_n]$$

Now assume that $E[u_i u_j] = 0$ for all $i \neq j$, then this last expression becomes:

$$E[w_1^2 u_1^2 + w_2^2 u_2^2 + \ldots + w_n^2 u_n^2]$$

Finally, assuming $E[u_i^2] = E[u_j^2] = \sigma^2$ we have:

$$E[w_1^2 u_1^2 + w_2^2 u_2^2 + \ldots + w_n^2 u_n^2] = \sigma^2 E[w_1^2 + w_2^2 + \ldots + w_n^2] = \sigma^2 \Sigma w_i^2$$

## PROOF THAT $\hat{\beta}_0$ IS BEST

It is straightforward to show that $\hat{\beta}_0 (= \bar{Y} - \hat{\beta}_1 \bar{X})$ is the best estimator of $\beta_0$. Since $\bar{Y}$, $\bar{X}$, and $\hat{\beta}_1$ are efficient estimators of the true $\bar{Y}$, $\bar{X}$, and $\beta_1$, then $\hat{\beta}_0$ will be an efficient estimator of $\beta_0$. This is because $\hat{\beta}_0$ is a linear combination of these three efficient estimators.

# 9 Multicollinearity

## THE NATURE OF MULTICOLLINEARITY

In a multivariate regression there are two or more explanatory variables. At times, some of these variables will be highly linearly related—a condition known as multicollinearity. Multicollinearity means that some or all of the explanatory variables move in lockstep, or near lockstep. In this situation, regression analysis struggles to disentangle the effect each explanatory variable has on the dependent variable.

## PERFECT MULTICOLLINEARITY

Perfect multicollinearity is when the explanatory variables in a regression are perfectly linearly related. Consider X1 and X2 below:

| X1 | X2 |
|------|------|
| 10.0 | 6.0 |
| 17.0 | 2.5 |
| 12.0 | 5.0 |
| 21.0 | 0.5 |

You might stare at these numbers for a long time before realizing that X2 = 11 − 0.5 X1. In other words, X2 is a perfect linear re-write of X1. The two variables are perfectly collinear. Notice that if the first observation on X1 was 10.1 instead of 10.0, then the two variables would be highly linearly related, but no longer perfectly collinear.

DOI: 10.4324/9781003213758-9

When the explanatory variables in a regression are perfectly collinear, the structural parameters are undefined. Consider the regression:

$$Y_i = \hat{\beta}_0 + \hat{\beta}_1 X1_i + \hat{\beta}_2 X2_i + e_i$$

The formulas for $\hat{\beta}_1$ and $\hat{\beta}_2$ are:

$$\hat{\beta}_1 = \frac{(\Sigma y_i x_{1i})(\Sigma x_{2i}^2) - (\Sigma y_i x_{2i})(\Sigma x_{1i} x_{2i})}{(\Sigma x_{1i}^2)(\Sigma x_{2i}^2) - (\Sigma x_{1i} x_{2i})^2};$$

where $y_i = Y_i - \bar{Y}$;   $x_{1i} = X1_i - \bar{X}1$;   $x_{2i} = X2_i - \bar{X}2$

and

$$\hat{\beta}_2 = \frac{(\Sigma y_i x_{2i})(\Sigma x_{2i}^2) - (\Sigma y_i x_{1i})(\Sigma x_{1i} x_{2i})}{(\Sigma x_{1i}^2)(\Sigma x_{2i}^2) - (\Sigma x_{1i} x_{2i})^2};$$

where $y_i = Y_i - \bar{Y}$;   $x_{1i} = X1_i - \bar{X}1$;   $x_{2i} = X2_i - \bar{X}2$

It can be shown that the denominators of both of these equations are equal to zero when X1 and X2 are perfectly collinear. With the denominators equal to zero, both $\hat{\beta}_1$ and $\hat{\beta}_2$ are undefined. Therefore, $\hat{\beta}_0 = \bar{Y} - \hat{\beta}_1 \bar{X}1_i - \hat{\beta}_2 \bar{X}2_i$ is undefined as well.

You may wonder why a researcher would include perfectly collinear variables in a regression. Usually it happens by mistake. For instance, in a regression explaining grade point average (GPA) a researcher might include study time per day (ST/DAY) and study time per week (ST/WK) before realizing that ST/WK = 0 + 7 ST/DAY.

In another example, a regression explaining the wage rate (WAGES) may include the number of unemployed people (#UNEM), the unemployment rate (UNEMRATE), and the number of people in the labor force (LFORCE).

$$WAGES_i = \hat{\beta}_0 + \hat{\beta}_1 \, \#UNEM_i + \hat{\beta}_2 UNEMRATE_i + \hat{\beta}_3 LFORCE_i + e_i$$

In this case, the UNEMRATE = #UNEM/LFORCE. A linear combination of two of the explanatory variables equals the third explanatory variable. This is perfect multicollinearity and the structural parameters are undefined.

There is only one thing to do in the face of perfect multicollinearity— remove one of the collinear variables.

## MULTICOLLINEARITY DEFINED

Multicollinearity is when the explanatory variables in a regression are highly, but not perfectly, linearly related. In this case, the structural parameters and all the residual statistics can be calculated with the usual formulas.

The OLS estimators are BLUE in the presence of multicollinearity. There is no other linear estimator that will yield estimates that vary less in repeated sampling. However, the standard errors of the estimators will be larger than if there were no multicollinearity.

To understand this more clearly, consider the following regression:

$$Y_i = \hat{\beta}_0 + \hat{\beta}_1 X1_i + \hat{\beta}_2 X2_i + e_i$$

The standard error of $\hat{\beta}_1$ in the following regression can be written as:

$$SE(\hat{\beta}_1) = \sqrt{\frac{\Sigma e_i^2/(n-k)}{\Sigma(X1_i - \bar{X}1)^2(1 - r_{12}^2)}}$$

$r_{12}^2$ is the square of the correlation coefficient between X1 and X2. It measures the degree of collinearity between X1 and X2 on a scale from 0 to 1. The more collinear X1 and X2, the closer $r_{12}^2$ gets to 1. As $r_{12}^2$ approaches 1, $SE(\hat{\beta}_1)$ increases. If $r_{12}^2 = 1$, then $SE(\hat{\beta}_1)$ is undefined.

Thus, the more collinear X1 and X2, the larger the standard error of $\hat{\beta}_1$. In other words, the more severe the multicollinearity, the larger the standard errors of the estimators.

## CONSEQUENCES OF MULTICOLLINEARITY

Multicollinearity does not violate any of the assumptions of the Classical Linear Regression Model. Therefore, OLS estimators are unbiased and best in the presence of multicollinearity. "Best" means minimum variance. No other technique for estimating the structural parameters of a regression yields lower standard errors than OLS, even when the regression suffers from multicollinearity. However, if we could somehow remedy the multicollinearity, the variance of the OLS estimators would be even lower.

The main consequence of multicollinearity is inflated (but still minimum) standard errors of the structural parameters. This will lead to further problems. Since the t-ratios are calculated from the standard errors they will be smaller in absolute value than if there were no multicollinearity. This makes hypothesis testing precarious. Similarly, p-values will be larger because of multicollinearity.

Artificially anemic t-ratios and inflated p-values can lead to more TYPE II errors.

In addition, the bloated standard errors can cause parameter estimates to be sensitive to model specification. Dropping an irrelevant variable, let alone a relevant one, can cause large swings in parameter estimates under multicollinearity. Model selection becomes tricky when multicollinearity is severe.

If two independent variables in model are collinear, then all of the estimators are affected as described above. The effects are not limited to the coefficients attached to the two collinear variables.

## DETECTING MULTICOLLINEARITY

There are a few techniques available to detect multicollinearity. The simplest and most common technique is to check the correlation coefficient between the explanatory variables:

$$r = \frac{\Sigma(X1_i - \bar{X}1)(X2_i - \bar{X}2)}{SD(X1)\,SD(X2)}; \quad \text{where SD is the standard deviation}$$

r ranges between plus and minus unity. $|r| > 0.7$ means severe multicollinearity. If there are three independent variables in the regression, then three separate r's will have to be checked. Econometric packages typically do this at the touch of a button.

A more formal procedure for detecting multicollinearity requires the calculation of a set of variance inflation factors (VIFs). To find the VIFs: (1) regress each explanatory variable on all the others in a bank of auxiliary regressions and (2) calculate VIF for each regression.

As an example, consider the regression:

$$Y_t = \hat{\beta}_0 + \hat{\beta}_1 X1_t + \hat{\beta}_2 X2_t + \hat{\beta}_3 X3_t + e_t$$

The required auxiliary regressions are:

$$X1_t = \hat{\beta}_0 + \hat{\beta}_1 X2_t + \hat{\beta}_2 X3_t + e_t$$
$$X2_t = \hat{\beta}_0 + \hat{\beta}_1 X1_t + \hat{\beta}_2 X3_t + e_t$$
$$X3_t = \hat{\beta}_0 + \hat{\beta}_1 X1_t + \hat{\beta}_2 X2_t + e_t$$

The three $R^2$'s from these regressions are each in turn plugged into:

$$VIF = \frac{1}{1 - R^2}$$

VIF's range from 1 to infinity. It is unusual to have absolutely no multicollinearity, but in that case VIF = 1. If any VIF > 10, then the original regression suffers from severe multicollinearity. VIFs between 1 and 10 indicate increasing degrees of multicollinearity.

## REMEDIES FOR MULTICOLLINEARITY

Once it has been detected, there are several things to consider when working with regressions that suffer from multicollinearity. Often, doing nothing is the best response. The OLS estimators are still BLUE. The consequences of multicollinearity are not totally debilitating and can be taken into account. For instance, hypothesis testing should be conducted with a mind toward the fact that TYPE II errors are more likely to occur. That means increasing the critical level of hypothesis tests to perhaps 10% or higher depending on the severity of the multicollinearity. Estimators with p-values greater than 0.05% might be considered significant.

It is probably not a good idea to drop one of the collinear explanatory variables. This would be done only if it was determined that the variable could be removed without causing an underspecified model. But then why was this irrelevant variable in the model in the first place?

Sometimes moving to an alternate functional form can alleviate the multicollinearity. Notice that it does not pay to change into an inappropriate functional form since the consequences of being in the wrong form are much worse than the consequences of multicollinearity. Regressions in the wrong functional form yield biased parameter estimates.

A better option would be to somehow combine the collinear variables. Sometimes it is possible to form ratios or differences of the collinear variables and thereby avoid dropping the information that belongs in the regression. With time-series data, using the change in the variables from one period to the next, rather than their levels, can relieve multi-collinearity.

Dealing with multicollinearity is much like dealing with a common cold. There are some things that can alleviate the symptoms, but most of the time they simply must be endured. And like the common cold, the consequences of having multicollinearity usually are not life threatening.

## TERMS

Correlation coefficient (r)—A statistic ranging between –1 and +1 that estimates the degree of linear relationship between two variables

Multicollinearity—When the explanatory variables in a regression are highly linearly related

Perfect multicollinearity—When the explanatory variables in a regression are perfectly linearly related

Variance inflation factor (VIF)—A statistic used to detect multicollinearity

## CHAPTER 9 PROBLEMS

(1) Use the data in CONSUMP.XLS and statistical software to run the following regression:

$$RCONPC_t = \hat{\beta}_0 + \hat{\beta}_1 REALYDPC_t + \hat{\beta}_2 REALR_t + \hat{\beta}_3 CC_t + e_t$$

where RCONPC = real consumer spending in the USA per capita
REALYDPC = real disposable income per capita
REALR = real interest rate on one-year Treasury Bonds
CC = University of Michigan Index of Consumer Confidence

(A) Which explanatory variables do not obtain their expected signs?

(B) According to the correlation coefficients between the explanatory variables, would you classify the multicollinearity in this regression as severe, moderate, mild, or non-existent? Explain.

(C) According to the correlation coefficients between the explanatory variables, which two variables are most collinear?

(D) Calculate the three VIFs for this regression. Would you classify the multicollinearity in this regression as severe, moderate, mild, or non-existent? Explain.

(E) Run the regression in first difference form. Which explanatory variables do not obtain their expected signs?

(F) According to the correlation coefficients between the explanatory variables, would you classify the multicollinearity in this regression as severe, moderate, mild, or non-existent? Explain.

(G) Calculate the three VIFs for this regression. Would you classify the multicollinearity in this regression as severe, moderate, mild, or non-existent? Explain.

(H) Based on your look into this matter, what do you recommend doing about the multicollinearity in the original regression? Explain.

(2) Use the data in ANMACRO.XLS and statistical software to run a regression where the demand for money (m2) is explained by a constant term, income (ngdp), interest rates (aaa), and prices (cpi).

| Variable | Description |
|----------|-------------|
| m2 | Demand for m2 |
| ngdp | Nominal GDP |
| aaa | aaa corporate bond rate |
| cpi | Consumer price index |

(A) Which explanatory variables do not obtain their expected signs?

(B) According to the correlation coefficients between the explanatory variables, would you classify the multicollinearity in this regression as severe, moderate, mild, or non-existent? Explain.

(C) According to the correlation coefficients between the explanatory variables, which two variables are most collinear?

(D) Calculate the three VIFs for this regression. Would you classify the multicollinearity in this regression as severe, moderate, mild, or non-existent? Explain.

(E) Run the regression in first difference form. Which explanatory variables do not obtain their expected signs?

(F) According to the correlation coefficients between the explanatory variables, would you classify the multicollinearity in this regression as severe, moderate, mild, or non-existent? Explain.

(G) Calculate the three VIFs for this regression. Would you classify the multicollinearity in this regression as severe, moderate, mild, or non-existent? Explain.

(H) Based on your look into this matter, what do you recommend doing about the multicollinearity in the original regression? Explain.

(3) Discuss the pros and cons of the following remedies for multicollinearity:

(A) Drop a variable

(B) Try an alternate functional form such as the reciprocal form

(C) Do nothing

(4) Use the following equation to argue that the $SE(\hat{\beta}_1)$ is undefined under perfect multicollinearity between X1 and X2:

$$SE(\hat{\beta}_1) = \sqrt{\frac{\Sigma e_i^2/(n-k)}{\Sigma(X_{i1} - \bar{X}_1)^2(1 - r_{12}^2)}}$$

where $r_{12}^2$ is the correlation coefficient between X1 and X2 squared.

(5) Use the following equation to argue that the VIF is undefined when there is perfect multicollinearity between two explanatory variables:

$$VIF = \frac{1}{1 - R^2}$$

(6) Mark each of the following statements TRUE or FALSE:

(A) $\hat{\beta}_1$ is BLUE in the presence of multicollinearity.

(B) In the presence of multicollinearity, $\hat{\beta}_1$ will be inefficient.

(C) With perfect multicollinearity, the OLS estimators are undefined.

(D) Consider $Y_i = \hat{\beta}_0 + \hat{\beta}_1 X1_i + \hat{\beta}_2 X2_i + \hat{\beta}_3 X3_i + \hat{\beta}_4 X4_i + e_i$. If X1 and X2 are highly collinear, then the standard errors of $\hat{\beta}_1$ and $\hat{\beta}_2$ will be inflated, but not those of $\hat{\beta}_3$ and $\hat{\beta}_4$.

(E) A VIF (variance inflation factor) less than 5 means multicollinearity is non-existent.

# 10 Heteroskedasticity

## WHAT IS HETEROSKEDASTICITY?

Heteroskedasticity literally means different (hetero) spread (skedasticity). It occurs when the error terms from a population regression do not all have the same variance. This is a direct violation of assumption 4 of the Classical Linear Regression Model, which states that the error terms all have the same variance: $E[u_i^2] = E[u_j^2] = \sigma^2$.

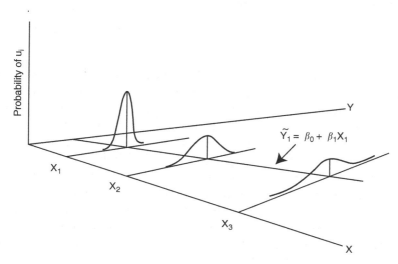

**Figure 10.1** Heteroskedasticity.

DOI: 10.4324/9781003213758-10

Cross-sectional data are most likely to be heteroskedastic. The example below considers the relationship between the spending (CONS) and disposable income (INC) of 50 families.

$$CONS_i = 9929.78 + 0.76 \ INC_i + e_i$$

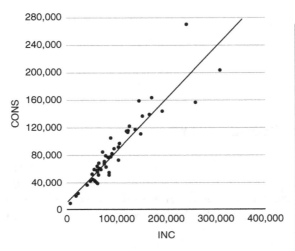

**Figure 10.2** Suspected heteroskedasticity.

The regression line for this scattergram is a consumption function.

The slope of the consumption function is 0.76, the coefficient attached to INC.

The marginal propensity to consume is estimated to be 0.76.

When family income is low, the regression errors tend to be relatively small. As income increases, so does the magnitude of the residuals. Intuitively, this makes sense. When a family has low income, it is easy to predict their spending. It is probably not much different than their income since it is difficult to save much with low income. However, there is more room for error when predicting the savings of a family with high income.

Heteroskedasticity is not the larger errors associated with higher levels of income. It is the wider frequency distributions of the residuals at higher levels of income. The difference is subtle but important. As income increases, the observations become more erratic and therefore not as trustworthy. The remedy for this situation is to give the observations at higher levels of income less credence.

More generally, as the X-variable increases, heteroskedasticity occurs when the frequency distributions of the population regression errors widen, narrow, or vary in manner.

## CONSEQUENCES OF HETEROSKEDASTICITY

The structural parameters of a regression suffering from hetero-skedasticity are not best. Since assumption 4 (the error terms all have the same variance: $E[u_i^2] = E[u_j^2] = \sigma^2$) of the CLRM is violated, it is impossible to get through the Gauss-Markov proof. It is, however, possible to prove that the structural parameters are linear and unbiased.

The estimated SER, the estimated standard errors of the structural parameters, and therefore the t-ratios, the $R^2$, and F-statistics are all biased. So hypothesis testing of any sort is precarious in the presence of heteroskedasticity.

## DETECTION

In practice, heteroskedasticity is detected by checking to see if the magnitude of the residuals varies with one of the explanatory variables. Larger residuals are evidence of wider frequency distributions. Notice that it is the residuals, the $e_i$'s, that are being inspected. But hetero-skedasticity is when the population errors, the $u_i$'s, have frequency distributions that vary in width. The hope is that the sample regression residuals mimic the population errors. A variety of tests are available to detect heteroskedasticity. Three are introduced here.

### The Graphical Approach

The graphical method involves plotting the squared residuals from a regression against the "culprit" variable. The culprit variable is the explanatory variable that gives rise to heteroskedasticity. In $CONS_i = 9929.78 + 0.76\ INC_i + e_i$ there is only one explanatory variable and therefore INC is the only possible culprit.

To test that regression for heteroskedasticity plot the residuals are squared $(e_i^2)$ against income:

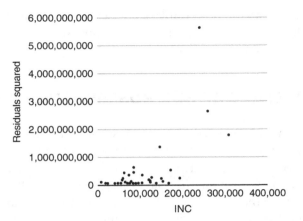

**Figure 10.3** The residuals are plotted against the culprit variable.

The squared residuals become larger as income increases. In general, any pattern to the squared residuals indicates heteroskedasticity. The chart on the left below shows no pattern, while the one on the right is indicative of heteroskedasticity.

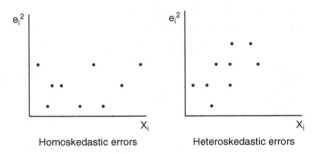

**Figure 10.4** Hypothetical graphs indicating homoskedastic and hetero-skedastic residuals.

### The Park Test

The Park test (Park 1966) is a more formal way to look for patterns in the squared residuals. To test if $Y_i = \hat{\beta}_0 + \hat{\beta}_1 X_i + e_i$ suffers from heteroskedasticity, square the residuals and regress them on the explanatory variable, which gives rise to heteroskedasticity.

$$\ln(e_i^2) = \alpha_0 + \alpha_1 \ln(X_i) + \varepsilon_i$$

If $\alpha_1$ is statistically significant, then heteroskedasticity is present. Use the double-log form if possible. The natural log of 0 is undefined, so it is not possible to log the $e_i^2$'s if $e_i^2 = 0$. Similarly, if any of the $X_i$'s are zero or negative, then the natural logs of those observations are undefined. In either of those situations the Park test is run taking natural logs only where valid.

To test if $CONS_i = 9929.78 + 0.76 INC_i + e_i$ suffers from heteroskedasticity, square the residuals and regress them on the explanatory variable giving rise to heteroskedasticity:

$$\ln(e_i^2) = 7.37 + 0.90 \ln(INC_i) + \varepsilon_i$$
$$(1.70) \qquad \leftarrow t - ratio \quad n = 50$$

(1) Ho: $\alpha_1 = 0$ (no hetero) Ha: $\alpha_1 \neq 0$ (hetero exists)
(2) 5%
(3) If |t-ratio| > $t^c$, reject Ho
(4) 1.70 < 2.011 (d.f. = n – k = 50 – 2 = 48)
(5) Do Not Reject Ho; heteroskedasticity is not suspected

The Park test contradicts what we suspected from the graphical analysis and finds no evidence of heteroskedasticity. Notice that if there are more than one explanatory variables in the model, a Park test will have to be run for each.

### The White Test

One of the most popular tests for heteroskedasticity is the White test (White 1980). Let's add another explanatory variable to the example so that we may put the White test to full use.

$$Y_i = \hat{\beta}_0 + \hat{\beta}_1 X1_i + \hat{\beta}_2 X2_i + e_i$$

Two Park tests are required to check this regression for heteroskedasticity since there are two independent variables, either one of which may be the culprit:

$$\ln(e_i^2) = \alpha_0 + \alpha_1 \ln(X1_i) + \varepsilon_i$$
$$\ln(e_i^2) = \alpha_0 + \alpha_1 \ln(X2_i) + \varepsilon_i$$

One White test covers both possible culprit variables. To conduct the test, run the following auxiliary regression:

$$e_i^2 = \alpha_0 + \alpha_1 X1_i + \alpha_2 X1_i^2 + \alpha_3 X2_i + \alpha_4 X2_i^2 + \alpha_5(X1_i)(X2_i) + \varepsilon_i$$

The $e_i^2$'s from the regression being tested are regressed on the independent variables, the squares of those variables, and the cross terms. Cross terms are pairs of explanatory variables multiplied by each other. This test has one cross term, namely $(X1_i)(X2_i)$. If at least one of the coefficients $\alpha_1$ through $\alpha_5$ is significant, then heteroskedasticity is evident.

As an example, run a regression where family spending (CONS) is explained by income (INC) and family size (SIZE). The variable SIZE is the number of people in the family. This regression tests the theory that larger families spend more, holding income constant. SIZE turns out to be insignificant, throwing cold water on the theory.

$$CONS_i = 11{,}491.12 + 0.76\ INC_i - 358.27\ SIZE_i + e_i$$
$$\qquad\quad (0.22)\quad\ (0.00)\qquad\quad (0.84)\qquad \leftarrow p - values$$

To test if this regression suffers from heteroskedasticity, run the auxiliary regression:

$$e_i^2 = \alpha_0 + \alpha_1 INC_i + \alpha_2 INC_i^2 + \alpha_3 SIZE_i + \alpha_4 SIZE_i^2 + \alpha_5(INC_i)(SIZE_i) + \varepsilon_i$$
$$n = 50; \quad R^2 = .42$$

The test for significance of at least one of the coefficients $\alpha_1$ through $\alpha_5$ is distributed as a chi-squared $(\chi^2)$.

(1) Ho: no hetero                       Ha: hetero exists
    $(\alpha_1 = \alpha_2 = \alpha_3 = \alpha_4 = \alpha_5 = 0)$     $(\alpha_1$ and/or $\alpha_2$ and/or $\alpha_3$ and/or $\alpha_4$
                                                     and/or $\alpha_5 \neq 0)$
(2) 5%
(3) If $nR^2 > \chi^2 c$, then reject Ho
(4) $50(.42) = 21.0; \chi^2 c = 11.07$ (d.f. $= k - 1$ from the auxiliary regression $= 5$)
(5) Reject Ho; heteroskedasticity is suspected

This White test finds evidence of heteroskedasticity in the multiple regression of INC and SIZE on CONS. To look up $\chi^2 c$, go online or use a

table such as the one in the back of this book. Be sure the table corresponds to the critical level of the test. The degrees of freedom are equal
to k – 1 in the auxiliary regression. In this example, k = 6: $\alpha_0$, $\alpha_1$, $\alpha_2$, $\alpha_3$,
$\alpha_4$, and $\alpha_5$.

# REMEDIES

Unlike multicollinearity, econometricians typically take remedial measures against heteroskedasticity. The estimates of the structural parameters are unbiased, but not the residual statistics. This means t-ratios
and p-values are biased and hypothesis testing is invalid. In addition, the
structural parameters are not best. Given these consequences, something
should be done.

### *Weighted Least Squares*

The structural parameters are inefficient in a regression suffering from
heteroskedasticity. There is an estimation technique that yields structural parameters that vary less in repeated sampling than OLS. That
technique is weighted least squares. It can be shown that weighted least
squares is the best, linear, unbiased estimation technique in the presence
of heteroskedasticity. The trick is finding the appropriate weights to
correct for the non-constant variance of the error terms.

Suppose the error terms from $CONS_i = \beta_0 + \beta_1 INC_i + u_i$ are heteroskedastic in that the variance of the error terms varies with INC.
Multiply through the original regression by 1/INCOME.

$$\frac{CONS_i}{INC_i} = \beta_0 \frac{1}{INC_i} + \beta_1 \frac{INC_i}{INC_i} + \frac{u_i}{INC_i}$$

Note that $INC_i/INC_i = 1$, giving:

$$\frac{CONS_i}{INC_i} = \beta_0 \frac{1}{INC_i} + \beta_1 + \frac{u_i}{INC_i}$$

Applying OLS to this is the weighted least squares technique. The new
error terms are $\frac{u_i}{INC_i}$. They will be homoskedastic if the variance of the
$u_i$'s is proportional to the square of INC.

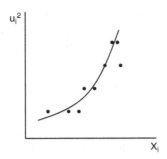

**Figure 10.5** Squared error terms proportional to income squared.

If the variance of the error terms is proportional to INC, rather than the square of INC, then multiplying through by $1/\sqrt{INC_i}$ will result in homoskedastic errors:

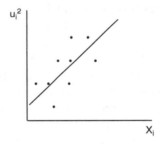

**Figure 10.6** Squared error terms proportional to income.

$$\frac{CONS_i}{\sqrt{INC_i}} = \beta_0\left(\frac{1}{\sqrt{INC_i}}\right) + \beta_1\left(\frac{INC_i}{\sqrt{INC_i}}\right) + \frac{u_i}{\sqrt{INC_i}}$$

Again, applying OLS to the weighted data mentioned earlier is known as weighted least squares. The error terms in the weighted least squares regression ($\frac{u_i}{\sqrt{INC_i}}$) are homoskedastic only if the variance of the $u_i$'s is proportional to INC.

Most econometric software packages apply weighted least squares on command. The researcher only needs to specify the weights. Typically, this is the reciprocal of the explanatory variable giving rise to the heteroskedasticity or the reciprocal of the square root of the culprit variable.

With proper weights specified, the structural parameters in a weighted least squares regression are BLUE. Finding the proper weights is a hit and miss proposition. Therefore, it is important to test any weighted least squares regression to ensure the heteroskedasticity has been remedied.

### Newey-West Standard Errors

Newey and West (1987) developed a better formula to estimate the standard errors of coefficients when a regression suffers from heteroskedasticity. The Newey-West standard errors are still biased, but less so than the usual estimates of the standard errors.

The Newey-West technique leaves the OLS parameter estimates untouched. Remember that the OLS parameter estimates are unbiased in the presence of heteroskedasticity. The standard errors of the parameter estimates, however, are biased. The Newey-West technique corrects for this bias.

$$\text{Newey} - \text{West } SE(\hat{\beta}_1) = \text{OLS } SE(\hat{\beta}_1)$$

$$+ \text{ adjustment based on the degree of heteroskedasticity}$$

This technique is so popular that many econometric software packages use these "robust" standard errors for every regression, whether heteroskedasticity is present or not. There is no harm in this approach. If heteroskedasticity is absent, then the Newey-West standard errors equal the OLS standard errors.

There is no reason to leave heteroskedastic regressions untreated. It can be difficult to find the appropriate weights to apply weighted least squares. In that case, or perhaps as a premier remedy, Newey-West standard errors can be applied.

Newey-West is perhaps the most popular of all the standard errors developed to eliminate the bias caused by heteroskedasticity. Other examples of so-called robust standard errors, or heteroskedasticity-consistent standard errors, include those of Huber (1967) and White (1980).

## TERMS

Culprit variable—The independent variable causing heteroskedasticity
Heteroskedasticity—The error terms of a regression do not all have the same variance

Newey-West technique—Formulas for the standard errors of the estimators that are less biased in the presence of heteroskedasticity

Robust standard error (Heteroskedasticity-consistent standard
error)—a formula for calculating the standard error of an estimator
that reduces the bias caused by heteroskedasticity

Weighted least squares—A technique that remedies heteroskedasticity
by dividing the data by some version of the culprit variable

## CHAPTER 10 PROBLEMS

(1) Given $Y_i = \hat{\beta}_0 + \hat{\beta}_1 + X1_i + \hat{\beta}_2 X2_i + e_i$
   (A) Write the auxiliary regression required for the Park test
       assuming X2 is the "culprit" variable.
   (B) Suppose n = 23 and the t-ratio on X2 in the auxiliary regression
       is –2.222. Is heteroskedasticity present? Show the five-step
       procedure for the Park test.
   (C) Write the auxiliary regression required for the White test.
   (D) Suppose n = 23 and the R-squared on the auxiliary regression is
       0.55. Is heteroskedasticity present? Show the five-step proce-
       dure for the White test.
   (E) Write the weighted least squares regression that would remedy
       the heteroskedasticity if it were proportional to X2.
(2) Use the data in EQUATOR.XLS and statistical software to run the
    following regression:

$$GDPCAP_i = \hat{\beta}_0 + \hat{\beta}_1 ED_i + \hat{\beta}_2 DISEQ_i + e_i$$

   Where GDPCAP is a nation's GDP per capita in US$
         ED is the nation's literacy rate
         DISEQ is the distance from the nation's capital to the
         equator in miles
   (A) What is your explanation for the positive sign on $\hat{\beta}_2$?
   (B) Plot the squared residuals from the regression against ED. Does
       the plot show evidence of heteroskedasticity? Explain.
   (C) Plot the squared residuals from the regression against DISEQ.
       Does the plot show evidence of heteroskedasticity? Explain.
   (D) Do a Park test for heteroskedasticity assuming ED is the
       "culprit" variable. Does the test indicate the presence of
       heteroskedasticity? Show the five-step procedure.

(E) Do a Park test for heteroskedasticity assuming DISEQ is the "culprit" variable. Does the test indicate the presence of heteroskedasticity? Show the five-step procedure.

(F) Perform White's test for heteroskedasticity. Does the test indicate the presence of heteroskedasticity? Show the five-step procedure.

(G) Run the original regression using weighted least squares. Assume the variance of the $u_i$'s is proportional to the square of ED so that 1/ED (variance of ED) is the correct weight. Then apply White's test for heteroskedasticity to the errors from this weighted regression. Does the test indicate the presence of heteroskedasticity? Show the five-step procedure.

(H) Run the original regression using weighted least squares. Assume the variance of the $u_i$'s is proportional to ED so that $1/\sqrt{ED_i}$ (standard deviation of ED) is the correct weight. Then apply White's test for heteroskedasticity to the errors from this weighted regression. Does the test indicate the presence of heteroskedasticity? Show the five-step procedure.

(I) Run the original regression using weighted least squares. Assume the variance of the $u_i$'s is proportional to the square of DISEQ so that 1/DISEQ (variance of DISEQ) is the correct weight. Then apply White's test for heteroskedasticity to the errors from this weighted regression. Does the test indicate the presence of heteroskedasticity? Show the five-step procedure.

(J) Run the original regression using weighted least squares. Assume the variance of the $u_i$'s is proportional to DISEQ so that $1/\sqrt{DISEQ_i}$ (standard deviation of DISEQ) is the correct weight. Then apply White's test for heteroskedasticity to the errors from this weighted regression. Does the test indicate the presence of heteroskedasticity? Show the five-step procedure.

(K) Use the Newey-West technique to obtain heteroskedasticity-corrected standard errors with the original regression. Did heteroskedasticity appear to be biasing the standard errors of the structural parameters very much? Explain.

(3) Use the data in ALCO5.XLS and statistical software to run a regression where drinks is explained by a constant term, gpa, male, ofage, cig, pot, intra, and white.

| Variable | Description |
|---|---|
| drinks | Number of alcoholic drinks consumed per week |
| gpa | Grade point average 0–4 scale |
| male | 1 If the student is male; 0 otherwise |
| ofage | 1 If the student is 21 or older; 0 otherwise |
| cig | 1 If the student uses tobacco; 0 otherwise |
| pot | 1 If the student uses marijuana; 0 otherwise |
| intra | 1 If the student participates in intramural athletics; 0 otherwise |
| white | 1 If the student is white; 0 otherwise |

(A) Which variables do not attain their expected signs
(B) Which variables are not significant at the 5% critical level?
(C) Plot the squared residuals from the regression against gpa. Does the plot show evidence of heteroskedasticity? Explain.
(D) Do a Park test for heteroskedasticity assuming gpa is the "culprit" variable. Show the five-step procedure.
(E) Perform White's test for heteroskedasticity. Show the five-step procedure.
(F) Run the original regression using weighted least squares. Assume the variance of the $u_i$'s is proportional to the square of gpa so that 1/gpa (variance of gpa) is the correct weight. Then apply White's test for heteroskedasticity to the errors from this weighted regression. Does the test indicate the presence of heteroskedasticity? Show the five-step procedure.
(G) Run the original regression using weighted least squares. Assume the variance of the $u_i$'s is proportional to gpa so that $1/\sqrt{gpa_i}$ (standard deviation of gpa) is the correct weight. Then apply White's test for heteroskedasticity to the errors from this weighted regression. Does the test indicate the presence of heteroskedasticity? Show the five-step procedure.
(H) Use the Newey-West technique to obtain heteroskedasticity-corrected standard errors with the original regression. Did heteroskedasticity appear to be biasing the standard errors of the structural parameters very much? Explain.

(4) Linear probability models are prone to heteroskedasticity. Use the data in BINGE.XLS and statistical software to run a regression where BINGE is explained by a constant term, cig, class, intra, male, pot, and white.

| Variable | Description |
| --- | --- |
| binge | 1 If the student binged in the last two weeks; 0 otherwise |
| cig | 1 If the student uses tobacco; 0 otherwise |
| class | 1 If first year; 2 if soph; 3 if jr; 4 if senior |
| intra | 1 If the student participates in intramural athletics; 0 otherwise |
| male | 1 If the student is male; 0 otherwise |
| pot | 1 If the student uses marijuana; 0 otherwise |
| white | 1 If the student is white; 0 otherwise |

(A) Which variables do not attain their expected signs?

(B) Which variables are not significant at the 5% critical level?

(C) Perform White's test for heteroskedasticity. Show the five-step procedure.

(D) Apply the Newey-West technique to obtain heteroskedasticity-corrected standard errors with the original regression. Did heteroskedasticity appear to be biasing the standard errors of the structural parameters very much? Explain.

(5) Mark the following statements TRUE or FALSE:

(A) $E[u_i^2] \neq E[u_j^2]$ for all $i \neq j$ is the definition of heteroskedasticity.

(B) The "culprit variable" is the dependent variable in a heteroskedastic regression.

(C) In the presence of heteroskedasticity, tests of significance must be carried out with caution since the T-ratios of the structural parameters are biased.

(D) Application of the Newey-West technique will alter the estimate of the SER.

(E) Application of the Newey-West technique will alter the estimates of the structural parameters.

# 11 Serial Correlation

## WHAT IS SERIAL CORRELATION?

Serial correlation, also known as autocorrelation, is when the error terms from a population regression are related to one another.

The assumption is that the error terms are related in a first-order Markov scheme:

$$u_t = \rho \ u_{t-1} + \varepsilon_t$$

where $-1 \leq \rho \leq +1$ and $\varepsilon_t$ is white noise (i.e., $\varepsilon_t \sim N(0, \sigma^2)$ for all t).

Positive autocorrelation is when $\rho > 0$; negative autocorrelation is when $\rho < 0$.

Autocorrelation occurs frequently with time-series data. Second-order serial correlation is less frequently encountered. Second-order serial correlation is when the current error term is related to the two prior error terms: $u_t = \rho_1 u_{t-1} + \rho_2 u_{t-2} + \varepsilon_t$

## CONSEQUENCES OF SERIAL CORRELATION

Serial correlation is a direct violation of assumption 3 of the Classical Linear Regression Model: The error terms are not related to one another: $E[u_i \ u_j] = 0$ for all $i \neq j$. Recall that assumption 3 was required to prove that the estimators are best, but not unbiased.

Therefore, in the presence of autocorrelation the structural parameters are not best. In addition, the residual statistics from the regression are biased:

DOI: 10.4324/9781003213758-11

$$\text{SER,} \quad \text{S.E. } (\beta\text{'s}), \quad \text{t-ratios,} \quad \text{F,} \quad R^2$$
$$\underline{\phantom{-}}\; - \qquad \underline{\phantom{-}}\; - \qquad\quad + \qquad\quad + \qquad +$$

The signs under each statistic indicate the direction of the bias. Notice that each statistic is biased in a way that makes it appear stronger. For instance, the standard error of the regression (SER) indicates a good fit when it is low and it is biased downward in the presence of auto-correlation. Similarly, estimators are significant when their standard errors are low and S.E. ($\beta$'s) is biased downward.

The consequences of serial correlation are the same as those of het-eroskedasticity with one small difference. In the presence of serial cor-relation, the direction of the bias in the residual statistics is known. With heteroskedasticity, the direction of the bias is unknown.

Since the standard errors and t-ratios are biased, hypothesis tests must be carried out with extreme caution in the presence of serial correlation. TYPE I errors will be more likely because the standard errors are biased downward.

In summary, the structural parameters are inefficient and the residual statistics are biased in the presence of serial correlation.

## DETECTION

Many techniques are available to detect serial correlation. Three of them are presented here. All of the detection techniques analyze the $e_t$'s, while autocorrelation concerns the $u_t$'s. The $u_t$'s are not available to researchers using sample regressions. The hope is that the $e_t$'s mimic the $u_t$'s.

### The Graphical Approach

Since serial correlation is when one error term from a time-series re-gression is related to its predecessor, it can be detected by looking for patterns in the error terms. One way to see these patterns is to make a graph of the residuals from the regression over time.

Consider the regression: $CON_t = \hat{\beta}_0 + \hat{\beta}_1 \, DPI_t + e_t$

where CON = annual real consumer spending in the United States;
       DPI = annual real disposable income in the United States.
Here are the residuals from the regression plotted over time:

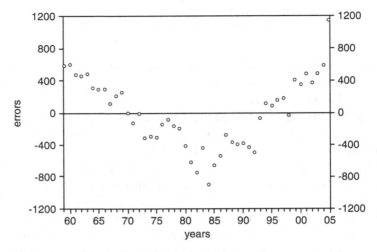

**Figure 11.1** The residuals from a time-series regression.

The pattern revealed here is indicative of positive serial correlation: $e_t = \rho e_{t-1} + \varepsilon_t$ and $\rho > 0$. Since $\rho$ is positive, any residual is likely to have the same sign as the one before it. This holds in the graph presented. From 1959 through 1970, every $e_t$ is positive. Once the residuals become negative in 1971, there is a run of negative values until 1994 when they once again become positive. These long runs of positive and negative values are characteristic of positive serial correlation.

Another type of graph also can be helpful in detecting autocorrelation. Here the residuals from the same regression are plotted against their lagged values:

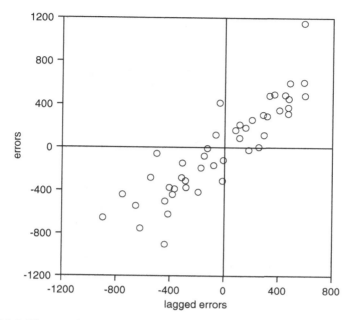

**Figure 11.2** The residuals from a time-series regression plotted against their previous values.

Almost all of the observations lie in the first and third quadrants. This implies that when an error term is positive, the one before it is as well. And when an error term is negative, so is its predecessor. In other words, error terms tend to have the same sign as their predecessors. This implies a positive $\rho$ in the first-order Markov scheme ($e_t = \rho e_{t-1} + \varepsilon_t$) and positive serial correlation.

How would the two types of graphs look if there was negative autocorrelation?

The graph on the left plots the residuals over time. Their values zigzag from positive to negative in sequence. If the current residual is positive, the subsequent residual is very likely to be negative.

The graph on the right plots the residuals against their previous values. Most of the observations lie in the second and fourth quadrants indicating that if the current error term is positive, the subsequent error term is very likely to be negative.

How do the graphs look when there is no serial correlation?

SERIAL CORRELATION

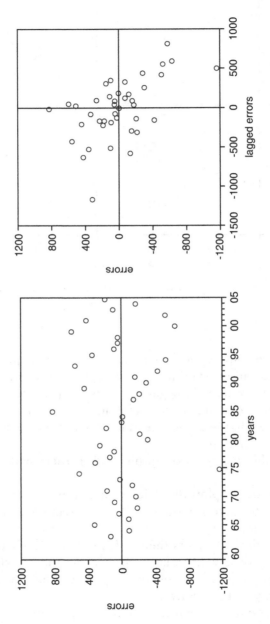

**Figure 11.3** Residuals reflecting negative serial correlation.

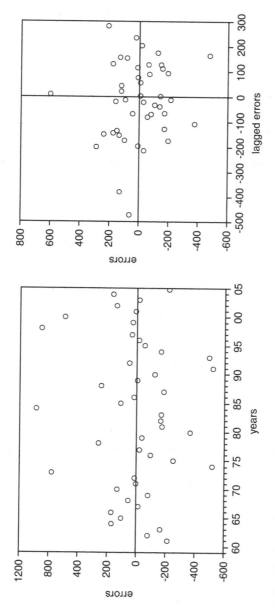

**Figure 11.4** Residuals reflecting no serial correlation.

The graph on the left shows no pattern, but a random splay of errors over time. The observations on the graph on the right are almost evenly divided between all four quadrants.

One problem with the graphical method for detecting autocorrelation is that patterns can be difficult to discern. In practice, the graphs usually are not as clear-cut as the ones shown here.

### The Durbin-Watson Test

The most popular technique for detecting serial correlation is the Durbin-Watson test (Durbin and Watson 1951). Econometric software packages routinely report the Durbin-Watson statistic. The test involves obtaining the residuals from the regression and calculating $d$, the test statistic:

$$d = \frac{\Sigma(e_t - e_{t-1})^2}{\Sigma e_t{}^2}$$

$d$ ranges between 0 and 4 and tends toward 2 if the residuals are not autocorrelated. If $d < 2$, suspect positive autocorrelation and apply the following five-step procedure:

(1) Ho: no positive auto  Ha: positive auto
(2) 5%
(3) If $d < d_L$, then reject Ho
    If $d_L < d < d_U$, then inconclusive
(4) Calculate $d$ and look up $d_L$ and $d_U$ in a Durbin-Watson 5% table
(5) Reject or Do Not Reject Ho

A Durbin-Watson table like the one in the back of this book is needed to look up $d_L$ and $d_U$. Be sure the table corresponds with the critical level of test, 5% in this case. To find the correct $d_L$ and $d_U$ look where n (the number of observations) and k (the number of structural parameters) intersect.

If $d > 2$, suspect negative autocorrelation and apply the following 5-step procedure:

(1) Ho: no negative auto  Ha: negative auto
(2) 5%
(3) If $4 - d_L < d$, then reject Ho
    If $4 - d_U < d < 4 - d_L$, then inconclusive
(4) Calculate $d$ and look up $d_L$ and $d_U$ in a Durbin-Watson 5% table
(5) Reject or Do Not Reject Ho

Examples:

(1)  $Y_t = 9734.2 - 3{,}782.2 \times 1_t + 2{,}815.3 \times 2_t + e_t$  n = 16 $d$ = 2.21

Since $d$ = 2.21, suspect negative autocorrelation:

(1) Ho: no negative auto Ha: negative auto
(2) 5%
(3) If $4 - d_L < d$, then reject Ho
   If $4 - d_U < d < 4 - d_L$, then inconclusive
(4) $d$ = 2.21 $d_L$ = 0.98 $d_U$ = 1.54 (n = 16; k = 3)
(5) Do Not Reject Ho; no negative auto

(2)  $Y_t = 0.568 + 0.907 \times 1_t + e_t$  n = 25 $d$ = 0.66

Since $d$ = 0.66, suspect positive autocorrelation:

(1) Ho: no positive auto Ha: positive auto
(2) 5%
(3) If $d < d_L$, then reject Ho
   If $d_L < d < d_U$, then inconclusive
(4) $d$ = 0.66 $d_L$ = 1.29 $d_U$ = 1.45 (n = 25; k = 2)
(5) Reject Ho; positive auto is present

The Durbin–Watson test is invalid in certain situations:

• The test is not valid in regressions without a constant term.
• The test is not valid for small samples (n < 15).
• The test is not valid for autoregressive models.

Autoregressive models are regressions that include the lagged dependent variable as an explanatory variable: $Y_t = \hat{\beta}_0 + \hat{\beta}_1 X_t + \hat{\beta}_2 Y_{t-1} + e_t$. The Durbin-Watson statistic is biased toward 2 in such models.

### The Breusch-Godfrey Test

Lagrange multiplier tests for serial correlation are increasingly popular since they overcome all the debilities of the Durbin-Watson test: they can be applied to small samples, autoregressive models, and models without a constant term. In addition, these tests for serial correlation have no inconclusive zone. The following Lagrange multiplier test is attributed to Breusch (1978) and Godfrey (1978):

If $Y_t = \hat{\beta}_0 + \hat{\beta}_1 X_t + \hat{\beta}_2 Y_{t-1} + e_t$ is suspected of suffering from serial correlation:

$$\text{Run: } e_t = \alpha_0 + \alpha_1 X_t + \alpha_2 Y_{t-1} + \alpha_3 e_{t-1} + \varepsilon_t$$

Then apply the following chi-squared $(\chi^2)$ test:

(1) Ho: no serial correlation  Ha: serial correlation exists
    $(\alpha_1 = \alpha_2 = \alpha_3 = 0)$        $(\alpha_1$ and/or $\alpha_2$ and/or $\alpha_3 \neq 0)$
(2) 5%
(3) If $nR^2 > \chi^2 c$, then reject Ho (d.f. = # of lagged residual terms = 1)
(4) Calculate $nR^2$ and look up $\chi^2 c$
(5) Reject or Do Not Reject Ho

Most econometric software packages can perform some form of Lagrange multiplier test for autocorrelation. To look up $\chi^2 c$, go online or use a table such as the one in the back of this book. Be sure the table corresponds to the critical level of the test. The degrees of freedom are equal to the number of lagged residual terms in the auxiliary regression. In this example, that regression has only one lagged residual term: $\alpha_3 e_{t-1}$.

### Testing for Second-Order Serial Correlation
All of the tests outlined earlier check for first-order serial correlation only. That is, the serial correlation is expected to follow a first-order Markov scheme: $e_t = \rho\, e_{t-1} + \varepsilon_t$. Second-order serial correlation ($e_t = \rho_1 e_{t-1} + \rho_2 e_{t-2} + \varepsilon_t$) is less common, but not unheard of, with economic data. It can be detected by running the following regression:

$$e_t = \hat{\beta}_1 e_{t-1} + \hat{\beta}_2 e_{t-2} + \varepsilon_t$$

This regression mimics a second-order Markov scheme. $\hat{\beta}_1$ and $\hat{\beta}_2$ are estimates of $\rho_1$ and $\rho_2$. If $\hat{\beta}_2$ is significant, then second-order autocorrelation is present.

## REMEDIES

Generalized least squares (GLS) is efficient in the presence of autocorrelation, OLS is not. GLS assumes the autocorrelated error terms follow a first-order Markov scheme. In order to apply GLS, $\rho$ from the first-order Markov scheme must be known. There are several methods for estimating $\rho$ and this leads to what appears to be a variety of remedies. However, there is only one remedy, GLS.

Consider a population regression with autocorrelated error terms:

$$Y_t = \beta_0 + \beta_1 X_t + u_t \quad (\text{where } u_t = \rho u_{t-1} + \varepsilon_t)$$

Lag the regression and multiply by $\rho$: $\rho Y_{t-1} = \rho \beta_0 + \rho \beta_1 X_{t-1} + \rho u_{t-1}$

Subtract the bottom equation from the top: $Y_t - \rho Y_{t-1} = \beta_0 - \rho \beta_0 + \beta_1$
$$X_t - \beta_1 \rho X_{t-1} + u_t - \rho u_{t-1}$$

Combine terms: $Y_t - \rho Y_{t-1} = \beta_0 (1 - \rho) + \beta_1 (X_t - \rho X_{t-1}) + u_t - \rho u_{t-1}$

This last equation is the generalized difference equation. The generalized differences of $Y_t$ ($=Y_t - \rho Y_{t-1}$) are regressed on the generalized differences of $X_t$ ($=X_t - \rho X_{t-1}$). When a regression is run using the generalized differences of the data, it is known as generalized least squares (GLS). The error terms ($u_t - \rho u_{t-1}$) in the GLS regression are free from serial correlation. This can be seen by substituting $u_t = \rho u_{t-1} + \varepsilon_t$ into ($u_t - \rho u_{t-1}$). The result is $\varepsilon_t$ which is white noise: a normally distributed stochastic variable that has a mean of zero, constant standard error, and is independently distributed (i.e., free from serial correlation).

In practice, when a regression suffers from serial correlation, the remedy is to run the regression using generalized differences. Most econometric software will do this on command. The results of a GLS regression are BLUE in the presence of autocorrelation and the residual statistics are unbiased.

GLS is the one and only remedy for autocorrelation. The problem in practice, is that $\rho$ is never known. It must be estimated. Four ways to estimate $\rho$ are presented here.

## OLS Technique

Suppose the residuals of the following regression are autocorrelated: $Y_t = \hat{\beta}_0 + \hat{\beta}_1 X1_t + e_t$. Estimate $\rho$ by regressing the residuals on their lagged values: $e_t = \hat{\beta}_1 e_{t-1} + \varepsilon_t$. This mimics a first-order Markov scheme. Notice there is no $\hat{\beta}_0$. $\hat{\beta}_1$ is the estimate of $\rho$. Now GLS may be applied with this estimate of $\rho$.

The OLS technique for estimating $\rho$ can check for second-order serial correlation:

Estimate $e_t = \hat{\beta}_1 e_{t-1} + \hat{\beta}_2 e_{t-2} + \varepsilon_t$. If $\hat{\beta}_2$ is significant, then second-order serial correlation is present. Strictly speaking, a second-order form of GLS is required to remedy second-order serial correlation. However, in practice GLS typically resolves both first and second-order serial correlation.

### Cochrane-Orcutt Iterative Procedure

Cochrane and Orcutt (1949) suggested an iterative process for settling on an appropriate value for $\rho$. This procedure estimates $\rho$ with a formula and then runs the GLS regression. However, it does not stop there. The GLS regression will have its own residuals, which can be plugged back into the formula for estimating $\rho$. Then GLS can be run again. Once again, the GLS residuals can be plugged into the formula for $\rho$ and GLS can be re-applied. This process iterates until sequential estimates of $\rho$ do not vary significantly.

(A) Estimate $\rho$ with this formula: $\rho = \frac{\Sigma e_t e_{t-1}}{\Sigma e_{t-1}^2}$

(B) Run GLS and obtain the new $e_t$'s.

(C) Go back to A.

(D) Stop when sequential estimates of $\rho$ do not vary by much.

### Hildreth-Lu Scanning Procedure

Once computer use became more widely available, Hildreth and Lu (1960) suggested scanning the entire grid of possible values for $\rho$. Since $\rho$ is expected to lie between plus and minus unity, a computer can easily check to see which value of $\rho$ gives the best fit in a GLS regression.

Assume $\rho = -1$; Run GLS; Assume $\rho = -0.9$; Run GLS; Assume $\rho = -0.8$; Run GLS;...; Assume $\rho = +0.9$; Run GLS; Assume $\rho = +1$; Run GLS. Of all these GLS regressions, use the one that has the best fit according to $R^2$ or SER.

### Maximum Likelihood Procedure

Most econometric software packages can estimate the parameters of GLS regressions using a maximum likelihood procedure. Basically, this procedure assigns initial values to $\hat{\beta}_0$, $\hat{\beta}_1$, and $\rho$, then evaluates the residuals from this GLS model. An algorithm is used to analyze the magnitude and pattern of the residuals, indicating adjustments to the initial values of $\hat{\beta}_0$, $\hat{\beta}_1$, and $\rho$. The residuals from the adjusted GLS model are put through the algorithm and used to make further adjustments to $\hat{\beta}_0$, $\hat{\beta}_1$, and $\rho$. The iterative process stops when sequential estimates of $\hat{\beta}_0$, $\hat{\beta}_1$, and $\rho$ do not vary significantly.

# FINAL THOUGHTS

Statistical software packages can correct for serial correlation on command. Econometricians understand that GLS is the remedy being employed, although the means of estimating $\rho$ can vary. Often the software allows for user specification of the method for estimating $\rho$.

Regressions that are underspecified or in the wrong functional form can test positive for serial correlation. When this occurs, it is known as pseudoautocorrelation. Graphs, the $d$-statistic, or Lagrange multiplier tests detect autocorrelation, but this is due to the regression missing an important explanatory variable or being in the wrong functional form. These misspecifications have worse consequences than autocorrelation. If autocorrelation is detected and remedial measures are ineffective, it is most likely pseudoautocorrelation.

Serial correlation has more serious consequences in autoregressive models. Remember, autoregressive models include the lagged dependent variable as an explanatory variable: $Y_t = \hat{\beta}_0 + \hat{\beta}_1 X1_t + \hat{\beta}_2 Y_{t-1} + e_t$. If an autoregressive model suffers from serial correlation, then the structural parameters are biased and so are the residual statistics. Remedies for autocorrelated, autoregressive models include instrumental variables and two-stage least squares. Those techniques are not covered here.

The Newey-West technique that is used to cope with heteroskedasticity is applicable in cases of autocorrelation as well. Newey-West standard errors are heteroskedasticity autocorrelation-consistent, or HAC. The technique corrects the biased standard errors of the structural parameters. This fixes the t-ratios and p-values and allows for hypothesis testing in the presence of serial correlation without recourse to GLS. The structural parameters are not changed by the Newey-West technique but it does not matter since they are unbiased. The residual statistics are biased in the presence of serial correlation and the Newey-West technique does not address that issue.

# TERMS

Autoregressive model—A regression that uses the lagged dependent variable as an explanatory variable.
Cochrane-Orcutt iterative procedure—A procedure to estimate $\rho$ for a generalized least-squares regression.
Durbin-Watson test—A test for serial correlation.

First-order Markov scheme ($u_t = \rho\, u_{t-1} + \varepsilon_t$)—A common way in which the error terms from a regression can be related.

Generalized least-squares (GLS)—A regression using the generalized differences of the data.

Heteroskedasticity autocorrelation-consistent standard errors (HAC)— The standard errors of the estimators are calculated by a formula that corrects for the bias caused by heteroskedasticity or auto-correlation such as the Newey-West technique.

Hildreth-Lu scanning procedure—A procedure to estimate $\rho$ for a generalized least-squares regression.

Lagrange multiplier test—A test for serial correlation.

Maximum likelihood procedure—A technique for estimating the structural parameters of an econometric model, such as a GLS model.

Newey-West technique—Formulas for the standard errors of the structural parameters of a regression that correct for the bias caused by serial correlation or heteroskedasticity.

Pseudoautocorrelation—When a regression tests positive for auto-correlation but the symptoms are due to underspecification or using the wrong functional form.

Second-order serial correlation ($u_t = \rho_1\, u_{t-1} + \rho_2\, u_{t-2} + \varepsilon_t$)—When the current error term is related to the two prior error terms.

Serial correlation (autocorrelation)—When the error terms from a regression are related to one another.

White noise—A normally distributed stochastic variable that has a mean of zero, constant variance, and is independently distributed (i.e., free from serial correlation).

## CHAPTER 11 PROBLEMS

(1) Complete the following table:

| Sample size | k | d-Stat | Autocorrelation present? |
|---|---|---|---|
| 20 | 2 | 0.83 | |
| 32 | 3 | 1.24 | |
| 45 | 4 | 1.98 | |
| 100 | 5 | 3.72 | |
| 150 | 7 | 1.71 | |

(2) Complete the following table:

| Sample size | k | d-Stat | Autocorrelation present? |
|---|---|---|---|
| 15 | 2 | 1.60 | |
| 25 | 3 | 1.80 | |
| 45 | 4 | 2.48 | |
| 100 | 6 | 2.72 | |
| 150 | 10 | 2.11 | |

(3) Use the data in CONSUMP.XLS and statistical software to run the following regression:

$$RCONPC_t = \hat{\beta}_0 + \hat{\beta}_1 REALYDPC_t + e_t$$

(A) Plot the error terms over time. Do you suspect serial correlation? Explain.
(B) Plot the error terms against their lagged values. Do you suspect serial correlation? Explain.
(C) Perform a Durbin-Watson test. Show the five-step procedure.

(4) Use the data in ANMACRO.XLS and statistical software to run the following regression:

$$m^2/cpi_t = \hat{\beta}_0 + \hat{\beta}_1 ngdp + cpi_t + e_t$$

where $m^2$ is the money supply
cpi is the consumer price index
ngdp is nominal gdp

(A) Plot the error terms over time. Do you suspect serial correlation? Explain.
(B) Plot the error terms against their lagged values. Do you suspect serial correlation? Explain.
(C) Perform a Durbin-Watson test. Show the five-step procedure.

(5) Use the data in CONSUMP.XLS and statistical software to run the following regression:

$$RCONPC_t = \hat{\beta}_0 + \hat{\beta}_1 REALYDPC_t + \hat{\beta}_2 REALR_t + \hat{\beta}_3 CC_t + e_t$$

Where RCONPC = real consumer spending in the USA per capita
       REALYDPC = real disposable income per capita
       REALR = real interest rate on one-year Treasury Bonds
       CC = University of Michigan Index of Consumer Confidence

(A) Plot the residuals from the regression over time. Does this plot suggest serial correlation is present? Positive or negative? Explain.

(B) Plot the residuals from the regression against their lagged values. Does this plot suggest serial correlation is present? Positive or negative? Explain.

(C) Does the regression suffer from serial correlation? Show the five-step procedure of the Durbin-Watson test.

(D) Estimate $\rho$ by regressing the residuals on their lagged values (no constant term). What is the estimate of $\rho$?

(E) Check for second-order serial correlation. Do you think it is present? Explain.

(F) Estimate $\rho$ and correct for first-order serial correlation using GLS with maximum likelihood estimation. What is this estimate of $\rho$?

(G) Did GLS remedy the serial correlation? Show the five-step procedure of the Breusch-Godfrey test.

(H) Compare the t-ratios from the original regression and the GLS regression. Are you surprised by which ones turn out to be larger? Explain.

(I) Apply the Newey-West technique to the original regression. Are you surprised at the new standard errors of the estimators? Explain.

(6) Use the data in ANMACRO.XLS and statistical software to run a regression where the demand for money $(m^2)$ is explained by a constant term, income (ngdp), interest rates (aaa), and prices (cpi).

(A) Plot the residuals from the regression over time. Does this plot suggest serial correlation is present? Positive or negative? Explain.

(B) Plot the residuals from the regression against their lagged values. Does this plot suggest serial correlation is present? Positive or negative? Explain.

(C) Does the regression suffer from serial correlation? Show the five-step procedure of the Durbin-Watson test.

(D) Estimate $\rho$ by regressing the residuals on their lagged values (no constant term). What is the estimate of $\rho$?

(E) Check for second-order serial correlation. Do you think it is present? Explain.

(F) Estimate $\rho$ and correct for first-order serial correlation using GLS with maximum likelihood estimation. What is this estimate of $\rho$?

(G) Did GLS remedy the serial correlation? Show the five-step procedure.

(H) Compare the t-ratios from the original regression and the GLS regression. Are you surprised by which ones turn out to be larger? Explain.

(I) Apply the Newey-West technique to the original regression. Are you surprised at the new standard errors of the estimators? Explain.

(7) Mark each of the following statements TRUE or FALSE.

(A) $u_t = \rho u_{t-1} + \varepsilon_t$ is a second-order Markov scheme.

(B) The standard error of the regression (SER) is biased upward in the presence of serial correlation.

(C) The standard error of $\hat{\beta}_1$ is biased downward in the presence of serial correlation.

(D) If $\rho > 0$, then the Durbin-Watson test should be for positive serial correlation.

(E) The Durbin-Watson test is invalid in autoregressive models.

# 12 Time-Series Techniques

## TIME-SERIES ECONOMETRICS

Time-series data can be any frequency. Most econometric software is set up to handle annual, quarterly, monthly, weekly, and daily figures. Testing economic ideas using time-series data has some special challenges and opportunities. For example, it is important that there are no missing observations when applying time-series techniques, whereas missing observations can be discarded with cross-sectional data.

Autocorrelation often afflicts time-series regressions. Cross-sectional data can be reordered with no effect on the regression results. The error terms would be in a different order and, hopefully, not autocorrelated.

But time-series techniques can be exploited when relationships occur sequentially. For instance, a large increase in consumer spending may be followed by a retrenchment the next period as consumers rebuild their savings balances. Or consider the idea that a decrease in the money supply may impact economic activity over the many periods going forward. Cross-sectional data cannot capture these effects.

## DISTRIBUTED LAG MODELS

A distributed lag model occurs when one or more of the independent variables is lagged one or more periods:

$$Y_t = \beta_0 + \beta_1 X_t + \beta_2 X_{t-1} + \beta_3 X_{t-2} + \beta_4 Z_t + \beta_5 Z_{t-1} + u_t$$

There are several justifications for using lags. For instance, changes in the explanatory variable may take time to impact the dependent variable.

DOI: 10.4324/9781003213758-12

Or the trend in the explanatory variable over several periods is what affects the dependent variable.

The permanent income hypothesis (PIH) offers an interesting application of a distributed lag model. The PIH asserts that consumer spending depends on expected future income, not actual income. It has been observed that consumer spending (CON) is smoother over time than actual income (DPI). One explanation for this is that windfalls do not change expected future income, so CON is relatively more stable than DPI.

The PIH predicts that CON is better explained by expected DPI (EXDPI) as opposed to actual DPI. In econometric terms:

$$\text{CON}_t = \hat{\beta}_0 + \hat{\beta}_1 \text{EXDPI}_t + e_t$$

The difficulty is that EXDPI is hard to measure especially for aggregate data. One of the first attempts to approximate aggregate EXDPI was to use the pattern of past actual incomes:

$$\text{CON}_t = \hat{\beta}_0 + \hat{\beta}_1 \text{DPI}_t + \hat{\beta}_2 \text{DPI}_{t-1} + \hat{\beta}_3 \text{DPI}_{t-2} + \hat{\beta}_4 \text{DPI}_{t-3} + e_t$$

Here a distributed lag model is used as a proxy for expected future income. The assumption in expected future income is based on a weighted average of actual incomes in the recent past. If the lagged values of DPI are significant, then the PIH is supported. It is not apparent how many lags of DPI are appropriate. Trial and error can be used to determine appropriate lag length.

Multicollinearity is typically a problem in distributed lag models. The correlation between DPI and $\text{DPI}_{t-1}$ is likely to be extreme. And distributed lag models can use up degrees of freedom.

### The Koyck Model

The Koyck model (Koyck 1954) is an ingenious way to employ a distributed lag model. Suppose current consumption (CON) is a weighted average of disposable personal income (DPI) going back many periods. Assume the weights decline geometrically by a factor of $\lambda$:

$$\text{CON}_t = \beta_0 + \beta_1 (\text{DPI}_t + \lambda \text{DPI}_{t-1} + \lambda^2 \text{DPI}_{t-2} + \lambda^3 \text{DPI}_{t-3} + \ldots \\ + \lambda^n \text{DPI}_{t-n}) + u_t$$

Lag this equation one period and multiply by $\lambda$:

$$\lambda\text{CON}_{t-1} = \lambda\beta_0 + \beta_1(\lambda\text{DPI}_{t-1} + \lambda^2\text{DPI}_{t-2} + \lambda^3\text{DPI}_{t-3} + \ldots + \lambda^n\text{DPI}_{t-n}) + \lambda u_{t-1}$$

Subtract the second equation from the first:

$$\text{CON}_t - \lambda\text{CON}_{t-1} = \beta_0 - \lambda\beta_0 + \beta_1\text{DPI}_t + u_t - \lambda u_{t-1}$$

Moving $\lambda\text{CON}_{t-1}$ to the other side and combining terms yields:

$$\text{CON}_t = \beta_0{}^* + \beta_1\text{DPI}_t + \lambda\text{CON}_{t-1} + \varepsilon_t \text{ where } \beta_0{}^* = \beta_0 - \lambda\beta_0 \text{ and } \varepsilon_t = u_t - \lambda u_{t-1}$$

This is a Koyck distributed lag model. By regressing CON on contemporaneous DPI and $\text{CON}_{t-1}$ it amounts to a regression where CON is explained by a distributed lag of DPI going back to the beginning of the data set. However, the weights attached to each lag of DPI decline geometrically. The data determine how fast the weights decline by estimating the value of $\lambda$. The coefficient on $\text{CON}_{t-1}$ is the estimate of the weight ($\lambda$) and is calculated like any regression coefficient. The short-run impact of DPI on CON is equal to $\beta_1$. The long-run impact is equal to $\beta_1/(1-\lambda)$.

In this model, a distributed lag of n periods is estimated with the loss of just one observation. Multicollinearity is usually reduced in the Koyck model compared to the regular distributed lag model.

Notice that the Koyck model is autoregressive, making the Durbin-Watson statistic invalid. Use a Lagrange multiplier test for serial correlation instead. Serial correlation has more serious consequences in autoregressive models and it is tricky to remedy. If an autoregressive model suffers from serial correlation, then the structural parameters are biased as well as the residual statistics. Remedies include instrumental variables and two-stage least squares, but we will not discuss those.

Using quarterly aggregate data from the US economy starting in 2002 allows for a comparison of a regular distributed lag model:

$$\text{CON}_t = \hat{\beta}_0 + \hat{\beta}_1\text{DPI}_t + \hat{\beta}_2\text{DPI}_{t-1} + \hat{\beta}_3\text{DPI}_{t-2} + \hat{\beta}_4\text{DPI}_{t-3} + \hat{\beta}_5\text{DPI}_{t-4} + e_t$$

with a Koyck model:

$$\text{CON}_t = \hat{\beta}_0 + \hat{\beta}_1\text{DPI}_t + \hat{\beta}_2\text{CON}_{t-1} + e_t$$

Dependent Variable is CON n = 70

|  | Model A | Model B |
|---|---|---|
| Constant | 1,059.46*** | 74.22 |
|  | (400.11) | (69.51) |
| DPI | 0.23*** | 0.09** |
|  | (0.04) | (0.04) |
| $DPI_{t-1}$ | 0.26*** |  |
|  | (0.04) |  |
| $DPI_{t-2}$ | 0.12** |  |
|  | (0.05) |  |
| $DPI_{t-3}$ | 0.12*** |  |
|  | (0.04) |  |
| $DPI_{t-4}$ | 0.09* |  |
|  | (0.05) |  |
| $CON_{t-1}$ |  | 0.90 |
|  |  | (0.04) |
| Adjusted $R^2$ | 0.99 | 0.99 |

Standard errors in parentheses:
*significant at 10%; **significant at 5%; ***significant at 1%

Model A features a distributed lag of four quarters. All the lags on DPI have the expected positive sign. The last lag is significant only at the 10% critical level, but this is allowed for due to the presence of multicollinearity. Had, say, the second lag on DPI been insignificant, it would not be dropped. It makes little sense to lag a variable four periods but omit the second period. The second period lag could very well be insignificant spuriously.

Model B is a Koyck lag. Rather than lag DPI any number of periods, the lagged dependent variable is added. This is akin to lagging DPI back many periods with each lag receiving less weight. The weight ($\lambda$) is 0.90, the coefficient on $CON_{t-1}$.

The short-term impact of DPI on CON is 0.09, the coefficient on $DPI_t$. That is to say, given an extra dollar, Americans typically increase spending nine cents in the current quarter. The long-run impact of DPI is $\hat{\beta}_1/(1 - \lambda) = 0.09/(1 - 0.90) = 0.90$. The interpretation here is: given an extra dollar, Americans typically spend 90 cents over the long run. In other words, the Koyck model estimates the short-run marginal propensity to consume (0.09) and the long-run marginal propensity to consume (0.90) in one regression.

## GRANGER TESTS

Often in time-series analysis, it pays to know if changes in one variable generally occur before changes in another. For instance, the accelerator theory of investment states that changes in business spending on plant and equipment (investment) are caused by changes in output (real GDP), and not the other way around (Samuelson 1939).

No doubt a variety of factors affect spending on plant and equipment. The accelerator theory posits that an increase in output this period would drive business spending higher in later periods. Moreover, the theory asserts that output is a critical factor affecting investment. If the accelerator theory is correct, then changes in output should occur before changes in investment.

Granger (1969) developed a test to determine precedence in time-series data. The following example uses quarterly data on the US economy. In order to determine if changes in output (RGDP) precede changes in investment (INV), run the following regression:

$$INV_t = \hat{\beta}_0 + \hat{\beta}_1 INV_{t-1} + \hat{\beta}_2 INV_{t-2} + \hat{\beta}_3 RGDP_{t-1} + \hat{\beta}_4 RGDP_{t-2} + e_t$$

$\hat{\beta}_3$ and/or $\hat{\beta}_4$ will be statistically significant if changes in RGDP do indeed precede changes in INV. The test for this is as follows:

(1) Ho: $\hat{\beta}_3$ and $\hat{\beta}_4$ = 0; RGDP does not precede INV
    Ha: $\hat{\beta}_3$ and/or $\hat{\beta}_4$ ≠ 0; RGDP precedes INV
(2) 5%
(3) If $F > F^C$, reject Ho
(4) 16.71 vs 2.25 (d.f. num. = R = 2; d.f. den. = n – k = 234 – 5 = 229)
(5) Reject Ho; changes in RGDP precede changes in INV

The F-statistic in this test is:

$$F = \frac{(SSR_R - SSR_U)/R}{SSR_U/(n-k)} = \frac{(207,128.50 - 180,749.00)/2}{180,749.00/(234-5)} = 16.71$$

where $SSR_U = \Sigma e_i^2$ from the unrestricted regression:
$$INV_t = \hat{\beta}_0 + \hat{\beta}_1 INV_{t-1} + \hat{\beta}_2 INV_{t-2} + \hat{\beta}_3 RGDP_{t-1} + \hat{\beta}_4 RGDP_{t-2} + e_t$$

$SSR_R = \Sigma e_i^2$ from the restricted regression:

$$INV_t = \hat{\beta}_0 + \hat{\beta}_1 INV_{t-1} + \hat{\beta}_2 INV_{t-2} + e_t$$

R is number of restrictions. (Two variables are left out of the restricted regression.)
n is number of observations in the unrestricted regression (234).
k is the number of structural parameters in the unrestricted regression (2).

The degrees of freedom are R in the numerator and n – k (from the unrestricted regression) in the denominator.

Fortunately, many econometric software packages will perform Granger tests on command and the user need only specify R—the number of restrictions. In this example, R = 2, but the number of restrictions and lag length are typically determined by trial and error. Trying various lag lengths helps determine if the results from any one Granger test are unusual.

The conclusion from this Granger test supports the accelerator hypothesis: changes in RGDP precede changes in INV. Regardless of how this test turns out, it is advisable to conduct the reverse Granger test by running the following regression:

$$RGDP = \hat{\beta}_0 + \hat{\beta}_1 RGDP_{t-1} + \hat{\beta}_2 RGDP_{t-2} + \hat{\beta}_3 INV_{t-1} + \hat{\beta}_4 INV_{t-2} + e_t$$

And then perform the following five-step procedure:

(1) Ho: $\hat{\beta}_3$ and $\hat{\beta}_4$ = 0; INV does not precede RGDP
    Ha: $\hat{\beta}_3$ and/or $\hat{\beta}_4$ ≠ 0; RGDP precedes INV
(2) 5%
(3) If F > $F^C$, Reject Ho
(4) 1.07 versus 2.25 (d.f. num. = R = 2; d.f. den. = n – k = 234 – 5 = 229)
(5) Do reject Ho; changes in INV do not precede changes in RGDP

The reverse Granger test indicates that changes in INV do not precede changes in RGDP. The initial Granger test showed that changes in RGDP precede changes in INV. The conclusion gleaned from both tests is that the precedence runs one way: from RGDP to INV. This supports the accelerator hypothesis.

If a Granger test and the reverse test both result in not rejecting Ho, then neither variable in the test can be said to precede the other. If the two Granger tests result in rejecting Ho, then the test is inconclusive since both variables seem to be preceding the other. There could be a feedback loop in effect.

Be careful not to attribute causality to any Granger test. Precedence does not necessarily imply causation. One observes many pedestrians carrying umbrellas before a rainstorm, but surely those umbrellas do not cause the rain. From the tests earlier we conclude that RGDP "Granger-causes" INV, but INV does not "Granger-cause" RGDP.

Granger tests are useful to test for reverse causality. The structural parameters in the following regression will be biased if Y has an impact on X:

$$Y_t = \beta_0 + \beta_1 X_t + u_t$$

In regression analysis, it is critical that changes in the explanatory variable (X) cause changes in the dependent variable (Y). However, if Y causes X, it is known as reverse causality. In such a case, it can be shown that the expected value of the error terms is not equal to zero given $X_i$: $E[u_i \mid X_i] \neq 0$. This violates assumption 2 of the CLRM and the structural parameters are biased.

## SPURIOUS CORRELATION, NONSTATIONARITY, AND COINTEGRATION

Spurious correlation is a strong relationship between variables that is the result of a statistical fluke, not an underlying causal relationship. This occurs often with economic data because economic variables tend to grow over time. Thus, variables that are not causally related have high correlation coefficients anyway.

As an example, the correlation coefficient between the money supply (M2) and per capita milk consumption in the United States is extreme at –.95. Yet it is highly unlikely that increases in the money supply cause people to consume less milk. The correlation between the two is merely coincidental.

Spurious correlations are common with time-series data since so many variables exhibit long-term trends. Special care must be taken when working with trended data because regression results can be biased as a result of spurious correlations.

In the best circumstances, time-series regressions will use only stationary data—time-series whose basic properties do not change over time. Specifically, a time-series, X, is said to be stationary if:

(1) the mean of X is constant over time
(2) the variance of X is constant over time
(3) the correlation between $X_t$ and $X_{t-k}$ (for all k) is constant

If one or more of these properties is not met, then X is nonstationary. The use of nonstationary time-series in regressions may result in spurious correlation and that means biased estimates of the structural parameters.

The graph here shows real GDP (RGDP) quarterly since 1960. This time-series exhibits a pronounced upward trend and therefore does have a constant mean. The mean of RGDP during the earlier years is lower than the mean in the later years.

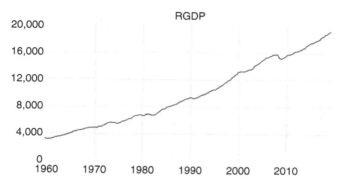

Figure 12.1 A time-series of real GDP.

Whether or not the variance of RGDP is constant over time is difficult to tell from visual inspection in this case. And there is no way to tell if observations a given distance apart have a constant correlation from visual inspection. Fortunately, there are tests for stationarity.

Econometricians can inspect the correlogram of a time-series to determine if it is stationary.

A correlogram is a chart that shows the degree to which observations k spaces apart are correlated. Correlograms that do not approach zero quickly indicate nonstationary data.

Econometric software packages typically produce correlograms on command. In the table here, r is the correlation coefficient between observations k spaces apart. Remember, $-1 \leq r \leq +1$ and extreme readings of r mean a high degree of linear correlation.

| k | r |
|---|---|
| 1 | 0.95 |
| 2 | 0.90 |
| 3 | 0.85 |
| 4 | 0.80 |
| 5 | 0.76 |
| 6 | 0.71 |
| 7 | 0.67 |
| 8 | 0.62 |

Given time-series data such as RGDP, take each pair of observations that are adjacent (k = 1). This means taking the first and second observation, the second and third, the third and fourth, and so on. Now calculate the correlation coefficient (r) between all these pairs.

Next take observations of RGDP that are a space apart (k = 2). These are observations one and three, two and four, three, and five, and so on. Now calculate the correlation coefficient (r) between all these pairs. Repeat this for all pairs of observations up to 8 spaces apart (k = 8).

Adjacent observations in RGDP are highly correlated (r = 0.95). Even observations eight years apart are highly correlated (r = 0.62). A chart of the table is a correlogram:

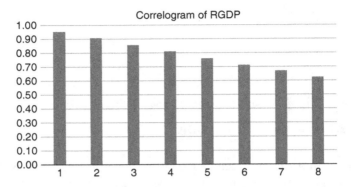

**Figure 12.2** A correlogram of real GDP.

The vertical axis of the correlogram reports the correlation coefficients from the table, while the horizontal axis corresponds to k. Correlograms that do not decay to r = 0 in 4 or 5 periods are typical of nonstationary time-series. The correlogram of RGDP here is indicative of a nonstationary time-series. At k = 8, the correlation is very far from zero. Regressions that use nonstationary data will most likely suffer from spurious correlation and yield biased results.

If a time-series is nonstationary, then it may be best to work with the first-differences of the data. First-differences are the change from one period to the next in the time-series, rather than the levels. The graph here depicts the first-differences in RGDP (FD1RGDP) over the years.

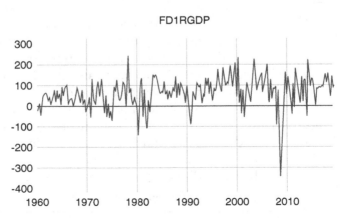

**Figure 12.3** The first-differences in real GDP.

Visual inspection suggests a constant mean (perhaps), but it appears as if the latter half of the line has a larger variance than the first half. It is a tough call. The correlogram here suggests significant correlations between observations at k = 1 and 2, but no further than that. In other words, FD1RGDP may be stationary since the correlations become insignificant after two lags.

| k | r |
|---|---|
| 1 | 0.41 |
| 2 | 0.11 |
| 3 | −0.03 |
| 4 | −0.02 |
| 5 | 0.07 |
| 6 | 0.06 |
| 7 | 0.14 |
| 8 | 0.12 |

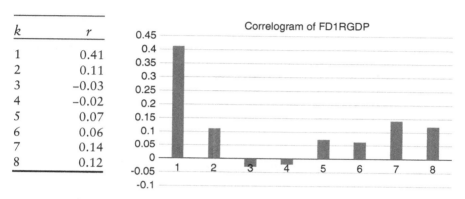

**Figure 12.4** A correlogram of the first-differences in real GDP.

In this case, it appears that the first-differences in RGDP are stationary. However, if a time-series and its first-differences are nonstationary, then second-differences may be called for. Second-differences in RGDP (FD2RGDP) are the differences in the first-differences, or the change in the change in RGDP.

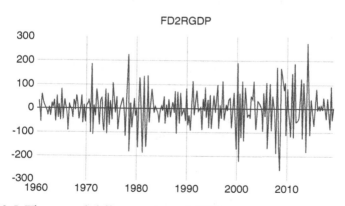

**Figure 12.5** The second-differences in real GDP.

The correlogram here suggests that the second-differences are stationary since they become insignificant after k = 3. At k = 8 the correlogram pops up to r = 0.21, but this is undoubtedly spurious.

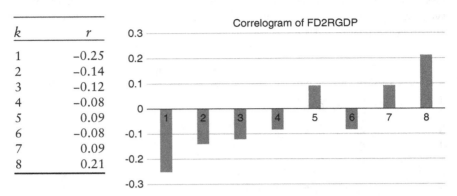

| k | r |
|---|---|
| 1 | −0.25 |
| 2 | −0.14 |
| 3 | −0.12 |
| 4 | −0.08 |
| 5 | 0.09 |
| 6 | −0.08 |
| 7 | 0.09 |
| 8 | 0.21 |

**Figure 12.6** A correlogram of the second-differences in real GDP.

Regressions that use RGDP are using a nonstationary variable. This is a serious allegation because the results of any such regressions are biased. The researcher can only hope that the bias is small. It would be better to use the first-differences in RGDP since they appear to be stationary according to a check of the correlogram. This means using the first-differences of all the variables in the regression.

Checking correlograms is not the premier test for stationarity. Econometricians prefer the Dickey–Fuller, or unit root, test (Dickey and Fuller 1979). To test if a time-series, $X_t$, is stationary:

(A) Run $(X_t - X_{t-1}) = \hat{\beta}_0 + \hat{\beta}_1 X_{t-1} + e_t$
(B) Perform a negative sign test on $\hat{\beta}_1$ as outlined here:
    (1) Ho: $\hat{\beta}_1 = 0$ (X is nonstationary) Ha: $\hat{\beta}_1 < 0$ (X is stationary)
    (2) 5%
    (3) If t-ratio < $-t^{c*}$, reject Ho
    (4) The t-ratio is the usual one, but $t^{c*}$ is about 60% higher than $t^c$ from the usual t table. As n approaches infinity, $t^{c*}$ approaches 2.86 from higher levels.
    (5) State the results of the test

Using the data on RGDP as an example, a Dickey-Fuller test is conducted here:

(A) $(RGDP_t - RGDP_{t-1}) = 25.92 + 0.03\ RGDP_{t-1} + e_t$
                      (5.72) ← t-ratio

(B) Negative sign test on $\hat{\beta}_1$:
  (1) Ho: $\hat{\beta}_1 = 0$ (X is nonstationary) Ha: $\hat{\beta}_1 < 0$ (X is stationary)
  (2) 5%
  (3) If t-ratio < $-t^{c*}$, reject Ho
  (4) 5.72 > -2.87, reject Ho
  (5) Do not reject Ho; RGDP is nonstationary

The t-ratio is taken from the regression in part A. The critical t, $t^{c*}$, can be found in a special Dickey–Fuller table, or the critical t from the usual table can be found and multiplied by 1.6. The degrees of freedom are n – k.

The test here finds RGDP to be nonstationary. Applying a Dickey–Fuller test to the first-differences in RGDP indicates that they are stationary:

(A) $(\text{RGDP}_t - \text{RGDP}_{t-1}) - (\text{RGDP}_{t-1} - \text{RGDP}_{t-2})$
  $= 90.68 - 0.51\ (\text{RGDP}_{t-1} - \text{RGDP}_{t-2}) + e_t$
  $\quad\ (-4.31)\quad \leftarrow \text{t-ratio}$

(B) Negative sign test on $\hat{\beta}_1$:
  (1) Ho: $\hat{\beta}_1 = 0$ (X is nonstationary) Ha: $\hat{\beta}_1 < 0$ (X is stationary)
  (2) 5%
  (3) If t-ratio < $-t^{c*}$, reject Ho
  (4) -4.31 < -2.87, reject Ho
  (5) Reject Ho; the first-differences in RGDP are stationary

The augmented Dickey–Fuller test adds a lagged dependent variable to the right-hand side of the unaugmented Dickey–Fuller regression:

$$(X_t - X_{t-1}) = \hat{\beta}_0 + \hat{\beta}_1 X_{t-1} + \hat{\beta}_2\ (X_{t-1} - X_{t-2}) + e_t$$

Augmented Dickey–Fuller tests in the case of RGDP yield the same results as the unaugmented tests: RGDP is nonstationary; FD1RGDP is stationary.

The lesson is clear: do not work with nonstationary time-series data. Instead, take first or second-differences in order make the data stationary and avoid spurious correlation.

However, it is unnecessary to difference nonstationary variables in a regression when they are cointegrated. Cointegrated variables are nonstationary to the same degree.

Consider a simple regression:

$$Y_t = \hat{\beta}_0 + \hat{\beta}_1\ X_t + e_t$$

Suppose X and Y are both nonstationary so that the regression may suffer from spurious correlation.

Further suppose that their first-differences are stationary. To determine if X and Y are cointegrated apply a Dickey-Fuller test to $e_t$:

(A) Run the regression: $Y_t = \hat{\beta}_0 + \hat{\beta}_1 X_t + e_t$
(B) Run the Dickey–Fuller regression on the error terms:
$(e_t - e_{t-1}) = \hat{\beta}_0 + \hat{\beta}_1 e_{t-1} + \varepsilon_t$
(C) Perform a negative sign test on $\hat{\beta}_1$:
    (1) Ho: $\hat{\beta}_1 = 0$ ($e_t$ is nonstationary) Ha: $\hat{\beta}_1 < 0$ ($e_t$ is stationary)
       (X and Y are not cointegrated) (X and Y are cointegrated)
    (2) 5%
    (3) If t-ratio $< -t^{c*}$, reject Ho.
    (4) The $t^c$ for the Dickey–Fuller test is about 60% higher than $t^c$ from the usual t table.
    (5) State the results of the test.

Cointegrated variables can be used "as is" in regressions without concern for spurious correlation.

As an example, let's go back to the accelerator hypothesis and run the following regression using quarterly time-series data for the United States. The hypothesis states that business spending on plant and equipment (INV) is explained by output (RGDP).

$$INV_t = \hat{\beta}_0 + \hat{\beta}_1 RGDP_t + e_t$$

As previously shown, RGDP is nonstationary although its first-differences are stationary. INV is the same: its levels are nonstationary, but its first-differences are stationary. Therefore, these two variables may be cointegrated. In that case, the regression mentioned earlier will not suffer from spurious correlation even if the levels of the variables are used.

To determine if the variables in $INV_t = \hat{\beta}_0 + \hat{\beta}_1 RGDP_t + e_t$ are indeed cointegrated, apply an augmented Dickey-Fuller test to $e_t$ by running the following regression:

$$(e_t - e_{t-1}) = \hat{\beta}_0 + \hat{\beta}_1 e_{t-1} + \hat{\beta}_2 (e_{t-1} - e_{t-2}) + \varepsilon_t$$

Then apply a negative sign test to $\hat{\beta}_1$:

(1) Ho: $\hat{\beta}_1 = 0$ ($e_t$ is nonstationary)   Ha: $\hat{\beta}_1 < 0$ ($e_t$ is stationary)
    (X and Y are not cointegrated)    (X and Y are cointegrated)

(2) 5%
(3) If t-ratio < –t$^{c}$*, reject Ho
(4) –1.76 > –2.87, reject Ho
(5) Do not reject Ho; the variables are not cointegrated

Unfortunately, the variables in the regression are not cointegrated. It would be best to take first-differences of both variables before running the regression in order to scrupulously avoid spurious correlation.

## ARIMA MODELS

Autoregressive integrated moving average (ARIMA) models are sometimes referred to as Box-Jenkins models after the authors of the seminal work on the topic (Box and Jenkins 1970). ARIMA models "look back" at past values of a time-series in order to determine patterns and consistencies. ARIMA models are a generalization of exponential smoothing models.

ARIMA models are a popular and expedient method for forecasting economic time-series. Patterns and correlations in the past values of a time-series are used to make forecasts of future values. Critics of the technique point out that any patterns discerned from the past are not likely to hold in the future.

### Autoregressive Models
An autoregressive model comprises the "AR" portion of an ARIMA model. An autoregressive model stipulates that the current value of a time-series is a linear function of its past values. For instance, the inflation rate (INFL) might depend on its own values in the previous three periods and is designated as AR(3):

$$INFL_t = \hat{\beta}_0 + \hat{\beta}_1 INFL_{t-1} + \hat{\beta}_2 INFL_{t-2} + \hat{\beta}_3 INFL_{t-3} + e_t$$

Purely autoregressive models can be estimated with ordinary least squares. It is important to test for serial correlation since serial correlation has more serious consequences in autoregressive models. The structural parameters are biased. Recall that the Durbin–Watson statistic is invalid in autoregressive models. Use an alternate test such as the Breusch-Godfrey test for serial correlation.

However, ARIMA modelers are usually not concerned about violating any assumptions of the Classical Linear Regression Model. Instead, the focus is on forecasting via patterns and correlations in the time-series. If the residuals are serially correlated, then that is a pattern that can be exploited.

### Moving Average Models

A moving average model comprises the "MA" portion of an ARIMA model. A moving average model stipulates that the current value of a time-series is a linear function of the past errors of the model. The model here is designated as MA(2):

$$INFL_t = \mu + \hat{\theta}_1 e_{t-1} + \hat{\theta}_2 e_{t-2} + e_t$$

where $\mu$ is the mean of INFL;
$e_t$ is the current error term;
$e_{t-1}$ and $e_{t-2}$ are error terms from the previous two periods;
$\hat{\theta}_1$ and $\hat{\theta}_2$ are structural parameters.

This model predicts the inflation rate this period is equal to the average inflation rate over the data set ($\mu$) plus $\hat{\theta}_1$ times the error from the previous period and $\hat{\theta}_2$ times the error from two periods ago. This prediction most likely will not be spot on and the difference between the actual inflation rate and the predicted rate in period t is $e_t$.

With $e_t$ in hand, the model can now make a prediction for the next period. In this manner, the error terms are determined sequentially. Therefore, all the $e_t$'s are not available when $\hat{\theta}_1$ and $\hat{\theta}_2$ are calculated. Indeed, the error terms cannot be determined until $\hat{\theta}_1$ and $\hat{\theta}_2$ are known. But $\hat{\theta}_1$ and $\hat{\theta}_2$ cannot be determined until the $e_t$'s are known. Therefore, OLS cannot be used to estimate $\theta_1$ and $\theta_2$. A nonlinear estimation technique, the maximum likelihood procedure, is used to estimate moving average models.

### Autoregressive Moving Average Models

Combining an autoregressive model (AR) with a moving average model (MA) creates an autoregressive-moving average model (ARMA). Here is an ARMA(3,2) model of the inflation rate:

$$INFL_t = \hat{\beta}_0 + \hat{\beta}_1 INFL_{t-1} + \hat{\beta}_2 INFL_{t-2} + \hat{\beta}_3 INFL_{t-3} + \hat{\theta}_1 e_{t-1}$$
$$+ \hat{\theta}_2 e_{t-2} + e_t$$

The inflation rate depends on its values in the past three periods and the errors of the ARMA model in the past two periods. In this manner, the ARMA model is "looking back" three periods for patterns and correlations that can be used to estimate the current inflation rate. Additionally, an ARMA model uses the past two prediction errors to improve the current prediction.

Future inflation rates can be forecasted AR models, MA models, and ARMA models. For instance, the ARMA(3,2) model can be used to predict next period's inflation rate, $\widehat{INFL}_{t+1}$:

$$\widehat{INFL}_{t+1} = \hat{\beta}_0 + \hat{\beta}_1 INFL_t + \hat{\beta}_2 INFL_{t-1} + \hat{\beta}_3 INFL_{t-2}$$
$$+ \hat{\theta}_1 e_t + \hat{\theta}_2 e_{t-1}$$

Next period's inflation rate, $\widehat{INFL}_{t+2}$, is determined by this period's inflation rate, the previous two inflation rates, this period's error, and the previous period's error. A forecast of the inflation rate two period's ahead ($\widehat{INFL}_{t+2}$) can be obtained as well:

$$\widehat{INFL}_{t+2} = \hat{\beta}_0 + \hat{\beta}_1 \widehat{INFL}_{t+1} + \hat{\beta}_2 INFL_t + \hat{\beta}_3 INFL_{t-1} + \hat{\theta}_1 e_{t+1} + \hat{\theta}_2 e_t$$

The forecast of INFL one period ahead ($\widehat{INFL}_{t+1}$) is used to help forecast INFL two periods ahead $\widehat{INFL}_{t+2}$. This process can continue to forecast INFL into the indefinite future. Perhaps it is precarious to build forecasts upon forecasts, but ARMA models compare favorably with other economic forecasting techniques. And ARMA forecasts are much more expedient than other economic forecasting methods. Only two things are required to generate ARMA forecasts for next period and beyond: a time-series of the variable to be forecasted and an ARMA modeler.

Building a good ARMA model is art, science, and craft. Typically trial and error is used to determine the appropriate number of autoregressive and moving average terms. Some of the data mining rules apply here. Include as many autoregressive and moving average terms as possible so long as they are significant. Marginally significant terms might be included if they improve the fit. There is less concern for appropriate signs on the coefficients. Usually, it is not clear what sign is appropriate. It is plausible that the inflation rate three periods ago has a positive or a negative effect on the current inflation rate.

Like MA models, ARMA models cannot be estimated with OLS. All the $e_t$'s are not available and yet the structural parameters ($\hat{\beta}_0$, $\hat{\beta}_1$, $\hat{\beta}_2$, $\hat{\beta}_3$, $\hat{\theta}_1$, and $\hat{\theta}_2$) require calculation. Indeed, the residuals cannot be determined until the structural parameters are known. A nonlinear estimation technique, such as the maximum likelihood procedure, is used to estimate the residuals and the structural parameters simultaneously.

Correlograms and their cousins, partial correlograms, can suggest how many autoregressive and moving average terms are appropriate for a given time-series. Remember, correlograms measure the degree to which observations k spaces apart are linearly correlated. Partial correlations are the degree to which observations k spaces apart are linearly correlated, net of the correlation explained by the intervening k − 1 observations. The patterns displayed by the correlogram and partial correlogram can be interpreted according to the table here:

| Correlogram/Partial Correlogram | Interpretation |
| --- | --- |
| Decays/Cuts off abruptly at k = 2 | AR terms only |
| Decays/Decays | AR and MA terms |
| No significant correlations/Decays | MA terms only |
| No significant correlations/Cuts off abruptly at k = 2 | White noise |

If the correlogram decays and the partial correlogram cuts off at k = 2, then a purely autoregressive model is indicated. If both the correlogram and the partial correlogram decay rather than cut off abruptly, then both AR and MA terms are indicated. A pure moving average model is indicated if there are no significant correlations and the partial correlogram decays. And finally, there are no patterns or correlations to exploit in a time-series that is white noise. No model is useful.

The models indicated by correlograms and partial correlograms are only starting points. Experimenting with ARMA models of various dimensions and zeroing in on the most appropriate model is the craft of time-series modeling.

### ARIMA Models

Statistical theory indicates that ARMA models applied to nonstationary time-series are invalid. Taking differences to attain stationarity is known as "integration" in time-series modeling. Thus an autoregressive moving average (ARMA) model becomes an autoregressive integrated moving average (ARIMA) model when the time-series to be modeled is differenced.

Suppose first-differences are required to make a time-series stationary. Working with the differenced series might lead to a model with two autoregressive terms and four moving average terms. The proper way to specify this model is ARIMA(2,1,4). There are two autoregressive terms, four moving average terms and the time-series has been differenced once to achieve stationarity.

It is still possible to obtain forecasts of the level of time-series even if it has been differenced. An ARIMA(2,1,4) model provides forecasts of the change in the time-series from one period to the next. The forecaster can simply apply that change to the known level of the time-series to get a forecast of the level in the next period.

If a time-series does not need differencing and is already stationary, then the ARMA model could be specified as ARIMA(2,0,4).

It is critical to apply ARIMA models only to stationary time-series. In addition, it is wise to work with seasonally adjusted data. ARIMA models are valid when applied to unadjusted data, but the dimensions of the model usually are higher since there are seasonal affects making patterns and correlations in the data. For example, a seasonally un-adjusted, monthly time-series on retail sales probably needs at least 12 autoregressive terms since there is a correlation between retail sales this December and December 12 months ago.

## THE MAXIMUM LIKELIHOOD PROCEDURE

OLS can be applied to AR models, but not to MA, and ARIMA models. Consider an ARIMA(3,0,2) model of the inflation rate:

$$INFL_t = \hat{\beta}_0 + \hat{\beta}_1 INFL_{t-1} + \hat{\beta}_2 INFL_{t-2} + \hat{\beta}_3 INFL_{t-3} + \hat{\theta}_1 e_{t-1}$$
$$+ \hat{\theta}_2 e_{t-2} + e_t$$

In order to apply OLS, data for all the independent variables for all periods need to be in hand. Only the time-series INFL, the dependent variable, is needed to obtain $INFL_{t-1}$, $INFL_{t-2}$, and $INFL_{t-3}$:

| Period (t) | $INFL_t$ | $INFL_{t-1}$ | $INFL_{t-2}$ | $INFL_{t-3}$ |
|---|---|---|---|---|
| 1960 | 1.7 | | | |
| 1961 | 1.0 | 1.7 | | |
| 1962 | 1.0 | 1.0 | 1.7 | |
| 1963 | 1.3 | 1.0 | 1.0 | 1.7 |
| 1964 | 1.3 | 1.3 | 1.0 | 1.0 |
| 1965 | 1.6 | 1.3 | 1.3 | 1.0 |
| 1966 | 2.9 | 1.6 | 1.3 | 1.3 |
| ⋮ | ⋮ | ⋮ | ⋮ | ⋮ |

The first three observations cannot be used since $INFL_{t-3}$ does not become available until 1963. After 1963, however, $INFL_{t-3}$ and the two previous lags of $INFL_t$ are available until the end of the data set.

But $e_t$ is not available and therefore neither of its two lags, $e_{t-1}$ and $e_{t-2}$, are available. $e_t$ cannot be determined until the structural parameters ($\hat{\beta}_0$, $\hat{\beta}_1$, $\hat{\beta}_2$, $\hat{\beta}_3$, $\hat{\theta}_1$, and $\hat{\theta}_2$) are determined. But the structural parameters cannot be determined until the $e_t$'s are determined.

Fortunately, techniques are available to estimate the error terms and the structural parameters simultaneously. Maximum likelihood estimation is the most popular technique for estimating ARIMA models. A maximum likelihood procedure estimates the structural parameters and the error terms simultaneously by using an algorithm to minimize a loss function.

(1) Select initial values for $\hat{\beta}_0$, $\hat{\beta}_1$, $\hat{\beta}_2$, $\hat{\beta}_3$, $\hat{\theta}_1$, and $\hat{\theta}_2$. Usually the modeler has no clue as to what the appropriate starting values might be so they are all set equal to 0.5, or some other arbitrary value, to begin with.
(2) Plug the starting values into the model and obtain the time-series $e_t$.
(3) Apply the maximum likelihood algorithm that uses the $e_t$'s to adjust $\hat{\beta}_0$, $\hat{\beta}_1$, $\hat{\beta}_2$, $\hat{\beta}_3$, $\hat{\theta}_1$, and $\hat{\theta}_2$ in order to minimize a loss function.
(4) Return to step (2) with the revised parameter estimates.
(5) The procedure stops when the revisions made to the parameter values in step (3) are insignificant.

The maximum likelihood procedure yields values for $\hat{\beta}_0$, $\hat{\beta}_1$, $\hat{\beta}_2$, $\hat{\beta}_3$, $\hat{\theta}_1$, and $\hat{\theta}_2$ that are most probable given the values of INFL and the model. Maximum likelihood procedures differ in the specific algorithm used to minimize the loss function. Nevertheless, all the algorithms end up with virtually identical estimators. One difference might be the number of iterations required to get there.

The maximum likelihood procedure can be applied to any regression. It is interesting to note that if the maximum likelihood procedure is applied to a typical regression such as

$$Y_t = \hat{\beta}_0 + \hat{\beta}_1 X_t + e_t$$

it yields the same parameter estimates as OLS.

## A COMPLETE EXAMPLE

Using quarterly aggregate data on real personal consumption expenditures (CON) from the US economy starting in 2002, a Dickey–Fuller test indicates the time-series is nonstationary:

$$(CON_t - CON_{t-1}) = -35.20 + 0.01 \ CON_{t-1} + e_t$$
$$(1.72) \quad \leftarrow \text{t-ratio}$$

(1) Ho: $\hat{\beta}_1 = 0$ (CON is nonstationary) Ha: $\hat{\beta}_1 < 0$ (CON is stationary)
(2) 5%
(3) If t-ratio < $-t^{c*}$, reject Ho
(4) If 1.72 > $-2.90^*$, reject Ho
(5) Do not reject Ho; CON is nonstationary

The first-differences in CON, however, appear to be stationary:

$$(CON_t - CON_{t-1}) - (CON_{t-1} - CON_{t-2}) = 90.68 - 0.51(CON_{t-1} - CON_{t-2}) + e_t$$
$$(-4.67) \leftarrow t\text{-ratio}$$

(1) Ho: $\hat{\beta}_1 = 0$ (CON is nonstationary) Ha: $\hat{\beta}_1 < 0$ (CON is stationary)
(2) 5%
(3) If t-ratio < $-t^{c*}$, reject Ho
(4) If $-4.67 < -2.90^*$, reject Ho
(5) Reject Ho; CON is stationary

Experimenting with ARIMA models of various dimensions leads to an ARIMIA(1,1,1):

**Dependent Variable Is D(CON) = $CON_t - CON_{t-1}$ n = 70**

|  | Model A (2,1,1) | Model B (1,1,2) | Model C (1,1,1) |
|---|---|---|---|
| Constant | 64.26*** | 64.23*** | 64.10*** |
|  | (17.55) | (16.89) | (17.60) |
| $DCON_{t-1}$ | 0.63** | 0.79*** | 0.85*** |
|  | (0.31) | (0.11) | (0.09) |
| $DCON_{t-2}$ | 0.18 |  |  |
|  | (0.21) |  |  |
| $e_{t-1}$ | -0.33 | -0.55*** | -0.49*** |
|  | (0.31) | (0.14) | (0.16) |
| $e_{t-2}$ |  | 0.23 |  |
|  |  | (0.17) |  |
| Adjusted $R^2$ | 0.30 | 0.31 | 0.30 |

Standard errors in parentheses:
*significant at 10%; **significant at 5%; ***significant at 1%

Model A is ARIMA(2,1,1): two autoregressive terms, and one moving average term. The second autoregressive term and the moving average term are insignificant. Model B is ARIMA(1,1,2). The second moving average term is insignificant. Model C is ARIMA(1,1,1). Everything is significant at the 1% critical level, making this model the most appropriate for forecasting CON. These are three of the dozen or so models considered during the selection process. Higher order models, such as

ARIMA(4,1,4) and ARIMA(5,1,1), were considered as well. In general, most economic time-series are best fit with lower order models such as in this example.

## TERMS

ARIMA model—A time-series model that may employ autoregressive and moving average terms in addition to being differenced any number of times.

Autoregressive model—A time-series model with the lagged dependent variable as an explanatory variable.

Cointegrated variables—When the time-series in a regression are non-stationary to the same degree.

Correlation—The degree to which two variables are linearly related.

Correlogram—A chart showing the correlations between observations in a time-series any given number of spaces apart.

Distributed lag model—A regression that lags one or more independent variables one or more times.

First-differences—The change from period to period in a time-series.

Granger test—A statistical test to determine if changes in one time-series precede changes in another.

Integration—When a time-series is differenced one or more times to make it stationary.

Koyck model—An autoregressive model used to mimic a distributed lag model with declining weights.

Maximum likelihood procedure—A procedure for estimating the parameters of a regression model.

Moving average term—The lagged error term of a regression used as an explanatory variable.

Partial autocorrelation—The degree to which observations in a time-series any given number of spaces apart are correlated net of the correlation of the intervening observations.

Partial correlogram—A chart showing the partial autocorrelations of a time-series for observations any number of spaces apart.

Second-differences—The change from period to period of the first-differences of a time-series.

Spurious correlation—A strong relationship between variables that is the result of a statistical fluke, not an underlying causal relationship.

Stationary time-series—A time-series with constant mean, variance, and correlation between observations k spaces apart, where k is any integer.

Time-series—Data on one phenomenon over time.

## CHAPTER 12 PROBLEMS

(1) Consider the following regression:

$$M_t = 2.00 - 0.10\ R_t + 0.70\ Y_t + 0.60\ M_{t-1} + e_t$$

$$\quad\quad\quad (0.10)\quad\quad (0.35)\quad\quad (0.10) \quad \leftarrow \text{standard errors}$$

$$\quad R^2 = .9 \quad\quad\quad\quad DW = 1.80 \quad\quad\quad\quad n = 26$$

where M is the demand for M1.
        R is the interest rate on ten-year treasuries
        Y is national income

(A) Do the variables attain their expected signs?
(B) What is the short-run impact of the interest rate (R) on money demand (M)?
(C) What is the long-run impact?

(2) Use the data in CONS.XLS and statistical software to run regressions of the following sort:

$$\text{cons}_t = \hat\beta_0 + \hat\beta_1 \text{dpi}_t + \hat\beta_2 \text{dpi}_{t-1} + \hat\beta_3 \text{dpi}_{t-2} + \hat\beta_4 \text{dpi}_{t-3} + \ldots + e_t$$
cons—the change in real consumer spending.
dpi—The change in real disposable income.

(A) What lag length seems appropriate? Explain.
(B) Is multicollinearity a problem in the regression with the appropriate lag length? Explain.
(C) Is serial correlation a problem in the regression with the appropriate lag length? Explain.
(D) Run the Koyck version of this distributed lag model. What is the short-run impact of a change in disposable income on consumer spending?
(E) What is the long-run impact?
(F) Does the Koyck version of the model suffer from multicollinearity? Explain.
(G) Does the Koyck version of the model suffer from autocorrelation? Show the five-step procedure.

(3) Use the data in QLEISCOIN.XLS and statistical software to do the following problems.

COIN—Percentage change in the composite index of coincident economic indicators.
LEIS—Percentage change in the composite index of leading economic indicators.

(A) Run a regression to determine if COIN is affected by LEIS and LEIS lagged 1 through 8 quarters. Do you think LEIS 8 quarters ago helps predict COIN this quarter? Explain.

(B) How many lags of the LEIS should be used to explain COIN? Explain how you came to this conclusion.

(C) Does the regression you settled on in (B) suffer from serial correlation according to the Durbin-Watson test? Show the five-step procedure.

(D) Does the regression you settled on in (B) suffer from serial correlation according to the Lagrange multiplier test? Show the five-step procedure.

(E) Does the regression you settled on in (B) suffer from multicollinearity? On what do you base your response?

(F) Employ a Koyck lag structure in the COIN/LEIS regression. Does this regression suffer from serial correlation according to the Lagrange multiplier test? Show the five-step procedure.

(G) Employ a Koyck lag structure in the COIN/LEIS regression. Does this regression suffer from multicollinearity? On what do you base your response?

(H) According to the Koyck model, a one-unit increase in LEIS implies COIN will be how much higher or lower in the short run?

(I) In the long run, the one-unit increase in LEIS implies COIN will eventually change how much?

(4) Use the data in MACRO.XLS and statistical software to determine if changes in real disposable personal income (RDPI) precede changes in real consumer spending (RCONS) or vice versa using lag lengths of 8 for both variables.

(A) Do you reject the null hypothesis that RDPI does not precede RCONS at the 5% critical level?

(B) Would you reject the null hypothesis that RDPI does not precede RCONS at the 10% critical level? Explain.

(C) Do you reject the null hypothesis that RCONS does not precede RDPI at the 5% critical level?

(D) Would you reject the null hypothesis that RCONS does not precede RDPI at the 10% critical level? Explain.

(5) Use the data in QLEISCOIN.XLS and statistical software to do Granger tests to determine if changes in the leading economic indicators (LEIS) precede changes in the coincident indicators (COIN).

    (A) Using lag lengths of 6, show the five-step procedure for the Granger test that changes in LEIS do not precede changes in COIN.

    (B) Using lag lengths of 6, show the five-step procedure for the Granger test that changes in COIN do not precede changes in LEIS.

    (C) Given your results in (A) and (B), can you unequivocally conclude that changes in LEIS precede changes in COIN?

    (D) Does your answer to (C) change when lag lengths of 10 are used?

    (E) Does your answer to (C) change when lag lengths of 12 are used?

(6) Use the data in MACRO.XLS and statistical software to run Granger tests to determine if reverse causality is a problem in the following regression:

$$RGDP_t = \hat{\beta}_0 + \hat{\beta}_1 \ RINV_t + e_t$$

where RGDP is real GDP; RINV is real business spending on plant and equipment.

    Is reverse causality a problem in the regression here? On what do you base your response?

(7) Use the data in MACRO.XLS and statistical software to run Granger tests to determine if changes in M2 Granger-cause INFL or vice-versa.

    (A) What are the appropriate lag lengths? Explain.

    (B) What do you conclude? Explain.

(8) Which of the following sets of variables are most likely to suffer from spurious correlation?

    (A) The population of America and the Dow Jones Industrial average

    (B) GDP and the unemployment rate

    (C) The inflation rate and government expenditures

    (D) The change in the money supply and the federal funds rate

(9) Using the data in MACRO.XLS and statistical software, which of the following variables appear to be nonstationary because of nonconstant means or nonconstant variances? Produce the graph

for each variable and say if the problem is a nonconstant mean or variance, both, or neither.

(A) Real investment (rinv)

(B) The first difference in real investment

(C) The second difference in real investment

(D) The first difference in the money supply (m2)

(E) Interest rate on AAA corporate bonds (aaa)

(10) Which variables from the this list appear to be nonstationary based on their autocorrelation functions? Produce the autocorrelation function for each variable and indicate if a variable is stationary, nonstationary, or questionable.

(11) Which variables from the list are nonstationary according to the Dickey–Fuller test? Show the five-step procedure for each variable.

(12) Use the data in RGDP.XLS to apply the augmented Dickey-Fuller test (one extra term) to real GDP (rgdp) and the first-differences in rgdp. Show the five-step procedure for each test.

(13) Use the data in AJ.XLS to replicate the famous Andersen-Jordan study by regressing a constant term, lagged money supply (m2), and the lagged standardized federal budget (fp) on GDP (ngdp):

$$\text{ngdp}_t = \hat{\beta}_0 + \hat{\beta}_1 \text{m2}_{t-1} + \hat{\beta}_2 \text{fp}_{t-1} + e_t$$

(A) Which explanatory variable has the more profound impact on nominal GDP? Explain.

(B) Which variables in the regression are nonstationary? Explain.

(C) Check for cointegration among the variables in the regression. Show the five-step Dickey–Fuller procedure.

(14) Use the data in RGDP.XLS and econometric software to answer the following:

(A) Produce a correlogram of SP500. Does it suggest the levels of SP500 are stationary? Explain.

(B) Produce a correlogram of the first differences of SP500. Does it suggest the first differences of SP500 are stationary? Explain.

(C) Do an augmented Dickey-Fuller test on the levels of SP500. Show the five-step procedure.

(D) Do an augmented Dickey-Fuller test on the first differences of SP500. Show the five-step procedure.

(E) Working with the first differences in SP500, what sort of model is suggested by the pattern of the correlogram and partial correlogram?

(i) purely autoregressive

(ii) purely moving average

(iii) autoregressive and moving average

(iv) neither autoregressive nor moving average since the time-series is white noise

(F) Find an appropriately specified ARIMA model for the first differences of SP500 and fill in your result here: ARIMA(?,1,?)

(15) Use the data in RGDP.XLS and econometric software to answer the following:

(A) Produce a correlogram of cpi. Does it suggest the levels of cpi are stationary? Explain.

(B) Produce a correlogram of the first differences of cpi. Does it suggest the first differences of cpi are stationary? Explain.

(C) Do an augmented Dickey-Fuller test (one extra term) on the levels of cpi. Show the five-step procedure.

(D) Do an augmented Dickey–Fuller test (one extra term) on the first differences of cpi. Show the five-step procedure.

(E) Working with the second differences in cpi, what sort of model is suggested by the pattern of the correlogram and partial correlogram?

(i) Purely autoregressive

(ii) Purely moving average

(iii) Autoregressive and moving average

(iv) Neither autoregressive nor moving average since the time-series is white noise

(F) Find an appropriately specified ARIMA model for the second differences of cpi and fill in your result here: ARIMA(?,2,?)

# 13 Panel Data Techniques

## PANEL DATA

When working with cross-sectional data, the convention in econometrics is to use the subscript "i" to denote the different entities. In this example, the crime rate in each state is explained by its unemployment rate. The subscript "i" stands for each state.

$$CRRATE_i = \hat{\beta}_0 + \hat{\beta}_1 UNRATE_i + e_i$$

| State | CRRATE | UNRATE |
|-------|--------|--------|
| Alabama | 524.2 | 3.9 |
| Alaska | 829.0 | 6.6 |
| Arizona | 508.0 | 4.8 |
| Arkansas | 554.9 | 3.7 |
| ⋮ | ⋮ | ⋮ |

where CRRATE is the violent crime rate in 2018

UNRATE is the unemployment rate in 2018

The subscript "t" is used when the data set is time-series. In this example, the crime rate in Alabama is explained by the unemployment. The "t" stands for each year.

DOI: 10.4324/9781003213758-13

$$CRRATE_t = \hat{\beta}_0 + \hat{\beta}_1 UNRATE_t + e_t$$

| Year | CRRATE | UNRATE |
|------|--------|--------|
| 1960 | 186.6  | 5.5    |
| 1961 | 168.5  | 6.7    |
| 1962 | 157.3  | 5.6    |
| 1963 | 182.7  | 5.6    |
| ⋮    | ⋮      | ⋮      |

where CRRATE is the violent crime rate in Alabama

UNRATE is the unemployment rate in Alabama

Panel data, also called longitudinal data, is a combination of cross-sectional and time-series data, such as annual data for each state. The convention with panel data is to use both "i" and "t" subscripts. The "i" stands for the state and the "t" stands for the year.

$$CRRATE_{it} = \hat{\beta}_0 + \hat{\beta}_1 UNRATE_{it} + e_{it}$$

| State | Year | CRRATE | UNRATE |
|-------|------|--------|--------|
| Alabama | 1976 | 388.8 | 6.8 |
| Alabama | 1977 | 414.4 | 7.3 |
| Alabama | 1978 | 419.1 | 6.3 |
| Alaska | 1976 | 540.1 | 7.5 |
| Alaska | 1977 | 443.2 | 9.9 |
| Alaska | 1978 | 441.9 | 10.6 |
| Arizona | 1976 | 455.3 | 9.7 |
| ⋮ | ⋮ | ⋮ | ⋮ |

where CRRATE is the violent crime rate by state and year

UNRATE is the unemployment rate by state and year

The panel data here are portrayed in the "stacked" manner. The time-series observations of each cross section are stacked one on top of the other. This method is best when there are more cross sections than years. Most econometric software packages use the stacked method.

Another possibility is the "wide" portrayal:

| State | Variable | 1976 | 1977 | 1978 |
|-------|----------|------|------|------|
| Alabama | CRRATE | 388.8 | 414.4 | 419.1 |
| Alabama | UNRATE | 6.8 | 7.3 | 6.3 |
| Alaska | CRRATE | 540.1 | 443.2 | 441.9 |
| Alaska | UNRATE | 7.5 | 9.9 | 10.6 |
| Arizona | CRRATE | 455.3 | 467.1 | 477.4 |
| Arizona | UNRATE | 9.7 | 10.0 | 10.2 |
| ⋮ | ⋮ | ⋮ | ⋮ | ⋮ |

Here the years, not the variables, run horizontally across the top row. If there were more than three years in this example, it would be apparent why this is called the wide method.

Ordinary least squares can be used on panel data. However, the distinct nature of panel data allows for the application of some special techniques. The key to panel data is that there is information for the same states over the same years. If that were not so, then these special panel data techniques would not be applicable.

Consider the situation where three years of data are available for all 50 states, but it is not the same three years for each state. This is not panel data. It is pooled data—data across various entities and over time, but the entities or the time periods do not match.

Another example of pooled data is spending and income figures for 25 families over the 10 years from 1966 to 1975. However, each year the 25 families change. OLS may be applied to pooled data, but the techniques shown in this chapter require panel data.

OLS may be applied to panel data and the results are BLUE so long as the assumptions of the CLRM are met. Panel data will often violate an important assumption of the CLRM: the expected value of the error terms is zero: $E[u_i | X_i] = 0$. This is due to heterogeneity, a special problem that crops up with panel data.

Suppose OLS is applied to panel data on a regression of crime rates on unemployment rates:

$$CRRATE_{it} = \hat{\beta}_0 + \hat{\beta}_1 UNRATE_{it} + e_{it}$$

An increase in the unemployment rate is expected to cause an increase in the violent crime rate. That is to say, $\hat{\beta}_1$ is expected to be positive. But the results may contradict this expectation because of the unique nature of panel data. Within a state a rise in the unemployment rate may indeed cause a rise in the crime rate. However, some states have higher crime rates in general because of greater population density which leads to more opportunities for criminals or perhaps some states have less strict law enforcement. Econometricians call these differences heterogeneity.

Therefore, the true relationship between unemployment and crime can be masked by demographic or enforcement differences between states. The true relationship can be unmasked by including variables that measure population density and the strictness of law enforcement in the regression.

However, it is not always possible to obtain data on the heterogenous variables. Consider that the strictness of law enforcement is difficult to measure. The number of police per capita may capture this effect, but not if the strictness comes from tough sentencing or very high bail amounts.

When heterogenous variables cannot be measured, or the researcher is not interested in them, fixed effects models can be used to account for them with panel data.

## CROSS-SECTIONAL FIXED EFFECTS MODELS

Consider the following panel data regression:
$$CRRATE_{it} = \hat{\beta}_0 + \hat{\beta}_1 UNRATE_{it} + e_{it}$$

where CRRATE is the violent crime rate by state and year
UNRATE is the unemployment rate by state and year and i = 1, 2, ..., n and t = 1, 2, ..., T

Assume the model is correctly specified in the sense that there are no other important variables affecting the crime rate in every state other than the unemployment rate. However, there may be factors particular to each state that effect the crime rate in those states. For instance, some states have higher incarceration rates than others. Or some states have more police per capita than others.

The assumption of cross-sectional fixed effects regressions is that there are omitted variables that affect the dependent variable across states but these factors do not affect the dependent variable over time within each state. In this example, the assumption is that various incarceration rates across the states explain why the crime rate differs from state to state, but incarceration rates in any given state do not change much from year to year. Incarceration rates are time-invariant within states.

Fixed effects, such as the incarceration rate or other heterogenous factors, can be accounted for by including a dummy variable for each state:

$$CRRATE_{it} = \hat{\beta}_0 + \hat{\beta}_1 UNRATE_{it} + \hat{\beta}_2 D2_i + \hat{\beta}_3 D3_i + ... + \hat{\beta}_n Dn_i + e_{it}$$

Notice there are 49 dummy variables since there are 50 states. One of the states will be the base state, so no dummy is needed for that state. Also notice that the dummy variables have only the subscript "i" since there are no dummies for the years. The dummies allow for different intercepts for each state but the slope of the relationship between UNRATE and CRRATE is forced to be the same across states. This slope is the value $\hat{\beta}_1$.

Rather than running a regression with a large number of dummy variables, most econometric software packages use "entity-demeaned" data for fixed effects regressions. Entity-demeaned estimation yields estimators equivalent to the dummy variable approach without actually including the dummies.

For this regression: $CRRATE_{it} = \hat{\beta}_0 + \hat{\beta}_1 UNRATE_{it} + e_{it}$, the demeaned cross-sectional fixed effects model is:

$$CRRATE_{it} - \overline{CRRATE}_t = \hat{\beta}_0 + \hat{\beta}_1 UNRATE_{it} - \overline{UNRATE}_t + e_{it}$$

The equation represents what is sometimes called the "within-transformation." Each observation is transformed by subtracting the mean of the three years for that state.

OLS is applied to the dummy-variable regression or the entity-demeaned regression. The results are exactly the same in either case. It may seem as if the demeaned regression will have more degrees of freedom since it lacks all the dummy variables. This is not so. The degrees of freedom are the same in both approaches since the demeaning transformation uses up the same number of degrees of freedom as the dummy-variables.

Standard errors, t-ratios, p-values, and all the usual OLS residual statistics can be obtained for cross-sectional fixed effects models. The estimators are BLUE if the assumptions of the CLRM hold.

## TIME FIXED EFFECTS MODELS

Again, consider the following panel data regression: $CRRATE_{it} = \hat{\beta}_0 + \hat{\beta}_1 UNRATE_{it} + e_{it}$ and assume the model is correctly specified in the sense that there are no other important variables affecting the crime rate in each state other than the unemployment rate. However, the impact on the crime rate in each state may differ as the unemployment rate changes each year. In other words, the unemployment rate affects the crime rate in every state, but the slope of the relationship differs across states. In order to allow each state's regression line to slope differently include dummies for each year except the base year:

$$CRRATE_{it} = \hat{\beta}_0 + \hat{\beta}_1 UNRATE_{it} + \hat{\beta}_2 D2_t + \hat{\beta}_3 D3_t + ... + \hat{\beta}_n DT_T + e_{it}$$

This is the time fixed effects model. Notice there would be only two dummies for the example data set shown earlier since there are three years of data for each state. One of the years will be the base year, so no dummy is needed for that year. Also notice that the dummy variables have only the subscript "t" since there are no dummies for the states. The dummies allow for different slopes for each state but the intercept of the relationship between UNRATE and CRRATE is forced to be the same across states. This intercept is the value $\hat{\beta}_0$.

An alternate technique that yields the exact same results as the dummy variable approach is "time-demeaned" estimation. For this regression: $CRRATE_{it} = \hat{\beta}_0 + \hat{\beta}_1 UNRATE_{it} + e_{it}$, the time-demeaned fixed effects model is:

$$CRRATE_{it} - \overline{CRRATE}_i = \hat{\beta}_0 + \hat{\beta}_1 UNRATE_{it} - \overline{UNRATE}_i + e_{it}$$

The equation represents what is sometimes called the "without-transformation." Each observation is transformed by subtracting the mean of the 52 states for that particular year.

OLS is applied to the dummy-variable regression or the time-demeaned regression. Despite appearances, the time-demeaned model has the same number of degrees of freedom as the dummy-variable model. The results are exactly the same regardless of the approach taken.

Standard errors, t-ratios, p-values, and all the usual OLS residual statistics can be obtained for time fixed effects models. Regardless of the estimation technique, the results are BLUE if the assumptions of the CLRM hold.

## RANDOM EFFECTS MODEL

The random effects model splits the difference between the cross-sectional fixed effects model and a straight-forward application of OLS to the panel data.

$$CRRATE_{it} - \hat{\lambda}\overline{CRRATE}_t = \hat{\beta}_0(1 - \hat{\lambda}) + \hat{\beta}_1 UNRATE_{it} - \hat{\lambda}\,\overline{UNRATE}_t + e_{it}$$
where $0 < \hat{\lambda} < 1$

If $\hat{\lambda} = 1$, then the random effects model is identical to the cross-sectional fixed effects model. If $\hat{\lambda} = 0$, then the random effects model is identical to applying OLS to the panel data with no effects. If $0 < \hat{\lambda} < 1$, then the random effects model is partially cross-sectionally demeaned.

$\hat{\lambda}$ is estimated by running a pooled regression on the panel data and then comparing the results with those from a fixed effects regression.

$$\hat{\lambda} = \sqrt{\frac{\hat{\sigma}_p^2}{\hat{\sigma}_p^2 + T\hat{\sigma}_{FE}^2}}$$

where $\hat{\sigma}_p^2$ is the sum of the squared residuals from the pooled regression

$\hat{\sigma}_{FE}^2$ is the sum of the squared residuals from the fixed effects regression

T is the number of periods in each cross section

The random effects model is a weighted-average of the fixed effects model and simply applying OLS to the panel data. The closer $\hat{\lambda}$ is to 0, the closer the random effects model is to the fixed effects model. When the random and fixed effects models yield similar results, the random effects model is superior because it is more efficient.

## ROBUST STANDARD ERRORS

Regressions that use cross-sectional data can suffer from hetero-skedasticity. Regressions that use time-series data can suffer from serially correlated errors. It is possible for regressions that use panel data to suffer from both heteroskedasticity and autocorrelation.

If a panel data regression has heteroskedasticity or autocorrelation or both, then the coefficients attached to the explanatory variables are unbiased, but the estimated standard errors of those coefficients are biased. Therefore, the t-ratios and p-values are biased as well.

Econometricians routinely use robust standard errors with panel data regressions. Robust standard errors are calculated with a different formula than usual. If the model suffers from either or both heteroskedasticity and autocorrelation, then the robust formula will correct the bias in the standard errors of the estimators. Examples of robust standard error formulas include those developed by Newey and West (1987), and White (1980). These examples are in a class of standard errors known as HAC—heteroskedasticity autocorrelation-consistent standard errors.

## HAUSMAN TEST

It can be difficult to determine if a fixed effects model, a random effects model, or neither is appropriate in any given situation. Moreover, a fixed effects model can be fixed cross- sectionally, across periods, or both. This is true of a random effects model as well. Perhaps the cross-sectional effects should be random and the time effects should be fixed.

Consider if the model is likely to have cross-sectional heterogenous effects. Is it likely that factors not accounted for by the explanatory variables affect the entities? For instance, the strictness of policing probably varies across states and no explanatory variable attempts to measure this effect. In this case, a cross-sectional fixed effects model is appropriate.

If a change in one of the explanatory variables is likely to affect the dependent variable to different degrees in different entities, then a time fixed effects model is warranted.

In many situations, there is no clue as to which model is appropriate. A Hausman test (1978) can help discern between random effects and fixed effects models. If an application of random effects results in coefficients that are very close to the coefficients in a fixed effects model, then a random effects model is more appropriate.

The question then becomes how close the coefficients of the two models have to be to suggest a random effects model. Put differently, how far apart do the coefficients have to be to suggest a fixed effects model? A Hausman test answers these questions.

To perform a Hausman test, run a random effects model, random cross-sectionally, or across periods, or both. Then run its fixed effects counterpart. Hausman's H-statistic compares the differences in the coefficients of both models.

(1) Ho: Random effects model     Ha: Fixed effects model
       superior to fixed effects           superior to random effects
(2) 5%
(3) If H > $\chi^2$c, then reject Ho
(4) Obtain H and $\chi^2$c (d.f. = k – 1)
(5) Reject or do not reject Ho

H is the Hausman test statistic. It is obtained by running a random effects model and fixed effects model. If the null hypothesis is correct, then the estimated coefficients of both models should be similar.

$$H = \frac{\Sigma((\hat{\beta}1_{FE} - \hat{\beta}1_{RE})^2 + (\hat{\beta}2_{FE} - \hat{\beta}2_{RE})^2 + \dots + (\hat{\beta}k_{FE} - \hat{\beta}k_{RE})^2)}{\begin{array}{c} \Sigma((VAR(\hat{\beta}1_{FE}) - VAR(\hat{\beta}1_{RE})) + (VAR(\hat{\beta}2_{FE}) \\ - VAR(\hat{\beta}2_{RE})) + \dots + (VAR(\hat{\beta}k_{FE}) - VAR(\hat{\beta}k_{RE}))) \end{array}}$$

where $\widehat{\beta 1}_{FE}$ is the estimator attached to X1 in the fixed effects regression

$\widehat{\beta 1}_{RE}$ is the estimator attached to X1 in the random effects regression

$VAR(\hat{\beta 1}_{FE})$ is the variance of $\widehat{\beta 1}_{FE}$

$VAR(\widehat{\beta 1}_{RE})$ is the variance of $\widehat{\beta 1}_{RE}$

If Ho is rejected, then the fixed effects model is superior to the random effects model.

## AN ILLUSTRATIVE EXAMPLE

Consider the panel data regression: $WAGE_{it} = \hat{\beta}_0 + \hat{\beta}_1 PROD_{it} + e_{it}$

where WAGE is the wage rate
and PROD is a measure of labor productivity

The data are annual for the same six US counties over the same 12 years. The regression tests the notion that labor productivity drives the wage rate. $\hat{\beta}_1$ is expected to be positive. Application of OLS to the panel data yields:

Pooled Model

$$WAGE_{it} = 675.6 + 0.002\ PROD_{it} + e_{it}$$
$$(18.7)\ (0.0002)\quad \leftarrow \text{standard errors}$$
$$R^2 = 0.21 \quad n = 72$$

WAGE is the wage rate
PROD is output per hours worked

The sign on PROD is appropriate and significant. There is nothing untoward in these results. However, there is a suspicion that the wage rates in various counties are affected by more than productivity alone. The missing variable or variables could be considered heterogenous, making a cross-sectional fixed effects model appropriate.

Cross-Section Fixed Effects Model

$$WAGE_{it} = 475.2 + 0.005\ PROD_{it} + e_{it}$$

$$(18.7)\quad (0.0006) \leftarrow \text{standard errors}$$

$$R^2 = 0.88 \quad n = 72$$

WAGE is the wage rate

PROD is output per hours worked

Again, the sign on PROD is appropriate and significant. The $R^2$ is much higher in this model, making it superior to the pooled regression. The time fixed effects model is almost as good:

Time Fixed Effects Model

$$WAGE_{it} = 685.3 + 0.002\ PROD_{it} + e_{it}$$

$$(18.7)\quad (0.0002) \leftarrow \text{standard errors}$$

$$R^2 = 0.76 \quad n = 72$$

WAGE is the wage rate

PROD is output per hours worked

Only the $R^2$ is slightly lower than the cross-sectional fixed effects model. Perhaps a model that uses both cross-sectional and time fixed effects is warranted:

Cross-Sectional and Time Fixed Effects Model

$$WAGE_{it} = 995.0 - 0.001\ PROD_{it} + e_{it}$$

$$(71.4)\quad (0.0009) \leftarrow \text{standard errors}$$

$$R^2 = 0.95 \quad n = 72$$

WAGE is the wage rate

PROD is output per hours worked

The sign on PROD is inappropriate but insignificant at the 5% critical level. This puts the model at a disadvantage versus its competitors despite its high $R^2$. The next model to try is cross-sectional random effects:

Cross-Sectional Random Effects

$$\text{WAGE}_{it} = 590.6 + 0.005 \text{ PROD}_{it} + e_{it}$$

$$(47.9) \ (0.0007) \leftarrow \text{standard errors}$$

$$R^2 = 0.41 \quad n = 72$$

WAGE is the wage rate
PROD is output per hours worked

Once again, the sign on PROD is appropriate and significant. The lower $R^2$ makes this an inferior model. However, a Hausman test will directly compare the cross-sectional random effects model with the cross-sectional fixed effects model:

(1) Ho: Random effects model      Ha: Fixed effects model
       superior to fixed effects         superior to random effects
(2) 5%
(3) If H > $\chi^2 c$, then reject Ho
(4) 7.15 > 3.84 (d.f. = k – 1 = 2 – 1 = 1)
(5) Reject Ho; the cross-sectional fixed effects model is superior

In this manner, the cross-sectional fixed effects model is settled on as the most appropriate. However, the model could suffer from heteroskedasticity, serial correlation, or both. Using heteroskedasticity autocorrelation-consistent (HAC), standard errors can shed light on this situation. The HAC standard errors eliminate the bias in the usual standard errors due to heteroskedasticity or serial correlation. The HAC standard errors are presented below the original standard errors.

Cross-Section Fixed Effects Model with HAC Standard Errors

$$\text{WAGE}_{it} = 475.2 + 0.005 \text{ PROD}_{it} + e_{it}$$

$$(18.7) \ (0.0006) \leftarrow \text{standard errors}$$

$$(71.1) \ (0.0008) \leftarrow \text{HAC standard errors}$$

$$R^2 = 0.88 \quad n = 72$$

WAGE is the wage rate
PROD is output per hours worked

In the results reported here, only the standard errors themselves change with the application of HAC standard errors. However, the t-ratios and the p-values change as well since they are based on the standard errors.

Since the HAC standard errors are quite a bit different than the usual standard errors, the model most likely has heteroskedastic or serially correlated errors, or both. However, the estimators are still highly significant. The cross-sectional fixed effects model appears to be the most appropriate for drawing inferences about the relationship between wages and productivity from these panel data.

## TERMS

Heterogenous effects—Factors causing differences across the entities in a panel data study.

Heteroskedasticity-autocorrelation consistent standard errors (HAC) —A class of estimators that gives unbiased estimates of the standard errors of regression coefficients even in the presence of heteroscedasticity or autocorrelation.

Panel data—A combination of cross-sectional and time-series data where the time periods are the same for each unchanging cross section.

Pooled data—A combination of cross-sectional and time-series data where the time periods or cross sections are not constant.

Robust standard errors—Unbiased estimates of the standard errors of regression coefficients even in the presence of heteroscedasticity or autocorrelation.

## CHAPTER 13 PROBLEMS

(1) Consider panel data on 10 nations for 7 years. If the data are annual, then
   (A) n = ?
   (B) i = ?
   (C) T = ?
   (D) How many dummy variables are added to run a cross-sectional fixed effects regression?
   (E) How many dummy variables are added to run a time fixed effects regression?
(2) Consider panel data on 50 households for 6 years. If the data are annual, then
   (A) n = ?

(B) i = ?

(C) T = ?

(D) How many dummy variables are added to run a cross-sectional fixed effects regression?

(E) How many dummy variables are added to run a time fixed effects regression?

(3) The table shows spending on recreation (RECEXP) by two households for three years.

| Household | Year | RECEXP | Entity-Demeaned RECEXP |
|---|---|---|---|
| 1 | 1976 | 100 | |
| 1 | 1977 | 150 | |
| 1 | 1978 | 200 | |
| 2 | 1976 | 60 | |
| 2 | 1977 | 50 | |
| 2 | 1978 | 40 | |

(A) n = ?

(B) i = ?

(C) T = ?

(D) Fill in the entity-demeaned values of RECEXP.

(E) Are entity-demeaned data used for cross-sectional or time fixed effects models?

(4) The table shows spending on recreation (RECEXP) by two households for three years.

| Household | Year | RECEXP | Time-Demeaned RECEXP |
|---|---|---|---|
| 1 | 1976 | 100 | |
| 1 | 1977 | 150 | |
| 1 | 1978 | 200 | |
| 2 | 1976 | 60 | |
| 2 | 1977 | 50 | |
| 2 | 1978 | 40 | |

(A) n = ?

(B) i = ?

(C) T = ?

(D) Fill in the time-demeaned values of RECEXP.

(E) Are time-demeaned data used for cross-sectional or time fixed effects models?

(5) Use the data in WAGES PANEL.XLS and statistical software to run the following regression:

$$LWAGE_{it} = \hat{\beta}_0 + \hat{\beta}_1 EX_{it} + \hat{\beta}_2 WKS_{it} + e_{it}$$

where LWAGE is the natural log of an individual's wages
     EX is the individual's years of work experience
     WKS is the number of weeks in the year the individual worked

The data set is a panel of 110 individuals for each of seven years.

(A) Run an OLS regression on the panel data. Which explanatory variable(s) is(are) insignificant?
(B) Run a time-period fixed effects regression. Which explanatory variable(s) is(are) insignificant?
(C) Run a time-period random effects regression. Which explanatory variable(s) is(are) insignificant?
(D) Perform a Hausman test. Show the five-step procedure.
(E) Using the model suggested by the Hausman test, apply White's HAC standard errors. Did the significance of either explanatory variable change with the new standard errors?

(6) Use the data in GROWTH PANEL.XLS and statistical software to run the following regression:

$$GRATE_{it} = \hat{\beta}_0 + \hat{\beta}_1 CAPRATE_{it} + \hat{\beta}_2 SECED_{it} + e_{it}$$

GRATE is the growth rate of the economy
CAPRATE is the growth rate of the capital stock
SECED is the average years of secondary schooling in the total population

The data set is a panel of 68 nations for each of 7 (five-year) periods.

(A) Run an OLS regression on the panel data. Which explanatory variable(s) is(are) insignificant?
(B) Run a cross-sectional fixed effects regression. Which explanatory variable(s) is(are) insignificant?
(C) Run a cross-sectional random effects regression. Which explanatory variable(s) is(are) insignificant?

(D) Perform a Hausman test. Show the five-step procedure.

(E) Using the model suggested by the Hausman test, apply White's HAC standard errors. Did the significance of either explanatory variable change with the new standard errors?

(7) Mark each of the following statements TRUE or FALSE.

(A) $CRRATE_{it} = \hat{\beta}_0 + \hat{\beta}_1 UNRATE_{it} + \hat{\beta}_2 D2_i + \hat{\beta}_3 D3_i + \ldots + \hat{\beta}_n Dn_i + e_{it}$ represents a time fixed effects model.

(B) $CRRATE_{it} - \hat{\lambda}\overline{CRRATE}_t = \hat{\beta}_0(1 - \hat{\lambda}) + \hat{\beta}_1 UNRATE_{it} - \hat{\lambda}\overline{UNRATE}_t + \varepsilon_{it}$ represents a random effects model.

(C) OLS can be applied to panel data, but the estimated coefficients are biased.

(D) Heterogenous effects refer to the consequences of heteroskedasticity.

(E) A cross-sectional fixed effects model can account for heterogeneity.

# Critical Values Tables

## CRITICAL VALUES OF THE T-DISTRIBUTION

| Two-tailed | | 20% | 10% | 5% | 2% |
|---|---|---|---|---|---|
| One-tailed | df | 10% | 5% | 2.5% | 1% |
| | 1 | 3.078 | 6.314 | 12.71 | 31.82 |
| | 2 | 1.886 | 2.920 | 4.303 | 6.965 |
| | 3 | 1.638 | 2.353 | 3.182 | 4.541 |
| | 4 | 1.533 | 2.132 | 2.776 | 3.747 |
| | 5 | 1.476 | 2.015 | 2.571 | 3.365 |
| | 6 | 1.440 | 1.943 | 2.447 | 3.143 |
| | 7 | 1.415 | 1.895 | 2.365 | 2.998 |
| | 8 | 1.397 | 1.860 | 2.306 | 2.896 |
| | 9 | 1.383 | 1.833 | 2.262 | 2.821 |
| | 10 | 1.372 | 1.812 | 2.228 | 2.764 |
| | 11 | 1.363 | 1.796 | 2.201 | 2.718 |
| | 12 | 1.356 | 1.782 | 2.179 | 2.681 |
| | 13 | 1.350 | 1.771 | 2.160 | 2.650 |
| | 14 | 1.345 | 1.761 | 2.145 | 2.624 |
| | 15 | 1.341 | 1.753 | 2.131 | 2.602 |
| | 16 | 1.337 | 1.746 | 2.120 | 2.583 |
| | 17 | 1.333 | 1.740 | 2.110 | 2.567 |
| | 18 | 1.330 | 1.734 | 2.101 | 2.552 |
| | 19 | 1.328 | 1.729 | 2.093 | 2.539 |
| | 20 | 1.325 | 1.725 | 2.086 | 2.528 |
| | 21 | 1.323 | 1.721 | 2.080 | 2.518 |
| | 22 | 1.321 | 1.717 | 2.074 | 2.508 |
| | 23 | 1.319 | 1.714 | 2.069 | 2.500 |

*(Continued)*

DOI: 10.4324/9781003213758-14

| | | | | |
|---|---|---|---|---|
| 24 | 1.318 | 1.711 | 2.064 | 2.492 |
| 25 | 1.316 | 1.708 | 2.060 | 2.485 |
| 26 | 1.315 | 1.706 | 2.056 | 2.479 |
| 27 | 1.314 | 1.703 | 2.052 | 2.473 |
| 28 | 1.313 | 1.701 | 2.048 | 2.467 |
| 29 | 1.311 | 1.699 | 2.045 | 2.462 |
| 30 | 1.310 | 1.697 | 2.042 | 2.457 |
| 40 | 1.303 | 1.684 | 2.021 | 2.423 |
| 50 | 1.295 | 1.676 | 2.009 | 2.403 |
| 60 | 1.296 | 1.671 | 2.000 | 2.390 |
| 80 | 1.292 | 1.664 | 1.990 | 2.374 |
| 100 | 1.290 | 1.660 | 1.984 | 2.364 |
| 1,000 | 1.282 | 1.646 | 1.962 | 2.330 |
| ∞ | 1.282 | 1.640 | 1.960 | 2.326 |

# CRITICAL VALUES OF THE F-DISTRIBUTION (5%)

The table here shows critical values of the F distribution at the 5% level of significance. For example, the critical F ($F^c$) for 3 degrees of freedom in the numerator and 25 degrees of freedom in the denominator is 2.99.

| Degrees of Freedom Denom. ↓ | Degrees of Freedom Numerator | | | | | | | | | | | | | | | | | | |
|---|---|---|---|---|---|---|---|---|---|---|---|---|---|---|---|---|---|---|---|
| | 1 | 2 | 3 | 4 | 5 | 6 | 7 | 8 | 9 | 10 | 12 | 15 | 20 | 24 | 30 | 40 | 60 | 120 | ∞ |
| 6 | 5.99 | 5.14 | 4.76 | 4.53 | 4.39 | 4.28 | 4.21 | 4.15 | 4.10 | 4.06 | 4.00 | 3.94 | 3.87 | 3.84 | 3.81 | 3.77 | 3.74 | 3.70 | 3.67 |
| 7 | 5.59 | 4.74 | 4.35 | 4.12 | 3.97 | 3.87 | 3.79 | 3.73 | 3.68 | 3.64 | 3.57 | 3.51 | 3.44 | 3.41 | 3.38 | 3.34 | 3.30 | 3.27 | 3.23 |
| 8 | 5.32 | 4.46 | 4.07 | 3.84 | 3.69 | 3.58 | 3.50 | 3.44 | 3.39 | 3.35 | 3.28 | 3.22 | 3.15 | 3.12 | 3.08 | 3.04 | 3.01 | 2.97 | 2.93 |
| 9 | 5.12 | 4.26 | 3.86 | 3.63 | 3.48 | 3.37 | 3.29 | 3.23 | 3.18 | 3.14 | 3.07 | 3.01 | 2.94 | 2.90 | 2.86 | 2.83 | 2.79 | 2.75 | 2.71 |
| 10 | 4.96 | 4.10 | 3.71 | 3.48 | 3.33 | 3.22 | 3.14 | 3.07 | 3.02 | 2.98 | 2.91 | 2.85 | 2.77 | 2.74 | 2.70 | 2.66 | 2.62 | 2.58 | 2.54 |
| 11 | 4.84 | 3.98 | 3.59 | 3.36 | 3.20 | 3.09 | 3.01 | 2.95 | 2.90 | 2.85 | 2.79 | 2.72 | 2.65 | 2.61 | 2.57 | 2.53 | 2.49 | 2.45 | 2.40 |
| 12 | 4.75 | 3.89 | 3.49 | 3.26 | 3.11 | 3.00 | 2.91 | 2.85 | 2.80 | 2.75 | 2.69 | 2.62 | 2.54 | 2.51 | 2.47 | 2.43 | 2.38 | 2.34 | 2.30 |
| 13 | 4.67 | 3.81 | 3.41 | 3.18 | 3.03 | 2.92 | 2.83 | 2.77 | 2.71 | 2.67 | 2.60 | 2.53 | 2.46 | 2.42 | 2.38 | 2.34 | 2.30 | 2.25 | 2.21 |
| 14 | 4.60 | 3.74 | 3.34 | 3.11 | 2.96 | 2.85 | 2.76 | 2.70 | 2.65 | 2.60 | 2.53 | 2.46 | 2.39 | 2.35 | 2.31 | 2.27 | 2.22 | 2.18 | 2.13 |
| 15 | 4.54 | 3.68 | 3.29 | 3.06 | 2.90 | 2.79 | 2.71 | 2.64 | 2.59 | 2.54 | 2.48 | 2.40 | 2.33 | 2.29 | 2.25 | 2.20 | 2.16 | 2.11 | 2.07 |
| 16 | 4.49 | 3.63 | 3.24 | 3.01 | 2.85 | 2.74 | 2.66 | 2.59 | 2.54 | 2.49 | 2.42 | 2.35 | 2.28 | 2.24 | 2.19 | 2.15 | 2.11 | 2.06 | 2.01 |
| 17 | 4.45 | 3.59 | 3.20 | 2.96 | 2.81 | 2.70 | 2.61 | 2.55 | 2.49 | 2.45 | 2.38 | 2.31 | 2.23 | 2.19 | 2.15 | 2.10 | 2.06 | 2.01 | 1.96 |
| 18 | 4.41 | 3.55 | 3.16 | 2.93 | 2.77 | 2.66 | 2.58 | 2.51 | 2.46 | 2.41 | 2.34 | 2.27 | 2.19 | 2.15 | 2.11 | 2.06 | 2.02 | 1.97 | 1.92 |
| 19 | 4.38 | 3.52 | 3.13 | 2.90 | 2.74 | 2.63 | 2.54 | 2.48 | 2.42 | 2.38 | 2.31 | 2.23 | 2.16 | 2.11 | 2.07 | 2.03 | 1.98 | 1.93 | 1.88 |
| 20 | 4.35 | 3.49 | 3.10 | 2.87 | 2.71 | 2.60 | 2.51 | 2.45 | 2.39 | 2.35 | 2.28 | 2.20 | 2.12 | 2.08 | 2.04 | 1.99 | 1.95 | 1.90 | 1.84 |
| 21 | 4.32 | 3.47 | 3.07 | 2.84 | 2.68 | 2.57 | 2.49 | 2.42 | 2.37 | 2.32 | 2.25 | 2.18 | 2.10 | 2.05 | 2.01 | 1.96 | 1.92 | 1.87 | 1.81 |
| 22 | 4.30 | 3.44 | 3.05 | 2.82 | 2.66 | 2.55 | 2.46 | 2.40 | 2.34 | 2.30 | 2.23 | 2.15 | 2.07 | 2.03 | 1.98 | 1.94 | 1.89 | 1.84 | 1.78 |
| 23 | 4.28 | 3.42 | 3.03 | 2.80 | 2.64 | 2.53 | 2.44 | 2.37 | 2.32 | 2.27 | 2.20 | 2.13 | 2.05 | 2.01 | 1.96 | 1.91 | 1.86 | 1.81 | 1.76 |
| 24 | 4.26 | 3.40 | 3.01 | 2.78 | 2.62 | 2.51 | 2.42 | 2.36 | 2.30 | 2.25 | 2.18 | 2.11 | 2.03 | 1.98 | 1.94 | 1.89 | 1.84 | 1.79 | 1.73 |
| 25 | 4.24 | 3.39 | 2.99 | 2.76 | 2.60 | 2.49 | 2.40 | 2.34 | 2.28 | 2.24 | 2.16 | 2.09 | 2.01 | 1.96 | 1.92 | 1.87 | 1.82 | 1.77 | 1.71 |
| 26 | 4.23 | 3.37 | 2.98 | 2.74 | 2.59 | 2.47 | 2.39 | 2.32 | 2.27 | 2.22 | 2.15 | 2.07 | 1.99 | 1.95 | 1.90 | 1.85 | 1.80 | 1.75 | 1.69 |
| 27 | 4.21 | 3.35 | 2.96 | 2.73 | 2.57 | 2.46 | 2.37 | 2.31 | 2.25 | 2.20 | 2.13 | 2.06 | 1.97 | 1.93 | 1.88 | 1.84 | 1.79 | 1.73 | 1.67 |
| 28 | 4.20 | 3.34 | 2.95 | 2.71 | 2.56 | 2.45 | 2.36 | 2.29 | 2.24 | 2.19 | 2.12 | 2.04 | 1.96 | 1.91 | 1.87 | 1.82 | 1.77 | 1.71 | 1.65 |
| 29 | 4.18 | 3.33 | 2.93 | 2.70 | 2.55 | 2.43 | 2.35 | 2.28 | 2.22 | 2.18 | 2.10 | 2.03 | 1.94 | 1.90 | 1.85 | 1.81 | 1.75 | 1.70 | 1.64 |
| 30 | 4.17 | 3.32 | 2.92 | 2.69 | 2.53 | 2.42 | 2.33 | 2.27 | 2.21 | 2.16 | 2.09 | 2.01 | 1.93 | 1.89 | 1.84 | 1.79 | 1.74 | 1.68 | 1.62 |
| 40 | 4.08 | 3.23 | 2.84 | 2.61 | 2.45 | 2.34 | 2.25 | 2.18 | 2.12 | 2.08 | 2.00 | 1.92 | 1.84 | 1.79 | 1.74 | 1.69 | 1.64 | 1.58 | 1.51 |
| 60 | 4.00 | 3.15 | 2.76 | 2.53 | 2.37 | 2.25 | 2.17 | 2.10 | 2.04 | 1.99 | 1.92 | 1.84 | 1.75 | 1.70 | 1.65 | 1.59 | 1.53 | 1.47 | 1.39 |
| 120 | 3.92 | 3.07 | 2.68 | 2.45 | 2.29 | 2.18 | 2.09 | 2.02 | 1.96 | 1.91 | 1.83 | 1.75 | 1.66 | 1.61 | 1.55 | 1.50 | 1.43 | 1.35 | 1.25 |
| ∞ | 3.84 | 3.00 | 2.60 | 2.37 | 2.21 | 2.10 | 2.01 | 1.94 | 1.88 | 1.83 | 1.75 | 1.67 | 1.57 | 1.52 | 1.46 | 1.39 | 1.32 | 1.22 | 1.00 |

# CRITICAL VALUES OF THE $X^2$-DISTRIBUTION

| d.f. | 10% | 5% | 1% |
| --- | --- | --- | --- |
| 1 | 2.71 | 3.84 | 6.63 |
| 2 | 4.61 | 5.99 | 9.21 |
| 3 | 6.25 | 7.81 | 11.34 |
| 4 | 7.78 | 9.49 | 13.23 |
| 5 | 9.24 | 11.07 | 15.09 |
| 6 | 10.64 | 12.53 | 16.81 |
| 7 | 12.02 | 14.07 | 18.48 |
| 8 | 13.36 | 15.51 | 20.09 |
| 9 | 14.68 | 16.92 | 21.67 |
| 10 | 15.99 | 18.31 | 23.21 |
| 11 | 17.29 | 19.68 | 24.72 |
| 12 | 18.55 | 21.03 | 26.22 |
| 13 | 19.81 | 22.36 | 27.69 |
| 14 | 21.06 | 23.68 | 29.14 |
| 15 | 22.31 | 25.00 | 30.58 |
| 16 | 23.54 | 26.30 | 32.00 |
| 17 | 24.77 | 27.59 | 33.41 |
| 18 | 25.99 | 28.87 | 34.81 |
| 19 | 27.20 | 30.14 | 36.19 |
| 20 | 28.41 | 31.41 | 37.57 |
| 21 | 29.62 | 39.67 | 38.93 |
| 22 | 30.81 | 33.92 | 40.29 |
| 23 | 32.01 | 35.17 | 41.64 |
| 24 | 33.20 | 36.42 | 42.98 |
| 25 | 34.38 | 37.65 | 44.31 |
| 26 | 35.56 | 38.89 | 45.64 |
| 27 | 36.74 | 40.11 | 46.96 |
| 28 | 37.92 | 41.34 | 48.28 |
| 29 | 39.09 | 42.56 | 49.59 |
| 30 | 40.26 | 43.77 | 50.89 |
| 40 | 51.81 | 55.76 | 63.69 |
| 50 | 63.17 | 67.50 | 76.15 |
| 60 | 74.40 | 79.08 | 88.38 |
| 80 | 96.58 | 101.90 | 112.30 |
| 100 | 118.50 | 124.30 | 135.80 |

# CRITICAL VALUES TABLES

**Critical Values for the Durbin-Watson Statistic**
**5 Percent Critical Level**

| | k = 2 | | k = 3 | | k = 4 | | k = 5 | | k = 6 | | k = 7 | | k = 8 | | k = 9 | | k = 10 | | k = 11 | |
|---|---|---|---|---|---|---|---|---|---|---|---|---|---|---|---|---|---|---|---|---|---|
| n | $d_L$ | $d_U$ | $d_L$ | $d_U$ | $d_L$ | $d_U$ | $d_L$ | $d_U$ | $d_L$ | $d_U$ | $d_L$ | $d_U$ | $d_L$ | $d_U$ | $d_L$ | $d_U$ | $d_L$ | $d_U$ | $d_L$ | $d_U$ |
| 16 | 1.11 | 1.37 | 0.98 | 1.54 | 0.86 | 1.73 | 0.73 | 1.94 | 0.62 | 2.16 | 0.50 | 2.39 | 0.40 | 2.62 | 0.30 | 2.86 | 0.22 | 3.09 | 0.16 | 3.30 |
| 17 | 1.13 | 1.38 | 1.02 | 1.54 | 0.90 | 1.71 | 0.78 | 1.90 | 0.66 | 2.10 | 0.55 | 2.32 | 0.45 | 2.54 | 0.36 | 2.76 | 0.27 | 2.98 | 0.20 | 3.18 |
| 18 | 1.16 | 1.39 | 1.05 | 1.54 | 0.93 | 1.70 | 0.82 | 1.87 | 0.71 | 2.06 | 0.60 | 2.26 | 0.50 | 2.46 | 0.41 | 2.67 | 0.32 | 2.87 | 0.24 | 3.07 |
| 19 | 1.18 | 1.40 | 1.07 | 1.54 | 0.97 | 1.69 | 0.86 | 1.85 | 0.75 | 2.02 | 0.65 | 2.21 | 0.55 | 2.40 | 0.46 | 2.59 | 0.37 | 2.78 | 0.29 | 2.97 |
| 20 | 1.20 | 1.41 | 1.10 | 1.54 | 1.00 | 1.68 | 0.89 | 1.83 | 0.79 | 1.99 | 0.69 | 2.16 | 0.60 | 2.34 | 0.50 | 2.52 | 0.42 | 2.70 | 0.34 | 2.89 |
| 21 | 1.22 | 1.42 | 1.13 | 1.54 | 1.03 | 1.67 | 0.93 | 1.81 | 0.83 | 1.96 | 0.73 | 2.12 | 0.64 | 2.29 | 0.55 | 2.46 | 0.46 | 2.63 | 0.38 | 2.81 |
| 22 | 1.24 | 1.43 | 1.15 | 1.54 | 1.05 | 1.66 | 0.96 | 1.80 | 0.86 | 1.94 | 0.77 | 2.09 | 0.68 | 2.25 | 0.59 | 2.41 | 0.50 | 2.57 | 0.42 | 2.74 |
| 23 | 1.26 | 1.44 | 1.17 | 1.54 | 1.08 | 1.66 | 0.99 | 1.79 | 0.90 | 1.92 | 0.80 | 2.06 | 0.72 | 2.21 | 0.63 | 2.36 | 0.55 | 2.51 | 0.47 | 2.67 |
| 24 | 1.27 | 1.45 | 1.19 | 1.55 | 1.10 | 1.66 | 1.01 | 1.78 | 0.93 | 1.90 | 0.84 | 2.04 | 0.75 | 2.17 | 0.67 | 2.32 | 0.58 | 2.46 | 0.51 | 2.61 |
| 25 | 1.29 | 1.45 | 1.21 | 1.55 | 1.12 | 1.65 | 1.04 | 1.77 | 0.95 | 1.89 | 0.87 | 2.01 | 0.78 | 2.14 | 0.70 | 2.28 | 0.62 | 2.42 | 0.54 | 2.56 |
| 26 | 1.30 | 1.46 | 1.22 | 1.55 | 1.14 | 1.65 | 1.06 | 1.76 | 0.98 | 1.87 | 0.90 | 1.99 | 0.82 | 2.12 | 0.74 | 2.25 | 0.66 | 2.38 | 0.58 | 2.51 |
| 27 | 1.32 | 1.47 | 1.24 | 1.56 | 1.16 | 1.65 | 1.08 | 1.75 | 1.00 | 1.86 | 0.93 | 1.97 | 0.85 | 2.09 | 0.77 | 2.22 | 0.69 | 2.34 | 0.62 | 2.47 |
| 28 | 1.33 | 1.48 | 1.26 | 1.56 | 1.18 | 1.65 | 1.10 | 1.75 | 1.03 | 1.85 | 0.95 | 1.96 | 0.87 | 2.07 | 0.80 | 2.19 | 0.72 | 2.31 | 0.65 | 2.43 |
| 29 | 1.34 | 1.48 | 1.27 | 1.56 | 1.20 | 1.65 | 1.12 | 1.74 | 1.05 | 1.84 | 0.98 | 1.94 | 0.90 | 2.05 | 0.83 | 2.16 | 0.75 | 2.28 | 0.68 | 2.40 |
| 30 | 1.35 | 1.49 | 1.28 | 1.57 | 1.21 | 1.65 | 1.14 | 1.74 | 1.07 | 1.83 | 1.00 | 1.93 | 0.93 | 2.03 | 0.85 | 2.14 | 0.78 | 2.25 | 0.71 | 2.36 |
| 31 | 1.36 | 1.50 | 1.30 | 1.57 | 1.23 | 1.65 | 1.16 | 1.74 | 1.09 | 1.83 | 1.02 | 1.92 | 0.95 | 2.02 | 0.88 | 2.12 | 0.81 | 2.23 | 0.74 | 2.33 |
| 32 | 1.37 | 1.50 | 1.31 | 1.57 | 1.24 | 1.65 | 1.18 | 1.73 | 1.11 | 1.82 | 1.04 | 1.91 | 0.97 | 2.00 | 0.90 | 2.10 | 0.84 | 2.20 | 0.77 | 2.31 |
| 33 | 1.38 | 1.51 | 1.32 | 1.58 | 1.26 | 1.65 | 1.19 | 1.73 | 1.13 | 1.81 | 1.06 | 1.90 | 0.99 | 1.99 | 0.93 | 2.09 | 0.86 | 2.18 | 0.80 | 2.28 |
| 34 | 1.39 | 1.51 | 1.33 | 1.58 | 1.27 | 1.65 | 1.21 | 1.73 | 1.14 | 1.81 | 1.08 | 1.89 | 1.02 | 1.98 | 0.95 | 2.07 | 0.89 | 2.16 | 0.82 | 2.26 |
| 35 | 1.40 | 1.52 | 1.34 | 1.58 | 1.28 | 1.65 | 1.22 | 1.73 | 1.16 | 1.80 | 1.10 | 1.88 | 1.03 | 1.97 | 0.97 | 2.05 | 0.91 | 2.14 | 0.85 | 2.24 |
| 36 | 1.41 | 1.53 | 1.35 | 1.59 | 1.30 | 1.65 | 1.24 | 1.72 | 1.18 | 1.80 | 1.11 | 1.88 | 1.05 | 1.96 | 0.99 | 2.04 | 0.93 | 2.13 | 0.87 | 2.22 |
| 37 | 1.42 | 1.53 | 1.36 | 1.59 | 1.31 | 1.66 | 1.25 | 1.72 | 1.19 | 1.80 | 1.13 | 1.87 | 1.07 | 1.95 | 1.01 | 2.03 | 0.95 | 2.11 | 0.89 | 2.20 |
| 38 | 1.43 | 1.54 | 1.37 | 1.59 | 1.32 | 1.66 | 1.26 | 1.72 | 1.20 | 1.79 | 1.15 | 1.86 | 1.09 | 1.94 | 1.03 | 2.02 | 0.97 | 2.10 | 0.91 | 2.18 |
| 39 | 1.44 | 1.54 | 1.38 | 1.60 | 1.33 | 1.66 | 1.27 | 1.72 | 1.22 | 1.79 | 1.16 | 1.86 | 1.10 | 1.93 | 1.05 | 2.01 | 0.99 | 2.09 | 0.93 | 2.16 |
| 40 | 1.44 | 1.54 | 1.39 | 1.60 | 1.34 | 1.66 | 1.29 | 1.72 | 1.23 | 1.79 | 1.18 | 1.85 | 1.12 | 1.92 | 1.06 | 2.00 | 1.01 | 2.07 | 0.95 | 2.15 |
| 45 | 1.48 | 1.57 | 1.43 | 1.62 | 1.38 | 1.67 | 1.34 | 1.72 | 1.29 | 1.78 | 1.24 | 1.84 | 1.19 | 1.90 | 1.14 | 1.96 | 1.09 | 2.02 | 1.04 | 2.09 |
| 50 | 1.50 | 1.59 | 1.46 | 1.63 | 1.42 | 1.67 | 1.38 | 1.72 | 1.34 | 1.77 | 1.29 | 1.82 | 1.25 | 1.88 | 1.20 | 1.93 | 1.16 | 1.99 | 1.11 | 2.04 |
| 55 | 1.53 | 1.60 | 1.49 | 1.64 | 1.45 | 1.68 | 1.41 | 1.72 | 1.37 | 1.77 | 1.33 | 1.81 | 1.29 | 1.86 | 1.25 | 1.91 | 1.21 | 1.96 | 1.17 | 2.01 |
| 60 | 1.55 | 1.62 | 1.51 | 1.65 | 1.48 | 1.69 | 1.44 | 1.73 | 1.41 | 1.77 | 1.37 | 1.81 | 1.34 | 1.85 | 1.30 | 1.89 | 1.26 | 1.94 | 1.22 | 1.98 |
| 65 | 1.57 | 1.63 | 1.54 | 1.66 | 1.50 | 1.70 | 1.47 | 1.73 | 1.44 | 1.77 | 1.40 | 1.81 | 1.37 | 1.84 | 1.34 | 1.88 | 1.30 | 1.92 | 1.27 | 1.96 |
| 70 | 1.58 | 1.64 | 1.55 | 1.67 | 1.53 | 1.70 | 1.49 | 1.74 | 1.46 | 1.77 | 1.43 | 1.80 | 1.40 | 1.84 | 1.37 | 1.87 | 1.34 | 1.91 | 1.31 | 1.95 |
| 75 | 1.60 | 1.65 | 1.57 | 1.68 | 1.54 | 1.71 | 1.52 | 1.74 | 1.49 | 1.77 | 1.46 | 1.80 | 1.43 | 1.83 | 1.40 | 1.87 | 1.37 | 1.90 | 1.34 | 1.94 |
| 80 | 1.61 | 1.66 | 1.59 | 1.69 | 1.56 | 1.72 | 1.53 | 1.74 | 1.51 | 1.77 | 1.48 | 1.80 | 1.45 | 1.83 | 1.43 | 1.86 | 1.40 | 1.89 | 1.37 | 1.93 |
| 85 | 1.62 | 1.67 | 1.60 | 1.70 | 1.58 | 1.72 | 1.55 | 1.75 | 1.53 | 1.77 | 1.50 | 1.80 | 1.47 | 1.83 | 1.45 | 1.86 | 1.42 | 1.89 | 1.40 | 1.92 |
| 90 | 1.64 | 1.68 | 1.61 | 1.70 | 1.59 | 1.73 | 1.57 | 1.75 | 1.54 | 1.78 | 1.52 | 1.80 | 1.49 | 1.83 | 1.47 | 1.85 | 1.45 | 1.88 | 1.42 | 1.91 |
| 95 | 1.65 | 1.69 | 1.62 | 1.71 | 1.60 | 1.73 | 1.58 | 1.76 | 1.56 | 1.78 | 1.54 | 1.80 | 1.51 | 1.83 | 1.49 | 1.85 | 1.47 | 1.88 | 1.44 | 1.90 |
| 100 | 1.65 | 1.69 | 1.63 | 1.72 | 1.61 | 1.74 | 1.59 | 1.76 | 1.57 | 1.78 | 1.55 | 1.80 | 1.53 | 1.83 | 1.51 | 1.85 | 1.48 | 1.87 | 1.46 | 1.90 |
| 150 | 1.72 | 1.75 | 1.71 | 1.76 | 1.69 | 1.77 | 1.68 | 1.79 | 1.67 | 1.80 | 1.65 | 1.82 | 1.64 | 1.83 | 1.62 | 1.85 | 1.61 | 1.86 | 1.59 | 1.88 |
| 200 | 1.76 | 1.78 | 1.75 | 1.79 | 1.74 | 1.80 | 1.73 | 1.81 | 1.72 | 1.82 | 1.71 | 1.83 | 1.70 | 1.84 | 1.69 | 1.85 | 1.68 | 1.86 | 1.67 | 1.87 |

Extracted from Savin and White (1977).

# Cited Works

Andersen, Leonall C., and Jordan, Jerry L. 1969. "Monetary and Fiscal Actions: A Test of Their Relative Importance in Economic Stabilization." *Federal Reserve Bank of St. Louis Review* 51(4): 12–16.

Box, George, and Jenkins, Gwilym. 1970. *Time Series Analysis: Forecasting and Control.* San Francisco: Holden-Day.

Breusch, T. S. 1978. "Testing for Autocorrelation in Dynamic Linear Models." *Australian Economic Papers* 17: 334–355.

Cochrane, D., and Orcutt, G. H. 1949. "Applications of Least Squares Regression to Relationships Containing Autocorrelated Error Terms." *Journal of the American Statistical Association* 44: 32–61.

Dasgupta, Susmita, Laplante, B., Wang, H., and Wheeler, D. 2002. "Confronting the Environmental Kuznets Curve." *Journal of Economic Perspectives* 16 (1): 147–168.

Dickey, D. A., and Fuller, W. A. 1979. "Distribution of the Estimators for Autoregressive Time Series with a Unit Root." *Journal of the American Statistical Association* 74: 427–431.

Durbin, J., and Watson, G. S. 1951. "Testing for Serial Correlation in Least-Squares Regression." *Biometrika* 38: 159–177.

Godfrey, L. G. 1978. "Testing against General Autoregressive and Moving Average Error Models When the Regressors Include Lagged Dependent Variables." *Econometrica* 46: 1293–1302.

Granger, C. W. J. 1969. "Investigating Causal Relations by Econometric Models and Cross-spectral Methods." *Econometrica* 37: 24–36.

Hausman, Jerry. 1978. "Specification Tests in Econometrics." *Econometrica* 46: 1251–1272.

Hildreth, C., and Lu, J.Y. 1960. "Demand Relations with Autocorrelated Disturbances." *Research Bulletin 276*, Michigan State University Agricultural Experiment Station.

Huber, P. J. 1967. "The Behavior of Maximum Likelihood Estimates under Nonstandard Conditions." In *Proceedings of the Fifth Berkeley Symposium on Mathematical Statistics and Probability* 1: 221–233. Berkeley, CA: University of California Press.

212CITED WORKS

Keynes, John Maynard. 1936. *The General Theory of Employment, Interest, and Money*. London: Macmillan.

Koyck, L. M. 1954. *Distributed Lags and Investment Analysis*. Amsterdam: North-Holland Publishing Company.

Levitt, S., and Dubner, S. 2006. *Freakonomics*. New York, NY: Harper Trophy.

Marshall, Alfred. 1890. *Principles of Economics*. London: Macmillan.

Newey, W. K., and West, K. D. 1987. "A Simple, Positive Semi-definite Heteroskedasticity and Autocorrelation Consistent Covariance Matrix." *Econometrica* 55(3): 703–708.

Okun, A. M. 1962. "Potential GNP: Its measurement and significance." In Proceedings of the Business and Economics Statistics Section American Statistical Association. 98–104. Washington, D.C.

Park, R. E. 1966. "Estimation with Heteroscedastic Error Terms." *Econometrica* 34(4): 888.

Samuelson, P. A. 1939. "Interactions between the Multiplier Analysis and the Principle of Acceleration". *Review of Economic Statistics* 21(2): 75–78.

Savin, N. E., and White, K. J. 1977. The Durbin-Watson test for serial correlation with extreme sample sizes or many regressors. *Econometrica* 45(8): 1989–1996.

Spector, Lee C., and Mazzeo, Michael. 1980. "Probit Analysis and Economic Education." *Journal of Economic Education* 11(2): 37–44.

Theil, Henri. 1971. *Principles of Econometrics*. New York: Wiley.

White, H. 1980. "A Heteroskedasticity Consistent Covariance Matrix Estimator and a Direct Test of Heteroskedasticity." *Econometrica* 48(4): 817–818.

# Index

definition of 42, 50
probability density function of 44
Trend variable 85, 91
t-statistic 42
Two-sided tests 43
Two-tailed tests 48
TYPE I error 41–42, 45, 50
TYPE II error 42, 50, 132

U
Unbiased estimators 65–66, 117–119,
  125, 131
Underspecification 63–64, 70, 122
Unit root test 176
Units of measurement and
  estimates 79–80

V
Variance 55–56
Variance inflation factors 132–134
Vertical change 6–7
VIFs. *See* Variance inflation factors

W
Weighted least squares 143–146
White noise 159, 162
White test 141–143
"Without-transformation," 197

X
X-variable 14

Printed in the United States
by Baker & Taylor Publisher Services